Rising Powers in International Conflict Management

Rising Powers in International Conflict Management locates rising powers in the international conflict management tableau and decrypts their main motives and limitations in the enactment of their peacebuilding role.

The book sheds light on commonalities and divergences in a selected group of rising powers' (namely Brazil, India, China, and Turkey) understanding and applications of conflict management and explains the priorities in their conflict management strategies from conceptual/theoretical and empirical aspects. The case studies point to the evolving nature of conflict management policies of rising powers as a result of their changing priorities in foreign and security policy and the shifts observed in the international order since the end of the Cold War. The country-specific perspectives provided in this study have also proven right the potentialities of rising powers in managing conflicts, as well as their past and ongoing challenges in envisaging crises in both their own regions and extra-regional territories.

Improving the understanding of the strengths and weaknesses of rising powers as conflict management actors and peacebuilders at regional and international levels, *Rising Powers in International Conflict Management* will be of great interest to scholars of international relations, conflict studies, and peacebuilding. The chapters were originally published as a special issue of *Third World Quarterly*.

Emel Parlar Dal is Professor of International Relations at Marmara University, Turkey. Her recent publications have appeared in SSCI journals including *Third World Quarterly*, *Global Policy*, *Contemporary Politics*, *International Politics*, *Turkish Studies*, and *International Journal*. *Middle Powers in Global Governance* and *Turkey's Political Economy in the 21st Century* are her most recent edited books.

ThirdWorlds
Edited by Shahid Qadir, *University of London, UK*

ThirdWorlds will focus on the political economy, development and cultures of those parts of the world that have experienced the most political, social, and economic upheaval, and which have faced the greatest challenges of the postcolonial world under globalisation: poverty, displacement and diaspora, environmental degradation, human and civil rights abuses, war, hunger, and disease.

ThirdWorlds serves as a signifier of oppositional emerging economies and cultures ranging from Africa, Asia, Latin America, Middle East, and even those 'Souths' within a larger perceived North, such as the U.S. South and Mediterranean Europe. The study of these otherwise disparate and discontinuous areas, known collectively as the Global South, demonstrates that as globalisation pervades the planet, the south, as a synonym for subalterity, also transcends geographical and ideological frontier.

The most recent titles include:

War Economies and Post-war Crime
Edited by Sabine Kurtenbach and Angelika Rettberg

Post-conflict Reconstruction and Local Government
Edited by Paul Jackson and Gareth Wall

Violence and the Third World in International Relations
Edited by Randolph B. Persaud and Narendran Kumarakulasingam

Studying the State
A Global South Perspective
Edited by Esteban Nicholls

Converging Social Justice Issues and Movements
Edited by Tsegaye Moreda, Saturnino M. Borras Jr., Alberto Alonso-Fradejas and Zoe W. Brent

Rising Powers in International Conflict Management
Converging and Contesting Approaches
Edited by Emel Parlar Dal

For more information about this series, please visit:
https://www.routledge.com/series/TWQ

Rising Powers in International Conflict Management

Converging and Contesting Approaches

Edited by
Emel Parlar Dal

Routledge
Taylor & Francis Group

LONDON AND NEW YORK

First published in paperback 2024

First published 2020
by Routledge
4 Park Square, Milton Park, Abingdon, Oxon OX14 4RN

and by Routledge
605 Third Avenue, New York, NY 10158

Routledge is an imprint of the Taylor & Francis Group, an informa business

British Library Cataloguing in Publication Data
A catalogue record for this book is available from the British Library

ISBN: 978-0-367-42922-5 (hbk)
ISBN: 978-1-03-283891-5 (pbk)
ISBN: 978-1-00-300015-0 (ebk)

DOI: 10.4324/9781003000150

Typeset in Myriad Pro
by Newgen Publishing UK

Contents

Citation Information

The chapters in this book were originally published in *Third World Quarterly*, volume 39, issue 12 (2019). When citing this material, please use the original page numbering for each article, as follows:

For any permission-related enquiries please visit:
www.tandfonline.com/page/help/permissions

Notes on Contributors

Ferit Belder is a research assistant at Marmara University in international relations and a PhD candidate at Istanbul University, Turkey. He received a bachelor's degree in political science and international relations at Marmara University, Turkey, in 2011. He received his MA in international relations at Istanbul University in 2013 and an MSc in international politics at SOAS, University of London, in 2015. His research interests include Turkish foreign policy, Middle Eastern politics, Israeli politics, and security studies.

Arka Biswas is an associate fellow at the Strategic Studies Programme, Observer Research Foundation and a former visiting fellow at the Stimson Center, USA. He is a physics graduate and has a master's in international relations. His work has appeared in the *Washington Quarterly*, *Comparative Strategy*, *Foreign Policy*, and *Bulletin of the Atomic Scientists*, among other platforms.

Charles T. Call is Associate Professor of International Peace and Conflict Resolution in the School of International Service at American University, USA. He is a non-resident senior fellow at the Brookings Institute. He served as senior external advisor to the UN–World Bank study Pathways for Peace in 2017. From 2012 to 2014, he was a senior advisor in the US State Department, and from 2012 to 2018, he served on the UN Secretary-General's Advisory Group on the UN Peacebuilding Fund.

Sandra Destradi is Professor of International Relations and Regional Governance at Helmut Schmidt University/University of the Federal Armed Forces Hamburg, Germany, and head of the research programme 'Power and Ideas' at the GIGA German Institute of Global and Area Studies.

Linnéa Gelot is a senior researcher at the Folke Bernadotte Academy, Sweden, and an associate professor in peace and development at the School of Global Studies, Gothenburg University, Sweden. Her research has focused on peace operations, with a specialisation in African-led conflict management efforts, institutionalism – especially the legitimacy of African organisations and the African Union – United Nations peace and security relationship, and militarism. Her research project 'African Union Waging Peace' has employed the concepts of militarisation and security practice theory to study militarising institutional discourses and practices within African peace and security institutions. Her most recent publication is 'Civilian Protection in Africa: How the Protection of Civilians Is Being Militarised by African Policymakers and Diplomats' in *Contemporary Security Policy* (2017).

Abigail Kabandula is a doctoral candidate in global governance and human security at the John W. McCormack Graduate School of Policy and Global Studies, USA. She holds dual master's degrees in global governance and human security from University of Massachusetts Boston, and historical studies from University of Cape Town (UCT), an honors degree in gender and transformation from UCT, and a bachelor of arts in history and English from the University of Zambia (UNZA). Abigail has worked as a researcher at the Centres for Conflict Resolution (CCR) and for Social Science Research (CSSR) in Cape Town, South Africa.

Hakan Mehmetcik is an assistant professor at the Department of International Relations, Marmara University, Turkey. He has a master's degrees in economics and Eurasian studies from Dalarna and Uppsala Universities, respectively, in Sweden. He obtained his PhD in international relations in 2017 from Yildiz Technical University in Turkey, and his research interests lie in the area of international political economy, regionalism, globalisation, and broader security studies. He has several major publications on middle powers, rising powers, and Turkish foreign policy. He teaches several thematic and theoretical courses including globalisation and regionalism, theories of international relations, theories of international political economy, and international security.

Harsh V. Pant is Head of the Strategic Studies Program at the Observer Research Foundation in New Delhi and a professor of international relations at King's College London UK. He is director of studies and head of strategic studies programme at the Observer Research Foundation in New Delhi. He is also an adjunct fellow with the Wadhwani Chair in US–India Policy Studies at the Center for Strategic and International Studies, Washington, DC. His current research is focused on Asian security issues.

Emel Parlar Dal is Professor of International Relations at Marmara University, Turkey. Her recent publications have appeared in SSCI journals including *Third World Quarterly*, *Global Policy*, *Contemporary Politics*, *International Politics*, *Turkish Studies*, and *International Journal*. *Middle Powers in Global Governance* and *Turkey's Political Economy in the 21st Century* are her most recent edited books.

Timothy M. Shaw is Visiting Professor in the PhD program in global governance and human security at the University of Massachusetts Boston, USA. He is an adjunct professor at Aalborg, Carleton, Stellenbosch, and the University of Ottawa, and teaches every summer in Beijing, China. Tim also edits a series on IPE for Palgrave Macmillan/Springer and Routledge.

Martin Welz is a senior research fellow at the Department of Politics and Public Administration and at the Center of Excellence 'Cultural Foundations of Integration' at the University of Konstanz, Germany. His research focuses on the African Union, the United Nations, and inter-organisational relationships, especially in the context of peace operations. He is also interested in Africa's role in the world, particularly with regard to the International Criminal Court. His publications include *Integrating Africa: Decolonization's Legacies, Sovereignty and the African Union* (2013), *Military Twists and Turns in World Politics: Downsides or Dividends for UN Peace Operations?* (2015), and *Multi-actor Peace Operations and Interorganizational Relations: Insights from the Central African Republic* (2016). He is currently working on a book on African history and politics.

Rising powers in international conflict management: an introduction

Emel Parlar Dal

ABSTRACT

This introductory article sheds light on commonalities and divergences in a selected group of rising powers' (namely Brazil, India, China and Turkey) understanding and applications of conflict management and attempts to explain the priorities in their conflict management strategies from conceptual/theoretical and empirical aspects. The case studies in this special issue point to the evolving nature of conflict management policies of rising powers as a result of their changing priorities in foreign and security policy and the shifts observed in the international order since the end of the Cold War. The country specific perspectives provided in this issue have also proven right the potentialities of rising powers in managing conflicts, as well as their past and ongoing challenges in envisaging crises in both their own regions and extra-regional territories. The article begins by decoding the driving factors of rising powers' conflict management strategies and their commonalities and divergences in peacebuilding policies. It then jumps into the theoretical and conceptual assessment of their conflict management approaches. In the third part, the issue delves into the evidence-based assessment their converging and differing conflict management policies depending on the nature of the conflict, its involving actors and its geographical location.

Introduction

What kind of actors are rising powers in international conflict management? Are they active or passive conflict resolution actors? Do they pursue similar conflict and crisis management policies at the regional and global level or do they have diverging discourses and practices in the management of international crises? These are fundamental questions in understanding the strengths and weaknesses of rising powers as conflict management actors and peacebuilders at the regional and international levels. As status-seeking actors in a changing international order, rising powers make use of a series of conflict management strategies including prevention, mediation, peacebuilding and adjudication. With the emergence of 'new wars', new security threats emanating from violent non-state actors and an increasing number of factors leading to civil war conditions across the world,[1] conflict is changing and thus needs to be managed differently by major and rising powers. In the contemporary complex security environment, rising powers face several challenges affecting both their approaches to conflict and what tools they use to manage these conflicts. The current volatile security environment requires stronger collaboration and cooperation in diplomatic and military coercion and global counter-terrorism. For instance, the ongoing civil war in Syria has highlighted several divergences among major powers and rising states in how they assess the gradual degradation of civil war conditions and seek a peaceful solution to the crisis. In contrast to expectations, rising powers failed to develop a common peacebuilding approach to the Syrian civil war and a unified position determining the conditions of a peaceful settlement in Syria.

Despite the existence of a robust literature on conflict management,[2] a very limited number of studies have dealt with the approaches and understandings of rising powers to international conflict management. This study aims to fulfil this lacuna by offering a holistic framework of the assessment of how rising powers approach and strategise conflict management. In fact, rising powers' strong criticism of the current international order and their willingness to upgrade their international status to become viable actors that may compete with major powers in global governance policy areas run in parallel with their increasing desire to actively participate in international conflict management. The second novelty of this paper is its examination of multiple rising powers such as India, Brazil, China and Turkey as conflict management actors engaged in sustaining regional and global peace by the use of their prioritised conflict management instruments.

With this in mind, this special issue aims to locate rising powers in the international conflict management tableau and to decrypt their main motives and limitations in the enactment of their peacebuilding role. In doing so, it delves into the analysis of their positioning towards international crises from a comparative perspective and attempts to understand the effectiveness and functionality of the conflict mechanisms and tools they utilise as part of their preferred peacebuilding strategy. In this vein, this introductory article begins by decoding the driving factors of rising powers' conflict management strategies and their commonalities and divergences in peacebuilding policies. It then jumps into the theoretical and conceptual assessment of conflict management approaches of rising powers. In the third part, the issue delves into the evidence-based assessment of a group of selected rising powers' converging and differing conflict management policies depending on the nature of the conflict, its involving actors and its geographical location.

1. Decrypting rising powers as international conflict management actors

In the current post-Western international order, almost all major actors, including rising powers, have begun to redefine their international roles and responsibilities in successfully responding to global challenges. Both traditional and rising powers pursue either convergent or divergent policies depending on their mutual and differing interests. Their responses to ongoing shifts in the international order also vary according to their differing expectations and gains from the existing multilateral mechanisms and rules of today's global governance. The last decade has also witnessed significant shifts in the status politics of emerging powers entering into global competition with traditional powers on multiple fronts such as economics-trade, diplomacy and hard and soft power.[3] In addition, rising powers' relative increase in material power sources and diplomatic leverage in global affairs has also drawn a great deal of attention to both their bilateral and multilateral relations with the rest of the world.[4] Moreover, rising powers' strong attachment to the Westphalian norms of sovereign equality and non-interference in internal affairs and their ongoing criticism of the unjust Western-dominated liberal order also impact the way they conceive and construct their role in sustaining international peace and security. Added to this are their own conceptions of the international order, the nature and the components of their strategic culture, and their self-perception of the international responsibilities they have committed to for sustaining peace and preventing conflict. These conceptions determine the willingness of rising powers to actively involve themselves in managing international conflicts.

The rising powers are not a homogeneous group of states with similar responses to international conflicts and, as such, it is not an easy task to holistically assess their conflict management approaches and strategies. However, four driving factors can be observed as determining the construction of their conflict management policies: self-interests-based preferences, status-seeking attitudes, cost-oriented normative approach and region-focused priorities. The second driving factor, status seeking attitudes, mean that international recognition and prestige also play a key role in the shaping of rising powers' approaches to international conflict. Here, status refers to the voluntary deference of others.[5] Rising powers may also engage in an active role in international conflict management in order to gain legitimacy and authority in the international system. The cost-oriented normative approach, the third driving factor, signifies that rising powers tend to comply with the existing norms within the existing institutions in conflict management if the costs of challenging them is high. When the costs of challenging the existing norms and institutions are low, however, they may revise or create new ones according to their interests.[6] As the forth driving point, region-focused priorities represent the importance of geographical proximity in the determination of rising powers' conflict management strategies.

Self-interests-based preferences

Self-interests-based preferences reflect that, while engaging in a conflict as a third actor aiming to find a peaceful resolution to the crisis, rising powers act in conformity with their national interests-based preferences. Departing from this, it can be claimed that rising powers aim to preserve their own interests at the economic, political and economic levels in international crises. Thus, the greater extent to which a conflict affects their interests, a nation shows greater willingness to take part in its management. In addition, rising powers seek to reduce the number of conflicts in the international system by involving other like-minded nations in their attempt to find a peaceful resolution to the crisis by the use of multilateral channels and institutions. Similar to middle-ranged powers, they attempt to pre-empt, contain and resolve conflicts. Rising powers also show grand inclination to play a mediation role in high profile international conflicts since the reduction of conflicts positively affect their political and economic well-being.

Rising powers show some similar behavioural patterns in the realm of conflict management as well. One of the most important patterns is free-riding. From a rationalist point of view, rising powers are generally inclined to act as free-riders to the traditional powers, even if their involvement in the conflict as a third party might damage their material interests. For instance, while China would free-ride on the US in the management of conflicts triggered in the Middle East, Japan and South Korea allegedly do the same for conflicts in East Asia.

Another aspect of free-riding of rising powers to major powers is closely related with the material gains that rising powers obtain from free-riding in case of their (dis)involvement in conflicts. There also exists some difficulties for major powers in cooperating with rising powers in conflict management mainly due to their differing values and interests in the preservation of the liberal world order. Even rising powers that are more democratic and Western-oriented may also break with their Western allies on many security-related and geopolitical issues (e.g. Turkey). In case of the existence of overriding interests, rising powers may cooperate with major powers in sustaining peace through conflict management. A closer assessment of the current international conflict landscape clearly proves how rising powers prioritise their self-interests during the involvement in international conflicts as third parties and peace brokers. For instance, China's mediation in the North Korean nuclear crisis and Russia's Syrian engagement are all closely linked with their material and ideational interests.

Status-seeking attitudes

Rising powers are generally inclined to achieve higher status and recognition in world politics and thus pursue active foreign policies in multiple fields of global governance, from peace-keeping to climate change. Their quest for status also turn them into transformative actors seeking reform and revision in the international system. Peacebuilding in general and conflict management in particular constitute important aspects of the status-seeking policies of rising powers.[7] In this regard, rising powers give support to UN-led and non-UN-led peace-keeping operations depending on their regional priorities as well as their ideational prefer-ences including their soft power strategies. In short, rising powers' status politics are also strongly informed by their differing approaches to peacebuilding. Given their differing his-torical experiences, geographic locations, cultural affinities and economic and political pri-orities, rising powers may give distinctive reactions to the same international conflicts. In line with this, they may cooperate to prevent, stop or transform conflicts if this would bring them enhanced status and prestige in the sphere of global governance. China's lead in the fight against climate change or its substantial cooperation against the proliferation of nuclear weapons by joining UN sanctions against North Korea are some contemporary examples of such status politics.

However, the status concerns of rising powers push them to increase their notoriety in many policy areas of international politics including conflict management and prevention. Almost all rising powers pursue status seeking behaviours in the realm of peacebuilding and this may affect the outcomes of their relations with major powers, formal and informal international organisations, less developed and developing countries, etc. Rising powers' demand for higher status and prestige is thus a key factor in their international security policies.

Cost-oriented normative approach

Another commonality of rising powers in the sphere of conflict management is their cost-oriented normative approach to conflicts. Despite their relatively weak institutional power and normative setting, rising powers have a general tendency to calculate costs before taking a new normative initiative such as the creation of new institutions. If the cost of creating new institutions or challenging them is high, rising powers prefer to comply with the existing structures or reform the existing institutions and their mechanisms but tend to change them by creating new ones if the relative costs are lower. This cost-based approach is not only valid in the field of conflict management. In many issue areas of global governance such as nuclear proliferation, climate change, international terrorism and economic and financial governance, rising powers have adopted policies based on cost calculations in the pursuit of their normative preferences. The establishment by BRICS (Brazil, Russia, India, China, South Africa) countries of the BRICS Development Bank and Contingent Reserve Fund demonstrates their level of discomfort with the existing global financial institutions dominated by traditional powers and can be regarded as an end-result of their cost-based normative policies. However, in the field of conflict management, especially at the regional level, rising powers prefer in most of cases to act alone or together with a small number of regional states. They rarely cooperate with major powers in regional crisis due to their strong commitment to the principle of non-interference in the internal affairs of third countries. The reluctance of rising powers like India, Brazil and, to a lesser extent, China in the involvement in the Syrian crisis is a good example of the cost-oriented normative approach in taking actions in the management of international crisis.

Region-focused priorities

Most of the current security threats impacting rising powers can be found and addressed at the regional level. The existence of negative security externalities and the use of regional conflict management tools such as the presence of institutional and normative settings and values are key to the success or failure of conflict management at the regional level. If the conflict's negative externalities are high, which means that the conflict has an overriding and significant negative impact on other regional countries, the incentive for conflict management will be higher. The more negative externalities spill over, the more conflict management efforts are initiated. However, in certain cases the existence of a high number of negative externalities could be detrimental to the effective use of conflict management tools due to the involvement of many actors in the conflict. A good example of this is the Syrian case where, as a result of the crisis' increasing negative externalities to regional countries, more actors have become involved in the conflict and this has complicated its management.

Here it must also be emphasised that rising powers have weaker capacities compared to traditional powers in setting out working institutional design for conflict management. The institutionalisation of conflict management as a norm is a difficult task since it requires uniting different identities, interests, priorities and values under a common peacebuilding system. Rising powers are either not a part of such effective international institutions or lack strong institution and norm-building capabilities. This lack of sufficient power capacities pushes them to deal more bilaterally than multilaterally with conflicts. They even engage in coercive power to limit the conflict's spillover to neighbouring regions. Rising powers give the impression of adopting a mix of two strategies for conflict management: bilateral or autonomous and multilateral. However, compared to traditional powers, rising powers seem to be more willing to take initiative within the existing international bodies to either prevent conflicts or find resolutions to conflicts. China's effort to initiate Six-Party Talks to address the North Korean nuclear crisis, and when it failed, to seek a solution to the Korean crisis through the UN Security Council, is one such example of rising powers' dual approach to conflicts. In regional conflicts, more specifically those in which national interests are under threat, rising powers do not hesitate to use coercive conflict management tools, making their conflict management strategy more autonomous and independent. However, conflict management necessitates a holistic multilateral approach to peacebuilding covering multiple policy applications from peace-keeping to mediation, from mediation to development cooperation, and from development cooperation to adjudication. Turkey's management of the Syrian crisis is a good example of rising powers' dual approach to conflict resolution based on a mix of bilateral and multilateral strategies. On a bilateral basis, Turkey uses both diplomatic and military tools to prevent the conflict's diffusion into its territories. At the regional level, its engagement in establishing an ad-hoc coalition with the other two regional states involved in the crisis (Russia and Iran), resulting in the launch of a series of Astana talks, also illustrates how its Syrian conflict management strategy's bilateral and autonomous components outweigh its multilateral ones.

2. Profiling rising powers in peacebuilding from theoretical and conceptual perspectives

In his article *Interests or Ideas? Explaining Brazil's Surge in Peacekeeping and Peacebuilding*, Charles T. Call assesses Brazil's increasing activism in peacebuilding since the 2000s from a theoretical approach. For Call, Brazil is one of several rising powers that have assumed greater protagonism in advancing peace on the global stage and in the global South beginning in the early 2000s. The author states that in Haiti, East Timor, Guinea-Bissau, Angola and Mozambique, Brazil expanded its peacekeeping deployments and leadership and exercised leadership on peacebuilding issues. More generally, it sought to lead efforts to reform and democratise the global order through the Security Council and South–South alliances such as the BRICS Alliance and IBSA. Its development cooperation tripled from 2003 to 2010 and it sought to shift norms on issues such as the Responsibility to Protect commitment.

In his article the author mainly investigates the reasons behind Brazil's increased activity in peace-related issues. He questions whether this activism can be best understood from the perspectives of the classic realist behaviour of middle powers seeking to rise in the global pecking order or of new liberal commitment to enhanced integrated approaches to global trade and order. Call continues by asking if post-colonial theories find support Brazil's proclaimed attempt to try to transform the Western-dominated overly militarised approach to global peace and security and if Brazil's identity as a developmental, non-interventionist middle power expressing solidarity with other former colonies helps explain its new peacebuilding policies.

The article tests the four core international relations theories of realism, liberalism, constructivism and post-colonial theory to explain the rise and content of Brazil's peacebuilding policies. Departing from the argument that Brazil has been vocal in its non-traditional approaches to peacekeeping and peacebuilding, the author examines the extent to which its rhetorical claims make sense and contends that this study can bring systematic theoretical thinking to a case whose empirics have been used to support each of the four main theoretical approaches.

In the final analysis based on literature on Brazil's operations and on personal interviews with senior Brazilian diplomats, Call argues that interest-based theories such as realism and liberalism best account for the emergence of Brazil's increased peacekeeping and peace-building initiatives in the early 2000s. However, idea-based constructivist and post-colonial approaches are necessary to account for the content of these approaches that reflect national identity and social and culturally historic experiences.

In their article *Pragmatic Eclecticism, Neoclassical Realism, and Post-Structuralism: Reconsidering the Libyan Crisis of 2011*, Gelot and Welz draw on Sil and Katzenstein's notion of 'analytical eclecticism' to analyse the botched African Union (AU) initiative to lead the management of the 2011 Libyan crisis. While the crisis for some render redundant the notion of 'African solutions to African problems' due to the AU's lack of internal cohesion, others emphasise the obstruction of the AU's Libya mediation plan by outside powers. Both views share the understanding that Africa's rise in political terms was curbed through the AU's inability to claim the lead mediator role in the Libyan crisis.

Gelot and Welz develop an original 'eclectic typology' by recombining theoretical and substantive elements from two distinct research traditions, post-structuralism and neoclassical realism, and identifying contact zones between them. The typology comprises the categories 'primacy of power, 'discourses' and 'images of leaders'. According to Gelot and Welz, both neoclassical realist and poststructuralist arguments as applied to AU's crisis management in Libya can be used to deconstruct the predominant narrative's advancement of liberal cosmopolitan motivations behind the intervention in Libya and is strongly related to the principle of the responsibility-to-protect (R2P). The authors show how the approach taken to Libya in 2011 depended on three justificatory moves linked to the three categories: a predominance of power towards a cosmopolitan liberal end, a legitimising discourse and the construction of an image of Gaddafi in world politics. For instance, the authors unpack the many contextual and multilevel factors involved in explaining why the AU's mediation plan was dismissed as out of sync with events and as dangerously naïve. Once the UNSC authorised the no-fly zone over Libya, a predominant discourse took hold that effectively limited the political choices at hand for the AU and African states.

Gelot and Welz also underline the fact that the image of Gaddafi as an intolerable and incorrigible tyrant helped advance the view among many Western powers that Libya faced a historic opportunity to liberalise and that the social forces demanding democracy and freedom in Libya needed outside assistance. The authors highlight the material and non-material power of states involved in side-lining the AU's opposition to forcible regime change. In their final analysis, the authors concluded that while the AU is an indispensable partner to major powers in many crisis situations in Africa today, the careful unpacking of many interrelated factors enabled by analytical eclecticism is important to explain why its crisis management role was so undesirable in Libya in 2011. In this regard, the politics of rouging/derouging Gaddafi depended more on geopolitics and economic realism than concern for the Libyan people and the unity among major powers to uphold and implement the R2P principle in Libya is open to critical investigation. In sum, the typology shows how insights from two or more theoretical perspectives can offer novel perspectives that satisfy both researchers and practitioners and such joint perspectives are more inclusive of contextual and multi-level factors.

In the essay *Reluctant Powers? Rising Powers' Contributions to Regional Crisis Management*, Sandra Destradi approaches the issue of rising powers' international conflict management initiatives by adopting the analytical lens of 'reluctance' and focusing on the regional level of analysis. She starts from the observation that rising powers have often been reluctant to engage in conflict management on both global terms and within their regions where they tend to be the predominant countries and where conflicts and instability often create dangerous security externalities. To capture the often ambivalent, indecisive approach of rising powers to regional conflict management, Destradi builds upon her previous work on reluctance in world politics.[8] In her contribution to this special issue, she develops a theorisation of the drivers of reluctance by focusing on difficulties in dealing with competing expectations: that rising powers address different (global, regional, domestic) constituencies at the same time and that by doing so they will pursue reluctant policies. The empirical analysis of India's and Brazil's varying reluctance in regional crisis management confirms this hypothesis.

According to the author, India has been a reluctant crisis manager in the South Asian region. Even under the stable government of Prime Minister Modi, who came to power with a large majority in 2014, India has been unable to contribute to the stabilisation of its region in a consistent manner. In Afghanistan, India has been divided between the expectations of the Afghan government, the US and the 'West' more generally to take over greater responsibilities in matters of security on the one hand and the need to not provoke its rival Pakistan by getting engaged too extensively on the other. In a constitutional crisis in neighbouring Nepal, India has similarly pursued an extremely reluctant, inconsistent approach, which Destradi traces back to competing expectations by domestic constituencies within Nepal and India.

In the case of Brazil, by contrast, the country under President Lula (2003–2011) has pursued a non-reluctant, consistent and responsive approach to regional conflict management as illustrated by the cases of its engagement in the MINUSTAH mission in Haiti as well as its role in the civil war in Colombia. According to Destradi, this was possible because, in the case of Haiti, global and regional actors supported Brazil's leadership and the Brazilian government was able to argumentatively sideline domestic critics of the mission. In the case of Colombia, Brazil's low-key offers of mediation and support were not contradicted by expectations of greater engagement in conflict management, thereby allowing Lula to pursue a coherent, non-reluctant policy. In the final analysis, the author contends that the analysis of India's and Brazil's varying reluctance in regional conflict management through its focus on competing expectations unveils some of the contradictions and tensions that rising powers are subjected to when they are asked to take over greater international responsibilities in matters of security.

3. From theory to practice rising powers in conflict management: case studies

In their article *Rising Powers and the Global Nuclear Order: The Case of India's Integration*, Harsh V. Pant and Arka Biswas ask why India's exceptional partial integration into the global nuclear order was possible and what explains the challenges that remain to India's complete integration. Their article attempts to address these two questions through a structural lens. It begins by laying out the process of India's partial integration into the global nuclear order to date. The article then employs the structural framework to explain how India's integration was possible. The third section examines the extent to which this framework also explains the challenges that remain to India's complete integration. Pant and Biswas depart from the common argument that India's relationship with the global nuclear order has been unique. The authors state that with its 'peaceful nuclear explosion' of 1974 and decision to not sign the Treaty on the Non-Proliferation of Nuclear Weapons (NPT) as a non-nuclear weapon state (NNWS), India was viewed by the global nuclear order and the larger international system as a pariah nuclear state for decades. The authors remind the reader that, much like other states that acquired nuclear weapons capability after 1 January 1967, India was subject to international criticism and sanctions. The relationship in question was expected to slide further downhill following India's nuclear tests of May 1998 and New Delhi's decision to operationalise its nuclear weapons capability, reflected through its draft nuclear doctrine of 1999 and the official doctrine of 2003. India, however, witnessed a dramatic turnaround in the following decade. In 2000, while the NPT held its review conference, India's then Minister of External Affairs, Jaswant Singh, noted in an address to the Indian Parliament that, while India would stay outside the NPT, it would uphold all principles enshrined in the Treaty, especially in curbing horizontal proliferation of nuclear weapons and related sensitive items.

As underlined by the authors, India's journey has indeed been exceptional, moving from isolation to the successful negotiation of a civil nuclear cooperation agreement with the US, the acquisition of a waiver from the Nuclear Suppliers Group (NSG), the definitions of condition for implementing full-scope safeguards to engage in global nuclear commerce in 2008, and membership in the Missile Technology Control Regime (MTCR), Wassenaar Arrangement (WA) and the Australia Group (AG) in 2016, 2017 and 2018, respectively. However, daunting challenges remain in the completion of India's integration into the global nuclear order and in the debate over India's membership application to the NSG, which forms a critical component of the global nuclear order.

The authors conclude that the structural framework holds credible explanatory power over India's rise in the global nuclear order as well as the challenges that remain to India's complete integration into the order. In the final analysis, the authors explicate what that means for the extant global nuclear order, especially as more rising nuclear powers challenge the order in future.

In her article *Assessing Turkey's Changing Conflict Management Role after the Cold War: Actorness, Approaches, and Tools*, Emel Parlar Dal attempts to profile Turkey as a rising power with its own conflict management understanding and practices. In doing so, the author uses a three-layered embedded framework built on conflict management *actorness*, *approaches* and *tools*. At the actorness level, the author looks at the historical trajectories of Turkey's active, passive or mixed conflict management approaches in international conflicts as a third party. At the second level of approaches, the author assesses Turkey's understanding of conflict management using Bercovitch and Regan's four categories of approaches to conflict management: threat-based, deterrence-based, adjudicatory and accommodationist. Thirdly, the author employs four conflict management tools drawn from Michael J. Butler's four-layered international conflict management applications framework: peacebuilding, mediation, peace enforcement and adjudication.

The author underlines that from the Republican era to the 2000s, Turkey could be considered a cautious and passive actor in international conflict management and distanced itself from regional and global crises, with few exceptions such as Cyprus and Kosovo. The successive Yugoslavian crisis represented a breaking point for Turkey's passive conflict management strategies as conflict management became an important issue policy and the 1990s saw a diversification of tools and practices. As indicated by the author, Turkey pursued both active and passive conflict management policies between the 1990s and early 2000s and became more active in international conflict management by shifting the nature of its conflict management practices from the military to more civilian-dominated between the 2000s and 2011. With the Syrian war most specifically, Turkey has followed a mix of active and passive conflict management strategies since 2011.

Parlar Dal reaches the following conclusion on Turkey's conflict management approaches: since actorness was largely shaped by its membership to NATO and its special relationship with the US, Turkey's approach to conflict management has generally been accommodationist. The only exception to Turkey's accommodationist understanding during the Cold War was the Cyprus crisis, during which Turkey followed the threat-based, deterrence-based and adjudicatory approaches. During the first decade following the end of the Cold War, Turkey employed traditional and non-traditional methods in managing conflicts from both accommodationist and adjudicatory perspectives. According to the author, with the Arab revolts and the Syrian War most specifically, Turkey began to pursue a mix of active and passive conflict management actorness based mostly on the threat-based and deterrence-based approach (especially with the two recent military operations in Syria).

The author concludes that while Turkey does not possess a coherent peacekeeping strategy, it has become a new player in international mediation utilising more hard than soft power instruments. Parlar Dal also points to the fact that Turkey's mediation in the Syrian war became more selective and less cosmopolitan, leaving Ankara as more an insider partial mediator than an outsider neutral one. The author underlines that, in recent years, peace enforcement has become a widely used conflict management tool. In the use of adjudicative mechanisms, Turkey follows a low-profile policy.

In the final analysis, the author concludes that, with the Syrian war and other regional developments, Turkey has gradually become more a regional than global conflict management actor and more of an autonomous peace provider and peace enforcement-oriented actor than a peacekeeper or a mediator.

In *China's Role in the Regional and International Management of Korean Conflict: An Arbiter or Catalyser?*, authors Hakan Mehmetçik and Ferit Belder look at different role conceptions of China using role theory. As the North Korean nuclear crisis continues, many diverging views on China's role in the conflict have emerged. China's role has been characterised as that of a bystander, arbiter, catalyser and mediator over the years. This chapter seeks to clarify where China stands on North Korea and assess the different phases of the Chinese approach to conflict resolution during the North Korean nuclear crisis. According to the authors, China's current duplicity stems from different priorities at different levels and thus role theory offers a distinct ability to explain this dual position. The authors state that role theory-related concepts have great use in elaborating China's changing role and the external expectations for China's role-taking and role-making patterns. First, it provides theoretically rich and analytically sound explanations. Second, by using role theory concepts we can plunge into spatial and temporal changes and the causes of those changes. To this end, the chapter starts with a conceptual analysis of the role theory and the way in which it can be beneficial to analyse the contending roles of China in the North Korean dispute and its effects on China's patterns of conflict resolution.

The main finding of this chapter is that the role of China within the North Korean conflict can only be assessed with a special focus on the several sets of China's conflicting ascribed and achieved/assumed roles. For the authors, the gap between China's ascribed and achieved/assumed roles has been closing over the years thanks to socialisation and other diplomatic mechanisms. However, as indicated by the authors, Chinese role adaptation and role contestation is a product of self-identification rather than of international pressures. North Korea races towards the nuclear finishing line and, although it has not already crossed that line, many analysts and politicians see China's role as being crucial to make pression on North Korea for halting its nuclear programme. In the eyes of the authors, this in reality is an immature assessment. In the final analysis, the authors contend that a closer assessment of China's role in the crisis from a role theory point of view shows that China has a limited interest and capacity in assuming the role of external expectations. China's changing role in the crisis basically derives from the fact that both China and other related actors have a high role adaptation. In this regard, this study enhances our theoretical and thematic understanding of China's conflict management strategies with regard to changes in its roles and role sets.

Abigail Kabandula and Timothy M. Shaw position rising powers at the centre of contemporary global politics and economics because they offer alternatives to the established unequal global order in *Rising Powers and the Horn of Africa: Conflicting Regionalism*. Understandably so, the global system is in flux as US global hegemony declines and nationalist (populist and protectionist) movements increase in Europe, the US and elsewhere, forcing Western regimes to prioritise domestic policies. The ongoing domestic turmoil and undiplomatic views of current US President Trump give impetus to middle and rising powers such as the BRICS and Turkey to continue seeking alternative and deeper partnerships in trade, development, peace, security and the environment at micro- and macro-regional levels.

With a focus on the complexities of the Horn of Africa, the authors investigate what exactly is a rising power? The authors explore two questions: what does the growing engagement of rising powers like Turkey entail for peace and security in the Horn of Africa region, and will rising inter-regional relations facilitate/exacerbate tensions? They argue that while rising and middle powers, especially China but also India and Brazil, have made significant contributions to overall trade and development in Africa, recent political engagement and regional expansion/inter-regionalism have contributed to the fragility of the Horn, thereby making the region susceptible to both intra- and inter-state conflicts. At the same time, conflict management processes, state stabilisation (Somalia) and human security have also been undermined as non-traditional security (hereafter NTS) policies that encourage these aspects of security are given less priority.

The authors posit that heightened Turkish (and allied) military activities in the Horn will lead to militarisation of the region, which inevitably reduces the priority previously given to NTS issues such as water, energy and food (the WEF nexus). NTS issues are the primary causes of both state and human insecurity as acute water and food shortages exacerbated by a rapidly growing population increase the likelihood of intra- and/or inter-state armed conflict as people scramble to survive on the limited resources available. The article also shows how this region, like most parts of Africa, faces new and complex NTS issues including terrorism, 'new wars' and climate change. The authors demonstrate how the advent of globalisation, particularly information technologies, has intensified and complicated NTS attempts and measures to promote security on the continent and the region. At the same time, information technologies have advanced the growth of spaces where states have limited, weak, contested or absent authority. Cyber, offshore and shadow banking institutions have been most challenging for states to exert control over because of the rise of powerful non-state actors, notably transnational corporations and networks that contest and sometimes undermine state authority and legitimacy. The authors argue that while rising and middle powers have contributed to the economy, increased military engagement in the region has unleashed a complex set of inter-regional relations and security challenges that further undermine both state and human security.

In the final analysis, the authors contend that situating and understanding the complexities of such meso- and micro-regionalisms require the juxtaposition of hitherto separate analytic and policy genres: from national and human development/security to old and new insecurities and rising and declining states and economies. Hence the relevance of treating Turkey and the BRICS as rising powers in the Horn: rising powers, regional and otherwise, are coming to disrupt post-Cold War assumptions and arrangements in northeast Africa and elsewhere, necessitating creative (Track Diplomacy 1/2/3) diplomacy and original analytic frameworks.[9]

In guise of conclusion

This collection of articles around the theme of rising powers in international conflict management seeks to analyse the different approaches and practices of a selected group of rising powers in international conflict management: Brazil, India, China and Turkey. This special issue sheds light on the commonalities and divergences in rising powers' understanding and applications of conflict management and attempts to explain the nuances and priorities in their conflict management strategies from conceptual/theoretical and empirical aspects. The case studies in this issue point to the evolving nature of conflict management policies of rising powers as a result of their changing priorities in foreign and security policy and the shifts observed in the international order since the end of the Cold War. The changing conflict management strategies of rising powers cannot be analysed without taking into consideration systematic changes observed in international politics since the 1990s. The decline since the 2000s in the willingness of major powers to play a leading role in the management of international conflicts associated with rising powers' pursuit of active peacebuilding policies as a part of their status politics seems to have changed how nations approach conflict management.

Moreover, it is clear that international conflict management does not follow a single policy or is able to be successfully carried out without the coordination of traditional and rising/middle powers in the global and regional institutional settings. In the current global governance structure, international conflict management now requires a new and much more effective institutional foundation, new concepts and a new distribution of roles among traditional and non-traditional actors. In this regard, UN or non-UN-based initiatives in sustaining peace using existing conflict management tools or the creation of new conflict management tools and mechanisms may help rising powers play much more operational and active roles in peacebuilding. The country specific perspectives provided in this special issue have also proven right the potentialities of rising powers in managing conflicts, as well as their past and ongoing challenges in envisaging crises in both their own regions and extra-regional territories. While Africa appears to be a common denominator in terms of geography in the majority of the rising powers' peacekeeping policies, other regions outside Africa, and their own regions in some cases, remain as geographies in which they pursue reluctant peacekeeping policies. However, not all rising powers actively contribute to UN peacekeeping operations as seen in the cases of Turkey and Russia. While Turkey prioritises NATO over the UN in its contributions to peacekeeping operations, Russia prefers to act autonomously in the sphere of peacekeeping and contributes to UN peacekeeping activities at a much lower level than other BRICS contributing countries. These differences in rising powers' approaches and practices clearly illustrate the difficulties of defining common objectives in international conflict management. However, the success stories of some rising powers in dealing with international crisis inside or outside the UN make it clear that these states are generally more prone to peace related cooperation either by the use of military or non-military methods/tools. Despite the differences in their strategies and priorities, rising powers all wish to appear as peace brokers in regional and international crises.

Another commonality among rising powers' conflict management policies is their willingness to link their security policies to development and development-related cooperation. Almost all rising powers seek to play active roles in development cooperation as an integral part of their status-seeking policies in global governance. In the last decade, countries such as China, India, Turkey, Brazil, Russia, South Africa and Mexico have gradually become important donors in the field of development cooperation and humanitarian assistance and have developed efficient policies in this niche diplomacy area at varying degrees. Given this, it must be underlined that any study on international conflict management and peacebuilding must certainly consider the security-development nexus and its increasing centrality in rising powers' conflict management and peacebuilding strategies and preferences. As seen clearly in the cases studies collected in this special issue, rising powers construct their conflict management policies on a mix of realpolitik and idealpolitik. This intermingled approach to conflict management may also help them adopt a holistic approach to development-cantered conflict prevention policies.

In conclusion, it is false to consider all rising powers a homogeneous or a unique bloc giving similar responses to international crises. Their conflict management understanding largely derives from their strategic culture, historical/cultural affinities to certain regions in the world, and national security and foreign policy interests and priorities. However, despite their differences in conflict management approaches and practices, rising powers have the capacity and potential to unite based on jointly defined global interests and under the auspice of international organisations, most specifically the UN. The research undertaken in this special issue and the findings derived from the different case studies justify this argument.

Disclosure statement

No potential conflict of interest was reported by the author.

Funding

This work was supported by Marmara University Scientific Research Project Coordination Unit-BAPKO A type project.

Notes

1. Oktav et al., *Violent Non-State Actors*.
2. Butler, *International Conflict Management*; Burton and Dukes, *Conflict*; Diehl and Lepgold, *Regional Conflict Management*.
3. Larson, "New Perspectives on Rising Powers"; Paul, Larson, and Wohlforth, *Status in World Politics*; Renshon, *Fighting for Status*.
4. Paul, "Global Peaceful Change and Accommodation"; Newman and Zala, "Rising Powers and Order Contestation"; Culp, "How Irresponsible Are Rising Powers?"; Patrick, "Irresponsible Stakeholders?"
5. Dafoe, Renshon, and Huth, "Reputation and Status as Motives for War."
6. Lipscy, *Renegotiating the World Order*.
7. Call, *Rising Powers and Peacebuilding*.
8. Destradi, "Reluctance in International Politics."
9. On UAE and Qatar as well as Turkey in Somalia/Somaliland, see *"Gulf Money in Somalia: A Storm Over a Port."*

Bibliography

Burton, John, and Frank Dukes. *Conflict: Readings in Management and Resolution*. Houndmills, Basingstoke, Hampshire and London: Springer, 1990.

Butler, Michael J. *International Conflict Management*. London; New York: Routledge, 2009.

Call, Charles T. *Rising Powers and Peacebuilding: Breaking the Mold?* 1st ed. New York, NY: Springer Berlin Heidelberg, 2017.

Culp, Julian. "How Irresponsible Are Rising Powers?" *Third World Quarterly* 37, no. 9 (September 2016): 1525–36. https://doi.org/10.1080/01436597.2016.1166046.

Dafoe, Allan, Jonathan Renshon, and Paul Huth. "Reputation and Status as Motives for War." *Annual Review of Political Science* 17, no. 1 (May 11, 2014): 371–93. https://doi.org/10.1146/annurev-polisci-071112-213421.

Destradi, Sandra. "Reluctance in International Politics: A Conceptualization." *European Journal of International Relations* 23, no. 2 (2017): 315–340.

Diehl, Paul F., and Joseph Lepgold. *Regional Conflict Management*. Lanham, MA: Rowman & Littlefield Publishers, 2003.

"Gulf Money in Somalia: A Storm Over a Port." *Economist* 14 April 2018: 40–41.

Larson, Deborah Welch. "New Perspectives on Rising Powers and Global Governance: Status and Clubs." *International Studies Review* 20, no. 2 (2018): 247–254. https://doi.org/10.1093/isr/viy039.

Lipscy, Phillip Y. *Renegotiating the World Order: Institutional Change in International Relations.* Cambridge, UK: Cambridge University Press, 2017.

Newman, Edward, and Benjamin Zala. "Rising Powers and Order Contestation: Disaggregating the Normative from the Representational." *Third World Quarterly* 39, no. 5 (2018): 871–888. https://doi.org/10.1080/01436597.2017.1392085.

Oktav, Özden Zeynep, Emel Parlar Dal, and Ali Murat Kurşun, eds. *Violent Non-State Actors and the Syrian Civil War: The ISIS and YPG Cases.* Cham, Switzerland: Springer International Publishing, 2018. www.springer.com/cn/book/9783319675275.

Patrick, Stewart. "Irresponsible Stakeholders? The Difficulty of Integrating Rising Powers." *Foreign Affairs* 89, no. 6 (2010): 44–53.

Paul, T. V. "Global Peaceful Change and Accommodation of Rising Powers: A Scholarly Perspective." *All Azimuth* 6, no. 2 (2017): 85.

Paul, Thazha V., Deborah Welch Larson, and William C. Wohlforth. *Status in World Politics.* Cambridge, UK: Cambridge University Press, 2014.

Renshon, Jonathan. *Fighting for Status: Hierarchy and Conflict in World Politics.* Princeton, NJ: Princeton University Press, 2017.

Reluctant powers? Rising powers' contributions to regional crisis management

Sandra Destradi ⓘ

ABSTRACT

Rising powers have often been characterised as 'reluctant' when it comes to their contributions to global governance. However, also within their regions they have sometimes pursued indecisive, muddling-through policies, including in the field of security. This paper addresses the puzzling issue of rising powers' reluctant approach to regional crisis management. It conceptualises reluctance as entailing the two constitutive dimensions of hesitation and recalcitrance, and it seeks to approach a theorisation of reluctance that focuses on a combination of international expectations and domestic preference formation. The empirical analysis addresses instances of regional crisis management by the democratic rising powers India and Brazil during phases of domestic political stability under the Modi (2014–2018) and the Lula (2003–2011) governments, respectively. The analysis of India's crisis management efforts in Afghanistan and Nepal, and of Brazil's leadership of the MINUSTAH mission and its approach to the civil war in Colombia, reveal that reluctance emerges if a government is faced with (competing) expectations articulated by international actors as well as with a range of domestic factors that lead to unclear preference formation.

Introduction: reluctant powers?

Great expectations have been associated with the emergence of 'new' powers in world politics since the beginning of the twenty-first century. Such expectations have come primarily from policy makers, who have expected rising powers to contribute to the provision of global public goods, given their success in terms of economic growth, their increasingly proactive foreign policy and their claims for great power status.[1] Academic debates have to a certain extent reflected this kind of discourse, with scholars discussing rising powers' often limited contributions to global governance – think of rising powers' insistence on common but differentiated responsibilities on climate governance or of their ambivalence on global crisis management. As Bisley suggests in this special issue, this might be due to them being 'poor great powers', lacking the capabilities to assume a managerial function in global politics. Or we could at least argue that rising powers are particularly careful about cost–benefit calculations in global public goods provision and tend to privilege domestic developmental needs. For example, rising powers have focused on the protection of their economies in global trade negotiations and they have long tended to prioritise industrialisation over climate change mitigation efforts.[2]

However, while the costs of burden sharing seem to be an important factor in explaining rising powers' high degree of reluctance towards contributing to public goods at the global level, things look different at the regional level. 'Rising powers' like India, Brazil or South Africa tend to be the dominant countries within their regions[3] and we could certainly expect them to have the capabilities to influence their regional neighbourhood as well as a high degree of interest in its stability. It is at the regional level that the costs of providing public goods are likely to be consistent with these countries' ability to provide them. We could therefore expect rising powers to contribute to the provision of regional public goods in a much more decisive and clear-cut manner as compared to the global level.

However, the empirical reality looks different: rising powers have sometimes been reluctant to engage in their regions,[4] including in the field of crisis management. This contribution builds upon a previous conceptualisation of 'reluctance' in world politics and develops it to flesh out its causal elements with the aim of theorising the drivers of reluctance. To explain varying reluctance, it focuses on a combination of international expectations and unclear domestic preferences. In the empirical analysis, the explanatory power of such a proto-theory of foreign policy reluctance is assessed with reference to four cases of regional crisis management by the democratic rising powers India and Brazil. The analysis focuses on periods in which these countries could be unequivocally considered as 'rising' and had stable governments, that is, on phases during which reluctance is particularly puzzling. For the case of India, it addresses regional crisis management under the government of Narendra Modi of the Bharatiya Janata Party (BJP) (2014–2018), which, together with its coalition partners in the National Democratic Alliance (NDA), has a stable majority in the lower house of Parliament (Lok Sabha); India at the same time has remained one of the few emerging powers with remarkably high growth rates. For Brazil, the focus is on regional crisis management during the years of President Luiz Inácio Lula da Silva of the Workers' Party (PT) (2003–2011), a period of domestic political stability during which Brazil increasingly came to be recognised as a rising power and pursued an active foreign policy.[5] The analysis confirms that reluctance emerges if there are obstacles to the formation of clear domestic preferences and international expectations cannot be met.

Reluctance and the impact of (competing) expectations and unclear preferences

Reluctance is ubiquitous in world politics. Indecisiveness, delaying, muddling through, disappointing the expectations of partners – these and similar attitudes are commonplace among international actors, but the phenomenon of reluctance has been largely ignored by the literature in the field of International Relations (IR). This is all the more surprising as the term is rather frequently used, not only with regard to rising powers, but also for example to the US.[6] Only recently, a conceptualisation of reluctance was developed,[7] but we still lack any kind of theorisation about what leads international actors to be reluctant. This contribution aims to flesh out such causal dimensions of the concept of reluctance. As Goertz points out in his seminal work, social science concepts always entail a causal dimension, and concept building is deeply interlinked with theorising.[8]

According to Destradi, reluctance can be understood as an analytical category that helps us grasp a 'peculiar *type* or *style* of foreign policy that can be found across issue areas and settings'.[9] Reluctance entails two constitutive dimensions, which are both necessary and jointly sufficient: hesitation and recalcitrance.[10] Reluctance is a relational concept that always refers to an interaction between different actors. While the dimension of hesitation is focused on the 'self' – on an actor's own internal dynamics – the second constitutive dimension of reluctance, recalcitrance, refers to an interplay with the 'other(s)'.

Hesitation describes an ambivalent, indecisive attitude and is operationalised as entailing at least one of the following indicators: a *lack of initiative*, which is particularly relevant if we want to analyse how rising powers react to crises in their regional neighbourhood where they are the predominant actors; *delaying*, which amounts to not sticking to a previously set time frame or to 'postponing important decisions in dealing with a specific issue or crisis';[11] or *flip-flopping*, which involves frequent or sudden changes in policies or statements, or contradictions, for example among the statements of members of the same government.

The second constitutive dimension of reluctance, recalcitrance, captures an unwillingness or inability to conform with the expectations articulated by others, and thereby reflects the elements of obstructionism and resistance that resonate with the notion of reluctance. Recalcitrance can be operationalised as entailing at least one of the following indicators: *ignoring requests* made by others or expectations articulated by others, in our specific analysis with reference to crisis management; *rejecting* such requests, that is, explicitly denying one's commitment; *obstructing others' initiatives* without providing a consistent alternative given one's parallel hesitation.[12]

Both dimensions, hesitation *and* recalcitrance, need to be in place in order to classify a policy as reluctant. Both of them can occur to different degrees, thereby entailing a continuum and making reluctance, as well, a continuous concept.[13] It has to be noted that, while reluctance in the political discourse is sometimes associated with a negative connotation, this contribution aims to use 'reluctance' as an analytical tool to grasp a particular type or style of foreign policy making that is not reflected in other existing concepts in IR. Importantly, reluctance does not simply amount to a passive foreign policy strategy. For example, a consistent refusal to get involved in a military dispute would not count as reluctant behaviour as it lacks the dimension of hesitation.[14] Japan and Germany's approach to the use of military force in the decades after World War II would similarly not count as reluctance according to this understanding since it was a clear and coherent policy course. Generally speaking, the opposite of reluctance would therefore be a determined and consistent (as opposed to hesitant) as well as responsive (as opposed to recalcitrant) foreign policy.[15]

Why does reluctance occur or, in other words, what leads governments to pursue reluctant policies? As suggested by Goertz, an explanation is inherent in the concept itself and, conversely, looking for such explanation helps us further develop the concept. In the case of reluctance, the two related but discrete constitutive dimensions of hesitation and recalcitrance play a causal role in explaining the occurrence of reluctance. The dimension of hesitation – with its indecisive, delaying, flip-flopping attitude – can be expected to contribute to the explanation of reluctance via domestic factors, which might prevent a government from following a determined and consistent course of action. The dimension of recalcitrance – that is, the fact of not conforming to others' expectations – implies that such expectations play a role in driving reluctance as well. In the field of international politics, we will focus on expectations by international actors. Importantly, as we will see, such domestic and international factors are deeply interrelated.

International expectations can be of different kinds. Particularly powerful states will be faced with an especially broad range of expectations given their potentially superior problem-solving ability, and particularly severe crises can be expected to generate more expectations concerning their resolution. Rising powers will be faced with expectations articulated by established powers, for example when it comes to participating in global public goods provision. At the same time, they will face expectations by their immediate regional neighbours, which might request them to commit to the solution of regional problems and the provision of regional public goods, but which might also feel threatened by their sheer power preponderance and wish that they avoid meddling with regional affairs.[16] Competing expectations by different international actors will be particularly challenging as compared to homogeneous expectations. As ultimately governments will always be the object of international expectations concerning their foreign policy, but as not all of them are always reluctant, international expectations do not seem to be a sufficient condition for the occurrence of reluctance. In fact, if such expectations meet clear domestic preferences, the government might choose to ignore them and to pursue a consistent course of action (or, as we will see below, it might pursue a reluctant policy in order to appease competing expectations).

Foreign-policy preferences will crystallise as a result of a domestic process and are analytically and '[…] by definition causally independent of the strategies of other actors and, therefore, prior to specific interstate political interactions, including external threats, incentives, manipulation of information, or other tactics'.[17] By choosing one policy option and by pursuing a determined and consistent course of action, the government will not be hesitant. It might be recalcitrant, if it disappoints some (or all) international expectations, but this will not be a sufficient condition for reluctance.

While clear domestic preferences that dovetail or clash with homogeneous international expectations will therefore lead to non-reluctant policies, we now need to specify under what conditions reluctance, understood as a combination of recalcitrance and hesitation, will emerge.

At the domestic level, there are several factors that might lead to hesitation. Among them is, first, simple government weakness. Lacking a clear majority or being dependent on coalition partners will make it more difficult to pursue consistent and determined courses of action. In this paper, the empirical analysis explicitly focuses on stable governments in order to control for this factor as far as possible.

Second, problems within the bureaucracy might have similar consequences.[18] Despite a robust majority, a government might end up being hesitant because its bureaucracy lacks capacity or preparedness, leading to coordination problems with the centre or simply to an inability to take initiatives or to delays in policy making. Moreover, even a capable bureaucracy might be overwhelmed by too much information, an 'increasing number of tasks', 'too many goals' and 'no agreement on the best means',[19] which will lead to the adoption of cognitive shortcuts to cope with complexity. It will be particularly likely in policy areas that are new to an emerging power or in severe crisis situations, since the bureaucratic and decision-making apparatus will likely lack the knowledge necessary to develop a clear policy position, while at the same time being forced to provide a quick response.

Finally, hesitation might emerge (and possibly be reinforced by international expectations) as a consequence of domestic arguing over competing norms.[20] We can identify indications of this explanation if we observe domestic actors using references to different normative foundations of foreign policy while they argue over the best course of action to follow. Such normative tensions are generally likely in rising powers as these countries try to adjust their policies to their changed (or changing) international status. Conformity with predominant international normative standards is likely to favour status gains, but might clash with established domestic norms, leading to sometimes contradictory, zig-zagging policies (hesitation). While this explanation of hesitation does not necessarily only apply to democracies, as such political struggles also take place within elites in authoritarian regimes, it nevertheless highlights that reluctant policies are often an outcome of a genuinely democratic political process of negotiation and perhaps reflect the very essence of democracy. However, normative tensions might also emerge as a result of path dependency in the way a country's bureaucracy conceives of foreign policy. For example, if a decades-old commitment to certain norms on the part of the bureaucracy clashes with a new normative approach on the part of the executive, this might lead to hesitant policies.

Since reluctance by definition involves a relational aspect, hesitation (driven by the above-mentioned domestic factors) needs to be paired with recalcitrance in the interaction with international actors. In other words, in order to be *reluctant*, foreign policy will involve not conforming to some international expectations. At the international level, a government might be faced with either homogeneous or competing expectations, depending on whether all relevant actors expect it to adopt the same kind of policy or whether different actors expect different things from it. Such actors can be, for example, international partners, relevant institutions or powerful competitors. If homogeneous expectations meet clear preferences, this will lead to non-reluctant policies, as was mentioned above. By contrast, homogeneous expectations in combination with unclear domestic preferences will lead to reluctance since extremely hesitant, flip-flopping policies will almost automatically disappoint international actors.[21]

If competing expectations by external actors meet unclear domestic preferences, we will obviously have a combination of recalcitrance and hesitation because the government will be torn apart between different expectations and will not have a clear own policy course.

To conclude, there is an additional explanation for reluctance, in which international expectations have a more explicit causal primacy. It refers to cases in which a government has a clear domestic preference, but is confronted with competing expectations. These might put it under such strong competing pressures that it will not be able to consistently implement its preferred policies; or it might consciously choose to pursue a hesitant policy (lack of initiative, delaying, flip-flopping) to conform to several of such different expectations. In other words, in the latter case, the government will try to appease, at least temporarily, as many actors as possible, but in that process, it will make contradictory decisions or adopt delaying tactics (hesitation). At the same time, as it will be impossible to appease everybody, recalcitrance about conforming to some of those expectations will inevitably emerge. The underlying assumption here is a rationalist one, and reluctance is used in a strategic manner. In fact, in some cases, reluctant policies help governments to keep international criticism and opposition at bay for a while by appeasing multiple competing expectations, or they allow them to buy time to collect additional information.

The following case studies of India and Brazil's regional crisis management will provide a first assessment of the plausibility of such explanations of reluctance focused on international expectations and domestic preferences.

India under Modi: still a reluctant crisis manager in South Asia

After an unsuccessful interventionist phase in its neighbourhood in the 1980s, India has pursued a much more low-key approach to regional crisis management in the South Asian region since the 1990s. South Asia is an extremely difficult regional context: it is one of the least institutionalised regions in the world, with the South Asian Association for Regional Cooperation (SAARC) confined to political irrelevance due to the conflict between India and Pakistan. At the same time, the region is characterised by a huge asymmetry between India and the other regional countries (Afghanistan, Bangladesh, Bhutan, the Maldives, Nepal and Sri Lanka), which has led to hostility and suspicion towards New Delhi on the part of its smaller neighbours.[22] Overall, India has not been able to contribute to regional cooperation in a meaningful way and has pursued reluctant policies in the management of several regional crises. Despite the introduction of his 'neighbourhood first' policy[23] and initial positive signals such as the invitation of all South Asian heads of state and government to his inauguration as prime minister,[24] Modi has not managed to reverse this trend.[25] In the following, the analysis will focus on India's reluctant approach to crisis management in Afghanistan and Nepal under Modi's government.

Afghanistan is the most conflict-ridden country in South Asia and, since the conclusion of the International Security Assistance Force (ISAF) mission and the handover of the responsibility for Afghanistan's security to the Afghan National Security Forces (ANSF) in 2014, the situation on the ground has worsened; the Taliban have expanded their presence again, and new groups such as the Islamic State-Khorasan (IS-K) have gained a foothold in the country.[26] Under the United Progressive Alliance governments of Manmohan Singh (2004–2009 and 2009–2014), India became Afghanistan's fifth-largest donor and was able to further expand the goodwill it enjoyed among the Afghan population through a mix of large-scale infrastructure projects (e.g. the Delaram-Zaranj highway, the Salma Dam and the new Parliament building in Kabul), small development projects and a well-established scholarship programme.[27] By contrast, in the field of security, India's policies were extremely reluctant as New Delhi pursued a hesitant (flip-flopping) and recalcitrant (rejecting and ignoring requests) approach on the provision of military equipment and cooperation requested by the Afghan government, including a failure to implement a 2011 Strategic Partnership Agreement in the subsequent years.[28]

Under Modi, not much has changed. India has a continued interest in the stabilisation of Afghanistan; it needs to avoid that the country becomes a base for terrorists able to carry out attacks against India, and it would like to see Afghanistan as a connectivity bridge to Central Asia.[29] However, Modi has not managed to bring about a substantive shift towards a more determined and responsive Indian policy. India's approach can still be classified as hesitant, as New Delhi did not take any initiatives to devise new ways to contribute to stabilising Afghanistan. While, in an apparently significant policy shift, India in 2015–2016 for the first time donated lethal military equipment to Afghanistan (four Mi-25 attack helicopters in addition to three HAL Cheetah light utility helicopters),[30] such support to the Afghan Air

Force came quite late, and in early 2018 all military helicopters delivered by India were reportedly grounded and needed repairs. According to Afghanistan's Ambassador to India, 'at times requests have been delayed for too long' to the disappointment of Kabul.[31] In March 2018, the Indian government agreed to buy four more refurbished Mi-24 helicopters for Afghanistan from Belarus,[32] and India has agreed to further support the Afghan Air Force through a trilateral cooperation with Russia, from where most spare parts need to be purchased.[33] However, requests for the delivery of other lethal military equipment have been denied so far.

In the case of Afghanistan, India's continued reluctance can be explained through the combination of competing international expectations and unclear domestic preferences. The Afghan government, with the exception of the initial months of Ashraf Ghani's presidency,[34] has been calling for greater engagement on the part of India in matters of weapons deliveries and of security more generally. Such requests were increasingly backed by Western countries, especially the US and the UK, which have been 'pushing India for a larger economic, but primarily military role'.[35] In particular, US President Trump went 'a step ahead [as compared to previous administrations] by openly inviting India to have an active role in Afghanistan'.[36] Such expectations however clash with those of Pakistan, which understands any kind of Indian engagement in Afghanistan as a vital threat to its own security.

Such competing international expectations have been met with unclear domestic preferences over Afghanistan in India. In fact, New Delhi is interested, on the one hand, in keeping its own influence on Afghanistan. On the other hand, it wants to limit Pakistan's influence over the country and therefore does not limit itself to an exclusively development-oriented approach. Instead, by signing a Strategic Partnership Agreement with Afghanistan, the Indian government has shown that it also aims to be engaged in matters of security. At the same time, the Indian government is aware that a more extensive security engagement would provoke its nuclear-armed rival Pakistan, which has long considered Afghanistan a hinterland that provides 'strategic depth' in the case of a war with India.[37] Pakistan and its proxies have in the past reacted violently to India's engagement in the country, as shown by repeated attacks on Indian personnel in Afghanistan. New Delhi's continued reluctance in conflict management in Afghanistan can therefore be explained by a combination of the need to balance between diametrically opposite international expectations (by the Afghan and Western governments, on the one hand, and by Pakistan, on the other) and unclear domestic preferences in India, which have prevented New Delhi from drastically curtailing its engagement. India's reluctance is not 'strategic' in the sense of appeasing competing expectations, as discussed above. It is rather a consequence of an interplay between international expectations and domestic arguing over competing norms. While there is a broad consensus among the Indian elite against any kind of 'boots on the ground' option,[38] other forms of engagement are debated rather explicitly by 'partisans' and 'conciliators' in the Indian establishment.[39] The Indian bureaucracy continues to stick to a 'Nehruvian' strategic culture focused on non-intervention, leading to a high degree of path dependency.[40] But at the same time, the BJP government of Prime Minister Modi has sought to side-line Nehruvian discourses and has rather relied on Hindu-nationalist ideology, which calls for a more 'muscular' approach to foreign policy. India's declining recalcitrance on the issue of lethal weapons supplies under Modi could be a first indicator of the formation of a more explicitly interventionist preference with regard to Afghanistan, which however still remains linked to the need to avoid outright war with Pakistan.

In the case of Nepal, the analysis focuses on a serious domestic political crisis related to the adoption of a new constitution. After the devastating earthquake of April 2015, Nepal's main political parties decided to speed up the constitutional process to replace the 2007 interim constitution, which had been adopted after the end of Nepal's civil war and the country's transition to democracy. The new constitution was passed on 20 September 2015, amid huge protests by disadvantaged groups dissatisfied with several of its provisions, which were considered to perpetuate the dominance of traditional upper caste hill elites.[41] Among the protesting groups were the Madhesis and Tharus of southern Nepal's Terai, a region that borders India and whose inhabitants have huge affinities toward their Indian neighbours. The protests went on for months, with over 50 casualties, mostly due to police firing into crowds. In that context, the otherwise open border between Nepal and India was closed for 135 days by Madhesi protesters, and the interruption of supplies originating from the blockade led to a humanitarian crisis.[42]

India's approach to crisis management in Nepal is almost a textbook case of reluctance understood as hesitation and recalcitrance. As Jha puts it, India's policy was characterised by 'inconsistency, ad-hoc policy making, multiplicity of power centres, conflicting messages, and absence of will'.[43] Moreover, India was recalcitrant all over again when it came to requests articulated by different political actors in Nepal, which were repeatedly disappointed. India has a long history of political meddling in Nepal and over the past decades has repeatedly struggled to keep its influence on that country, which in turn has sought to attenuate its dependence on India by seeking closer ties with China.[44] During the constitutional crisis, the Indian government followed an extremely contradictory policy. Initially, New Delhi supported the Madhesis' concerns and India's Foreign Secretary Jaishankar was sent to Kathmandu to put pressure on Nepal's government to delay the adoption of the new constitution and to make it more inclusive.[45] Later, India tacitly supported the blockade,[46] leading to disappointment and to a rapprochement with China on the part of the K. P. Oli government in Kathmandu. But the fear of losing its influence on Nepal to China ultimately led New Delhi to 'prod[…] the Madhesis to withdraw the blockade'.[47] In a new twist to its Nepal policy, in July 2016, India persuaded the Maoist leader Prachanda to withdraw from the governing coalition in Kathmandu, thereby side-lining the excessively China-friendly Prime Minister Oli, while it later 'pushed the Madhesi parties to participate in elections – even though they were deeply uncomfortable with the constitution, almost making a two year policy exercise futile'.[48] Ultimately, New Delhi's contradictory approach to Nepal under Prime Minister Modi led to a massive deterioration of bilateral relations and after the victory of the Left Alliance in Nepal's parliamentary elections in late 2017, India–Nepal relations reached a historical low.[49]

How can we explain India's highly reluctant policies in dealing with the crisis in Nepal? As opposed to the case of Afghanistan, domestic politics in Nepal were not a concern to the international community during the period analysed, so the only international expectations the Indian government was confronted with were those of different political actors in Nepal. But those expectations were highly divergent and, given the looming threat of growing Chinese influence in Nepal, they were taken seriously by the Indian government. Given India's long history of political influence on Nepal, any Indian move is an object of heated debate in Nepal, and India is the first international actor Nepalese parties and civil society seek help from, blame or just refer to, depending on the situation.[50] The political elites in Kathmandu therefore had expectations vis-à-vis India during the crisis (most notably, that it end its support for the Madhesi cause), the Nepalese government put pressure on India by 'playing the China card', and the marginalised groups in the Terai made use of their close relationship to the Indian population across the border to get New Delhi's support. Such competing expectations met unclear domestic preferences in India concerning the course to follow in Nepal. Some of them were related to a lack of bureaucratic capacity, which contributed to coordination problems in the way different sections of the Indian elite dealt with Nepal. Generally speaking, India's foreign policy capacity is limited by huge institutional deficiencies, including a tiny diplomatic corps[51] and individualistic decision making on the part of powerful foreign service officers.[52] Due to such capacity constraints and the ensuing lack of strategic planning, in cases like relations with Nepal, a range of actors who have direct ties to local elites tend to take over India's foreign policy.

Relatedly, in the case of Nepal there were underlying normative tensions among different constituencies in India. The Indian political landscape has long been fragmented in its approach to different sections of Nepal's society, from the hill elites to the army to the Maoists.[53] Within India, one particularly powerful constituency was the Hindu nationalist camp around the governing BJP, which had an interest in supporting Nepal's old elites (and even in reviving the Nepalese Hindu monarchy) to the detriment of the inclusion of minorities, especially the Madhesis.[54] However, as in the case of Afghanistan, the path-dependent Nehruvian notion of non-interference might have played a role in preventing India from openly intervening in a consistent manner. At the same time, the dramatically growing Chinese influence on Nepal and the need for India to counter it to keep its traditional sphere of influence (and against the backdrop of its declared 'neighbourhood first' policy) contributed to the difficulties in reaching a clear set of preferences vis-à-vis competing expectations from Nepal. As a result, the Modi government, despite its stability, ultimately pursued a reluctant approach.[55]

Brazil under Lula: determination and responsiveness in regional crisis management

Under President 'Lula' da Silva (2003–2011), Brazil became an increasingly active international player, with a clear intention to gain international recognition for its status as an emerging great power and a recognisable aspiration to regional leadership. Other than India, Brazil was not reluctant when it came to the management of conflicts and crises in its region. This analysis focuses particularly on Brazil's role in the United Nations Stabilization Mission in Haiti (MINUSTAH) from 2004, and on its engagement in the Colombian civil war between the Revolutionary Armed Forces of Colombia–People's Army (FARC) and the Colombian government during the years of the Lula presidency. Besides a range of domestic political crises in several South American countries, these were the two most severe crises in Brazil's extended neighbourhood during that period.

In the case of MINUSTAH, Brazil shed its initial reluctance, took over the leadership of this UN peacekeeping mission and pursued it without much hesitation or recalcitrance. A range of other South American countries participated in the mission under Brazilian leadership.[56] For the Brazilian government, crisis management in Haiti was a welcome opportunity to show its commitment to the United Nations – and government representatives explicitly depicted leadership in MINUSTAH as a way to gain international acceptance for Brazil's claim for a permanent seat in the UN Security Council.[57] At the same time, taking over the leadership of a UN peacekeeping mission was a remarkable development in Brazil's foreign and security policy, which had long been informed by a commitment to non-intervention.[58] In the case of MINUSTAH, the Brazilian government ultimately managed to pursue a predominantly consistent, non-reluctant policy course mainly because it could put forward a clear preference by allaying domestic fears and criticism in a process of arguing over the norms driving the mission, while at the same time aligning international expectations by global and regional actors.

At first, however, some elements of hesitation, and particularly some inconsistencies in Brazil's policies, could be observed in its approach to the crisis in Haiti. In fact, Brazil initially refused to participate in a Multinational Interim Force established with UNSC Resolution 1529 (on which it had voted in favour) citing this resolution's reference to Chapter VII, which allows for the use of force without the consent of the parties involved. Brazil's argument was that it could not participate in a mission to 'impose peace', among other things due to the provisions in Article 4 of its Constitution.[59] However, two months later Brazil agreed to participate in the multinational force under Resolution 1542, even though this resolution was equally based on Chapter VII.

The Brazilian government had initially been subjected to different international expectations. The US was not interested in further meddling with the situation in Haiti and its representatives were reportedly aware that a US presence in Haiti would be met with resistance.[60] France, the former colonial power, had similar concerns, and President Chirac called President Lula on the phone in March 2004 to ask for Brazil taking over the command of the UN mission – a wish that had the backing of UN Secretary General Kofi Annan.[61] While global-level actors therefore wanted Brazil to intervene, regional countries were very sceptical of such a mission (see, for example, criticism by countries like Chile and Argentina).[62] Domestically, the formation of a clear preference was initially hampered by a debate on the mission to Haiti, which was criticised (among others by intellectuals, MPs, representatives of unions and social movements, as well as by some members of Lula's PT) as an occupation force violating Haiti's sovereignty and reinforcing US hegemony.[63]

Ultimately, however, the Brazilian government managed to achieve a clear preference. A domestic coalition of diplomats and the military, which had an interest in Brazil's leadership of MINUSTAH as a tool to get international recognition and to 'maximize institutional gains',[64] respectively, managed to get support among the public and the parliament. Brazil therefore could pursue a determined, non-reluctant policy. The Brazilian government justified its bending to international pressure and its agreement to lead the multinational force under Resolution 1542 by arguing that in this Resolution, Chapter VII was mentioned only in one section and not in the introduction, and therefore it did not refer to the entire resolution.[65] Through this reinterpretation, the Brazilian government managed to frame MINUSTAH as a peacekeeping operation and to 'claim that [Brazil] was mostly concerned with humanitarian tasks and Haiti's development'.[66] This 'rhetorical exercise'[67] was an important move for reconciling contrasting international expectations and giving a direction to the domestic normative debate about Brazil's foreign engagement.[68]

The most virulent 'traditional' armed conflict in South America over the past decades has been the civil war in Colombia. Also in this case, the Brazilian government under Lula pursued a fairly consistent, not hesitant and thereby non-reluctant, approach to crisis management – albeit in a very different form, privileging low-key offers of mediation and support. Throughout the period analysed and even beyond, Brazil consistently defined the conflict as a domestic matter of Colombia, thereby refusing external interventions, and expressed support for a negotiated solution, in line with its own constitutionally-sanctioned foreign policy norms.[69] In that context, Brazil repeatedly offered to serve as a mediator and tried to portray itself as a neutral actor by condemning the FARC's crimes, but at the same time not declaring the FARC a terrorist organisation, which would have limited the room for negotiations.[70] Moreover, Brazil repeatedly provided logistical support in the liberation of hostages.[71] Overall, Brazil's interest in the conflict in Colombia was mostly related to the limitation of potential spill-over effects along the common border, given repeated cases of incursions by members of FARC into Brazilian territory and their connections to sections of the Brazilian drug mafia.[72]

Some elements of moderate recalcitrance were in place in Brazil's policy since Brazil was not ready to follow the Colombian government's call for labelling the FARC a terrorist organisation.[73] Brazil was also critical of US meddling with Colombia's affairs and of the militarisation related to Plan Colombia, and it wanted to avoid a further internationalisation of the conflict. However, under the Lula government, Brazil's approach to the Colombian civil war displayed no indicators of hesitation (lack of initiative, delaying or flip-flopping). Overall, therefore, Lula's Brazil followed a non-reluctant approach based on consistent but low-key offers of support. It could arguably do so because it developed a clear preference on the modalities of conflict resolution and, at the same time, it was not subject to competing international expectations. The Colombian government called for a labelling of the FARC as a terrorist organisation, but did not articulate other expectations concerning a more active Brazilian involvement in the conflict. This was mainly due to the ideological differences between Lula and Colombian President Uribe (2002–2010), which contributed to make the two countries 'distant neighbours'.[74] Only gradually did bilateral relations improve, as from 2009 Uribe got less support for his hard-line approach to the conflict from the US under the Obama administration, and therefore had to rely more on regional partners such as Brazil.[75] An indication of such improving relations was Uribe's decision to join the UNASUR Defence Council, which had been founded in 2009 at Brazil's initiative as a reaction to Colombian strikes against FARC camps on Ecuadorian territory.[76] This rapprochement, which continued under Colombia's president Santos, did not lead to specific calls for greater Brazilian engagement. Similarly, neither the US nor other international actors put pressure on the Brazilian government concerning crisis management in Colombia. In Brazil's domestic debate, conservative actors accused the Lula government of being too sympathetic to the FARC,[77] but generally there was a rather broad consensus among Brazil's political forces about pursuing a low-key approach to the Colombian conflict without getting enmeshed militarily.[78] All these factors ultimately allowed Brazil to pursue a non-reluctant approach to crisis management.

Conclusion

This contribution aimed to address the sometimes puzzling phenomenon of powerful countries that pursue hesitant, muddling-through, indecisive – 'reluctant' – courses of action when it comes to the management of crises in their neighbourhood that have the potential to adversely affect their interests and potentially even to destabilise them. To this end, the paper built upon a conceptualisation of reluctance based on the two necessary and jointly sufficient conditions of hesitation and recalcitrance, and it proposed an explanation for reluctance based on international expectations and domestic factors. In a first effort at theorising reluctance, it was hypothesised that governments will tend to adopt reluctant policies if they face expectations by international actors and, at the same time, do not have clear domestic preferences due to factors like government weakness, lack of bureaucratic capacity or domestic arguing over foreign policy norms. In the case of competing international expectations, they might also use a flip-flopping approach to temporarily appease different expectations. The empirical analysis focused on India and Brazil as 'rising powers' during phases of domestic political stability, and particularly on instances of regional crisis management by these two countries. It revealed that diametrically opposite expectations by international and regional actors concerning India's security engagement in Afghanistan, in combination with domestic normative debates and corresponding difficulties in devising clear preferences, have led to New Delhi's highly reluctant policy. In the case of Nepal's constitutional crisis, reluctance has been the outcome of competing expectations by different Nepalese actors, paired with lack of bureaucratic capacity (coordination problems) and normative disagreements in India. By contrast, Lula's Brazil was able to pursue a proactive and consistent policy towards Haiti by framing the mission in a way that allayed domestic concerns and aligned different international expectations. Brazil's approach to the conflict in Colombia reveals that a low-key engagement, if consistently pursued, does not amount to reluctance. In this case, Brazil had a clear preference for mediation and other forms of limited support, and it was not faced with competing international pressures.

Based on these initial findings on varying reluctance in India's and Brazil's regional crisis management efforts, further research will need to refine the proto-theory of reluctance developed in this contribution and to address a broader range of cases across different world regions. An analysis of longer-term trends is also a promising area of future research. In fact, reluctance might be deeply intertwined with rising powers' very process of 'rise', with its peculiar combination of increased international expectations (and sensitivity to them for status reasons) and domestic debates or insecurities about the new tasks related to growing power capabilities and international recognition. Further research will therefore need to study how reluctance varies over time and to what extent it might hamper rising powers' regional and global ambitions.

At the same time, reluctance is certainly not confined to rising powers or to the regional level of analysis. Powerful international actors, including established powers, often pursue hesitant and recalcitrant policies when it comes to global public goods provision. A better understanding of what drives reluctance in those cases could make a major contribution to addressing some of the most pressing problems of our time.

Disclosure statement

No potential conflict of interest was reported by the author.

Acknowledgements

I am grateful to Cordula Tibi Weber, without whose extensive and excellent research assistance this paper would not have been possible, and to Christoph Harig as well as to two anonymous reviewers for extremely helpful comments.

ORCID

Sandra Destradi (iD) http://orcid.org/0000-0001-7509-9349

Notes

1. On the notion that with power comes responsibility, see Zoellick, "Speech." The term 'rising powers' should be used carefully against the backdrop of massive domestic crises in countries like Brazil and South Africa. It will nevertheless be employed in this study as the focus of the empirical analysis is on periods that were generally considered to be phases of international ascendancy for rising powers.
2. Hochstetler and Milkoreit, "Responsibilities in Transition"; Narlikar, "Peculiar Chauvinism or Strategic Calculation?" On rising powers' likely impact on global governance, see Kahler, "Rising Powers and Global Governance."
3. On these countries as 'regional powers', see for example Nolte, "How to Compare Regional Powers."
4. For example, on Brazil's unwillingness to fully engage in South American regionalism, see Merke, "Neither Balance nor Bandwagon"; Burges, "Revisiting Consensual Hegemony." South Africa's engagement in southern Africa has similarly been described as 'full of ambiguities and contradictions'; Alden and Le Pere, "South Africa in Africa," 145.
5. Soares de Lima and Hirst, "Brazil as an Intermediate State"; Christensen, "Brazil's Foreign Policy Priorities."
6. Haass, *The Reluctant Sheriff*; Fehl, *Living with a Reluctant Hegemon*.
7. Destradi, "Reluctance in International Politics."
8. Goertz, *Social Science Concepts*, 5.
9. Destradi, "Reluctance in International Politics," 323.
10. Ibid., 325–8.
11. Ibid., 327.
12. Ibid., 328. Correspondingly, the indicators of hesitation refer to an actor's own policies, independent of interactions with others, while the indicators of recalcitrance always relate to an interaction with other actors. Indicators like 'delaying' and 'obstructionism' are therefore analytically distinct: delaying primarily refers to previously set own goals and timeframes, while obstructionism (whether it involves a temporal dimension or not) is explicitly aimed at initiatives promoted by others.
13. Ibid., 328.
14. Ibid., 325.
15. According to Destradi, reluctance does not have a single negative pole, but two negative poles: determination and responsiveness; Ibid., 324.
16. On the contestation of regional powers' policies, see Ebert et al., "Contestation in Asia."
17. Moravcsik, "Taking Preferences Seriously," 519. This is, of course, a simplification needed for analytical reasons.
18. I am grateful to an anonymous reviewer for highlighting this aspect to me.
19. Rathbun, "Uncertain About Uncertainty," 546.
20. Risse, "International Norms."

21. Competing expectations will by definition lead to recalcitrance, as not all of them can be addressed at the same time. But without the dimension of hesitation, this does not amount to reluctance.
22. Destradi, *India's Foreign and Security Policy in South Asia,* 56–61.
23. Passi and Bhatnagar, "India, India's Neighbourhood and Modi."
24. Swami, "Modi Invites Saarc Leaders."
25. On the more general issue of continuity and change under Modi, see Chatterjee Miller and Sullivan de Estrada, "India's Rise at 70"; Hall, "Is a 'Modi Doctrine' Emerging"; Hall, "Multialignment and Indian Foreign Policy."
26. International Crisis Group, "Afghanistan: Growing Challenges."
27. Sinha, "Rising Powers and Peacebuilding," 137–45.
28. Destradi, "India: A Reluctant Partner for Afghanistan."
29. Mahalingam, "India's Afghanistan Policy," 105.
30. Gady, "India's Plans to Buy Helicopter Gunships."
31. Haidar and Peri, "Afghan Army Chief Coming to India."
32. Laskar, "India Will Provide 4 Mi-24 Choppers."
33. Wagner, "India's Bilateral Security Relationship," 18.
34. Das, "Afghanistan's Relations with India and Iran."
35. Taneja, "India and the Afghan Taliban."
36. Ranade, "Trump's Afghanistan Strategy," 3.
37. Destradi, "India: A Reluctant Partner for Afghanistan," 106.
38. Ibid., 109.
39. Paliwal, *My Enemy's Enemy*, 206–10. The notion of 'uncertainty' in decision making does not seem to have much explanatory power as during the period analysed the situation in Afghanistan did not present entirely new challenges that might have caught the Indian bureaucracy or government off guard.
40. Hall, "The Persistence of Nehruvianism." Among the many works on strategic culture in India, see Tanham, "Indian Strategic Culture"; Bajpai, "Indian Strategic Culture."
41. Jha, "Nepal's Constitutional Politics."
42. International Crisis Group, "Nepal's Divisive New Constitution."
43. Jha, "How India Steadily Lost."
44. Destradi, *India's Foreign and Security Policy in South Asia,* 96–128.
45. Majumder, "Why India Is Concerned."
46. Jha, "India Must Firmly Push for Madhesi Inclusion."
47. Jha, "How India Steadily Lost."
48. Ibid.
49. Kaura, "Grading India's Neighborhood Diplomacy."
50. For details on India's involvement over the years, see Jha, "A Nepali Perspective."
51. Markey, "Developing India's Foreign Policy Software."
52. Chatterjee Miller, "India's Feeble Foreign Policy," 14–16.
53. For example, in 2005, towards the end of Nepal's civil war, the Indian government supported the Royal Nepalese Army through training in its fight against the Maoist rebels, while the Ministry of External Affairs gradually came to embrace the notion of including the Maoists in the political process, and Indian politicians ultimately mediated a peace agreement between the representatives of Nepal's democratic parties and the Maoists with the support of the Indian government; Destradi, *India's Foreign and Security Policy in South Asia*, 112–13.
54. Muni, "With the Left Alliance."
55. As for Afghanistan, the notion of 'uncertainty' in decision making does not necessarily apply to the case of Nepal since India has a long experience in dealing with the troubled politics of that country and was not confronted by an entirely new type of crisis that could be interpreted as challenging the cognitive ability of policy makers.
56. Argentina, Bolivia, Chile, Ecuador, Paraguay, Peru and Uruguay contributed troops. Colombia was among the contributors of civilian/police personnel.

57. Gauthier and John de Sousa, "Brazil in Haiti," 1. This connection was, however, denied by Brazil's Foreign Minister Amorim; Ministério das Relações Exteriores, "Entrevista Do Ministro Celso Amorim, 24/3/2008."
58. Christensen, "Brazil's Foreign Policy Priorities," 277.
59. Gauthier and John de Sousa, "Brazil in Haiti," 1.
60. Fernández Moreno et al., "Trapped between Many Worlds," 383.
61. Andrade, "Brasil Tem Tropa De 1.100 Militares."
62. Hirst, "La Intervención Sudamericana En Haiti."
63. cmi brasil, "Manifesto Da Campanha."
64. Harig and Kenkel, "Are Rising Powers Consistent or Ambiguous Foreign Policy Actors?" 636.
65. Ibid., 2.
66. Harig and Kenkel, "Are Rising Powers Consistent or Ambiguous Foreign Policy Actors?" 635.
67. Ibid.
68. Christensen, "Brazil's Foreign Policy Priorities," 277.
69. Ministério das Relações Exteriores, "Para Pinheiro Guimarães, AI Precisa De Um Plano Marshall."
70. Ministério das Relações Exteriores, "Íntegra Da Entrevista De Celso Amorim, 5/5/2008."
71. Candeas, "Brasil Y Colombia," 299.
72. Latinnews, "Tracking Trends."
73. Tarapués Sandino, "Colombia Y Brasil," 432.
74. Flemes, "Brasil-Colombia"; Soares de Lima and Hirst, "Brazil as an Intermediate State," 35.
75. Latinnews, "Colombia Reassesses Its Foreign Policy Priorities."
76. Ibid.
77. Latinnews, "Uribe's Diplomatic Influence Waxes."
78. Istituto de Estudos Socioeconômicos, "Tabelas."

Bibliography

Alden, Chris, and Garth Le Pere. "South Africa in Africa: Bound to Lead?" *Politikon* 36, no. 1 (2009): 145–169. doi:10.1080/02589340903155443.

Andrade, Renato. 2004. "Brasil Tem Tropa De 1.100 Militares Para Ir Ao Haiti." *gazeta digital*, March 5. http://www.gazetadigital.com.br/conteudo/show/secao/10/materia/30135.

Bajpai, Kanti. "Indian Strategic Culture." In *South Asia in 2020*, edited by Michael R. Chambers, 245–304. Carlisle, PA: Strategic Studies Institute, 2002.

Burges, Sean W. "Revisiting Consensual Hegemony: Brazilian Regional Leadership in Question." *International Politics* 52, no. 2 (2015): 193–207. doi:10.1057/ip.2014.43.

Candeas, Alessandro. "Brasil y Colombia: vecinos otrora distantes descubren el potencial de su relación." In *Colombia y Brasil: ¿Socios estratégicos en la construcción de Suramérica?*, edited by Eduardo Pastrana Buelvas, Stefan Jost, and Daniel Flemes, 283–308. Bogotá: Editorial Pontificia Universidad Javeriana, 2012.

Chatterjee Miller, Manjari, and Kate Sullivan de Estrada, eds. "Special Issue: 'India's Rise at 70.'" *International Affairs* 93, no. 1 (2017): 1–198. doi:10.1093/ia/iiw036.

Chatterjee Miller, Manjari. "India's Feeble Foreign Policy." *Foreign Affairs* 92, no. 3 (2013): 14–19.

Christensen, Steen Fryba. "Brazil's Foreign Policy Priorities." *Third World Quarterly* 34, no. 2 (2013): 271–86. doi:10.1080/01436597.2013.775785.

cmi brasil. 2004. "Manifesto Da Campanha: Não ao envio de tropas do Brasil ao Haiti." April 8. https://midiaindependente.org/pt/red/2004/04/277171.shtml.

Das, Nihar Ranjan. "Afghanistan's Relations with India and Iran: An Assessment of the Ghani Period." Indian Council of World Affairs Issue Brief, July 27, 2016.

Destradi, Sandra. "India: A Reluctant Partner for Afghanistan." *The Washington Quarterly* 37, no. 2 (2014): 103–117. doi:10.1080/0163660X.2014.926212.

Destradi, Sandra. "Reluctance in International Politics: A Conceptualization." *European Journal of International Relations* 23, no. 2 (2017): 315–40.

Destradi, Sandra. *India's Foreign and Security Policy in South Asia: Regional Power Strategies*. London and New York: Routledge, 2012.

Ebert, Hannes, Daniel Flemes, and Georg Strüver. "The Politics of Contestation in Asia: How Japan and Pakistan Deal with Their Rising Neighbors." *The Chinese Journal of International Politics* 7, no. 2 (2014): 221–260.

Fehl, Caroline. *Living with a Reluctant Hegemon: Explaining European Responses to US Unilateralism*. Oxford: Oxford University Press, 2012.

Fernández Moreno, Marta, Carlos Chagas Vianna Braga, and Maíra Siman Gomes. "Trapped between Many Worlds: A Post-Colonial Perspective on the Un Mission in Haiti (Minustah)." *International Peacekeeping* 19, no. 3 (2012): 377–392. doi:10.1080/13533312.2012.696389.

Flemes, Daniel. "Brasil-Colombia: ¿De vecinos distantes a socios estratégicos?" *Iberoamericana* XV, no. 60 (2015): 171–174.

Gady, Franz-Stefan. 2018. "India's Plans to Buy Helicopter Gunships for Afghanistan." *The Diplomat*, January 2. https://thediplomat.com/2018/01/indias-plans-to-buy-helicopter-gunships-for-afghanistan/

Gauthier, Amélie, and Sarah John de Sousa. "Brazil in Haiti: Debate over the Peacekeeping Mission." FRIDE Comment, November 2006.

Goertz, Gary. *Social Science Concepts: A User's Guide*. Princeton, NJ: Princeton University Press, 2006.

Haass, Richard N. *The Reluctant Sheriff: The United States after the Cold War*. New York: Council on Foreign Relations Press, 1997.

Haidar, Suhasini, and Dinakar Peri. 2016. "Afghan Army Chief Coming to India with Revised Wish List." *The Hindu*, July 25. https://www.thehindu.com/news/national/Afghan-Army-chief-coming-to-India-with-revised-wish-list/article14507929.ece

Hall, Ian. "Is a 'Modi Doctrine' Emerging in Indian Foreign Policy?" *Australian Journal of International Affairs* 69, no. 3 (2015): 247–252. doi:10.1080/10357718.2014.1000263.

Hall, Ian. "Multialignment and Indian Foreign Policy under Narendra Modi." *The Round Table* 105, no. 3 (2016): 271–286. doi:10.1080/00358533.2016.1180760.

Hall, Ian. "The Persistence of Nehruvianism in India's Strategic Culture." In *Strategic Asia 2016-17*, edited by Ashley J. Tellis, Alison Szalwinski, and Michael Wills, 141–167. Seattle: National Bureau of Asian Research, 2016.

Harig, Christoph, and Kai Michael Kenkel. "Are Rising Powers Consistent or Ambiguous Foreign Policy Actors? Brazil, Humanitarian Intervention and the 'Graduation Dilemma.'" *International Affairs* 93, no. 3 (2017): 625–641. doi:10.1093/ia/iix051.

Hirst, Mônica. "La intervención Sudamericana en Haiti." FRIDE Comentario, April 2007.

Hochstetler, Kathryn, and Manjana Milkoreit. "Responsibilities in Transition: Emerging Powers in the Climate Change Negotiations." *Global Governance* 21, no. 2 (2015): 205–226.

International Crisis Group. "Afghanistan: Growing Challenges." *Commentary/Asia*, April 30, 2017. https://www.crisisgroup.org/asia/south-asia/afghanistan/afghanistan-growing-challenges.

International Crisis Group. "Nepal's Divisive New Constitution: An Existential Crisis." Report no. 276/Asia, April 4, 2016. https://www.crisisgroup.org/asia/south-asia/nepal/nepal%E2%80%99s-divisive-new-constitution-existential-crisis.

Istituto de Estudos Socioeconômicos. "Tabelas." In *Plano Colômbia: Perspectivas do Parlamento Brasileiro*, 65–76. Brasília: INESC, 2002.

Jha, Prashant. "A Nepali Perspective on International Involvement in Nepal." In *Nepal in Transition: From People's War to Fragile Peace*, edited by Sebastian von Einsiedel, David M. Malone, and Suman Pradhan, 332–358. Cambridge: Cambridge University Press, 2012.

Jha, Prashant. 2015. "Nepal's Constitutional Politics: It's Time to Drop the Arrogance." *Hindustan Times*, August 25. https://www.hindustantimes.com/analysis/nepal-s-constitutional-politics-it-s-time-to-drop-the-arrogance/story-uAyhYTOeAcVvqQ2ftHDqCN.html

Jha, Prashant. 2017. "How India Steadily Lost All Its Leverage in Nepal." *Hindustan Times*, December 23. https://www.hindustantimes.com/opinion/how-india-steadily-lost-all-its-leverage-in-nepal/story-eyZcX3OOVJRVqJvP7EXH0O.html

Jha, Prashant. 2017. "India Must Firmly Push for Madhesi Inclusion with the Nepali President." *Hindustan Times*, April 18. https://www.hindustantimes.com/authors/india-must-firmly-push-for-madhesi-inclusion-with-the-nepali-president/story-WHz8glB8xIJSepSqf3Ccnl.html

Kahler, Miles. "Rising Powers and Global Governance: Negotiating Change in a Resilient Status Quo." *International Affairs* 89, no. 3 (2013): 711–729. doi:10.1111/1468-2346.12041.

Kaura, Vinay. 2018. "Grading India's Neighborhood Diplomacy." *The Diplomat*, January 1. https://the-diplomat.com/2017/12/grading-indias-neighborhood-diplomacy/

Laskar, Rezaul H. 2018. "India Will Provide 4 Mi-24 Choppers to Kabul, Says Afghan Envoy." *Hindustan Times*, March 27. https://www.hindustantimes.com/world-news/india-will-provide-4-mi-24-choppers-to-kabul-says-afghan-envoy/story-HGvDXi8b6D0fTT8unBwPMO.html

Latinnews. "Colombia Reassesses Its Foreign Policy Priorities." Latin American Regional Report, *Andean Group*, March 2009.

Latinnews. "Tracking Trends." Latin American Weekly Report, WR-10-21, 2010.

Latinnews. "Uribe's Diplomatic Influence Waxes." Latin American Regional Report, *Andean Group*, August 2008.

Mahalingam, V. "India's Afghanistan Policy." *CLAWS Journal* 15 (2016): 91–111.

Majumder, Sanjoy. 2015. "Why India Is Concerned About Nepal's Constitution." *BBC News*, September 22. https://www.bbc.com/news/world-asia-india-34313280

Markey, Daniel. "Developing India's Foreign Policy Software." *Asia Policy* 8 (2009): 73–96. doi:10.1353/asp.2009.0025.

Merke, Federico. "Neither Balance nor Bandwagon: South American International Society Meets Brazil's Rising Power." *International Politics* 52, no. 2 (2015): 178–192. doi:10.1057/ip.2014.49.

Ministério das Relações Exteriores. 2008. "Entrevista do Ministro Celso Amorim ao programa Roda Viva, 24/3/2008." http://www.itamaraty.gov.br/pt-BR/politica-externa/diplomacia-economi-ca-comercial-e-financeira/163-discursos-artigos-e-entrevistas/7961-entrevista-concedida-pelo-ministro-das-relacoes-exteriores-embaixador-celso-amorim-ao-programa-roda-viva-sao-paulo-sp-24-03-2008.

Ministério das Relações Exteriores. 2008. "Íntegra da entrevista de Celso Amorim (Entrevista do Ministro Celso Amorim ao repórter Luiz Carlos Azenha, 5/5/2008)." http://www.itamaraty.gov.br/pt-BR/discursos-artigos-e-entrevistas-categoria/ministro-das-relacoes-exteriores-entrevis-tas/7969-entrevista-concedida-pelo-ministro-das-relacoes-exteriores-embaixador-celso-amorim-ao-reporter-luiz-carlos-azenha-brasilia-df-05-05-2008.

Ministério das Relações Exteriores. 2008. "Para Pinheiro Guimarães, AL precisa de um Plano Marshall (Entrevista Secretário-Geral, Embaixador Samuel Pinheiro Guimarães, ao jornal Valor Econômico, 14/07/2008)". http://www.itamaraty.gov.br/discursos-artigos-e-entrevistas-categoria/secretario-geral-das-relacoes-exteriores-entrevistas/5924-para-pinheiro-guimaraes-al-precisa-de-um-plano-marshall-entrevista-secretario-geral-embaixador-samuel-pinheiro-guimaraes-ao-jornal-valor-economico-14-07-2008.

Moravcsik, Andrew. "Taking Preferences Seriously: A Liberal Theory of International Politics." *International Organization* 51, no. 4 (1997): 513–553. doi:10.1162/002081897550447.

Muni, S. D. 2017. "With the Left Alliance Now Dominant in Nepal, India Must Reach out with Positive Agenda." *The Wire*, December 16. https://thewire.in/external-affairs/nepal-left-alliance-uml

Narlikar, Amrita. "Peculiar Chauvinism or Strategic Calculation? Explaining the Negotiating Strategy of a Rising India." *International Affairs* 82, no. 1 (2006): 59–76. doi:10.1111/j.1468-2346.2006.00515.x.

Nolte, Detlef. "How to Compare Regional Powers: Analytical Concepts and Research Topics." *Review of International Studies* 36, no. 4 (2010): 889–993.

Paliwal, Avinash. *My Enemy's Enemy: India in Afghanistan from the Soviet Invasion to the US Withdrawal.* Noida: HarperCollins, 2017.

Passi, Ritika, and Aryman Bhatnagar. "India, India's Neighbourhood and Modi: Setting the Stage." In *Neighbourhood First: Navigating Ties under Modi*, edited by Aryman Bhatnagar and Ritika Passi, 3–12. New Delhi: ORF, 2016.

Ranade, Akshay. Trump's Afghanistan Strategy and Emerging Alignments in the Region: Implications for India. *ORF Issue Brief*, November 2017.

Rathbun, Brian C. "Uncertain About Uncertainty: Understanding the Multiple Meanings of a Crucial Concept in International Relations Theory." *International Studies Quarterly* 51, no. 3 (2007): 533–557. doi:10.1111/j.1468-2478.2007.00463.x.

Risse, Thomas. "International Norms and Domestic Change: Arguing and Communicative Behavior in the Human Rights Area." *Politics & Society* 27, no. 4 (1999): 529–559. doi:10.1177/0032329299027004004.

Sinha, Shakti. "Rising Powers and Peacebuilding: India's Role in Afghanistan." In *Rising Powers and Peacebuilding*, edited by Charles T. Call, and Cedric de Coning, 129–165. Cham: Springer, 2017.

Soares de Lima, Maria Regina, and Mônica Hirst. "Brazil as an Intermediate State and Regional Power: Action, Choice and Responsibilities." *International Affairs* 82, no. 1 (2006): 21–40. doi:10.1111/j.1468-2346.2006.00513.x.

Swami, Praveen. 2014. "In a First, Modi Invites SAARC Leaders for His Swearing-In." *The Hindu*, May 21. https://www.thehindu.com/news/national/in-a-first-modi-invites-saarc-leaders-for-his-swearingin/article6033710.ece

Taneja, Kabir. 2017. "India and the Afghan Taliban." *The Diplomat*, November 30. https://thediplomat.com/2017/11/india-and-the-afghan-taliban/

Tanham, George. "Indian Strategic Culture." *Washington Quarterly* 15, no.1 (1992): 129–142. doi:10.1080/01636609209550082.

Tarapués Sandino, Diego Fernando. "Colombia y Brasil en la lucha contra el crimen transnacional: una revisión a sus posturas, acciones y estrategias de seguridad." In *Colombia y Brasil: ¿Socios estratégicos en la construcción de Suramérica?*, edited by Eduardo Pastrana Buelvas, Stefan Jost; and Daniel Flemes, 423–52. Bogotá: Editorial Pontificia Universidad Javeriana, 2012.

Wagner, Christian. "India's Bilateral Security Relationship in South Asia." *Strategic Analysis* 42, no. 1 (2018): 15–28. doi:10.1080/09700161.2017.1418952.

Zoellick, Robert B. "Speech at George Washington University ahead of this Year's Annual Meetings Washington, United States." September 14, 2011. http://www.worldbank.org/en/news/speech/2011/09/14/the-world-bank-group-president-robert-b-zoellick-speech-at-george-washington-university-ahead-of-this-years-annual-meetings0.

Rising powers and the global nuclear order: a structural study of India's integration

Harsh V. Pant and Arka Biswas

ABSTRACT
The global nuclear order has been built around the Treaty on the Non-Proliferation of Nuclear Weapons (NPT), primarily aimed at addressing the challenges of nuclear non-proliferation. In the last two decades, this order has faced growing challenges from the demands of emerging nuclear powers which it has been unable to meet effectively. These powers have either been outside the order, like India, Israel and Pakistan, or withdrawn from it, like North Korea, or could leave in future due to arguably compelling security concerns, like Iran, Japan and South Korea. These nations and the challenges they pose to the global nuclear order are mostly considered unique and are treated as exceptional. This paper examines the case of India which has found partial acceptance into the extant order from being a pariah nuclear state outside the NPT to a de facto nuclear weapon state designated by the US–India civil nuclear cooperation pact of 2008. It explicates the ongoing process of its integration into the order, underlining why this task remains daunting. Other than factors unique to India, the case of its rise in the global nuclear order captures the structural shortcomings of the extant order. While these underlying shortcomings remain, new nuclear powers, with or without support from the established ones, are likely to challenge the order in future.

Introduction

India's relationship with the global nuclear order has been unique. With its 'peaceful nuclear explosion' of 1974 and with its decision to not sign the Treaty on the Non-Proliferation of Nuclear Weapons (NPT) as a non-nuclear weapon state (NNWS), India was viewed by the global nuclear order and the larger international system as a pariah nuclear state for decades. Much like other states that acquired nuclear weapons capability after 1 January 1967, India was subject to international criticism and sanctions.

The relationship in question was expected to slide further downhill following India's nuclear tests of May 1998 and New Delhi's decision to operationalise its nuclear weapons capability, reflected through its draft nuclear doctrine of 1999 and the official doctrine of 2003.[1] It, however, witnessed a dramatic turnaround in the following decade. In 2000, while the NPT held its review conference, India's then Minister of External Affairs, Jaswant Singh, in an address to the Indian Parliament, noted that while India would stay outside the NPT, it will uphold all the principles enshrined in the Treaty, especially in curbing horizontal proliferation of nuclear weapons and related sensitive items.

From there to the successful negotiation of the civil nuclear cooperation agreement with the US, acquiring waiver from the Nuclear Suppliers Group (NSG) to the condition of implementing full-scope safeguards to engage in global nuclear commerce in 2008, to joining the Missile Technology Control Regime (MTCR), the Wassenaar Arrangement (WA) and the Australia Group (AG) that broadly form part of the global nuclear order, in 2016, 2017 and 2018, respectively, India's journey has indeed been exceptional. Yet, daunting challenges remain in the completion of India's integration into the global nuclear order. The debate over India's membership application to the NSG, which forms a critical component of the global nuclear order, showcases the same. China's greater power in both the nuclear order and international system permits it to block India's path of further integration into the nuclear order.

Why was India's exceptional partial integration into the global nuclear order possible and what explains the challenges that remain to India's complete integration? This study attempts to address these two questions using realist theory. If liberalism postulates that international institutions are effective because they lead to positive gains for all states living under an anarchical international structure, constructivists believe that international institutions work as they engender a shared understanding among states based on similar norms and rules.[2] Realism, on the other hand, argues that international institutions, like all other aspects of international politics, are primarily an avenue of power politics and help codify existing power structures.[3] Change within institutions therefore does not emanate out of concerns of positive gains or an inclination to follow norms and rules; it is much more predicated upon interests of its constituents and the balance of power among them, both of which are subject to change. The India–US nuclear deal, in its essence, represented the change in both the interests and power of these two states in global politics.

The article begins by laying out the process of India's partial integration into the global nuclear order to date. The following section employs a realist framework to explain why India's integration was possible. The third section examines the extent to which this framework also explains the challenges that remain to India's complete integration. The study concludes that the structural framework holds credible explanatory power over India's rise in the global nuclear order as well as the challenges that remain to India's complete integration into the order. It also explicates what that means for the extant global nuclear order, especially as more rising nuclear powers challenge the order in future.

Two decades of India's partial integration

The process of India's integration with the global nuclear order commenced with the Indian government publicly announcing a change in its approach to the central pillar of that order – the NPT. As representatives of the states signatory to the NPT gathered for the Treaty's 2000 Review Conference, then India's Minister of External Affairs, Jaswant Singh, addressing the Indian Parliament, spoke of India's 'compliance' with the NPT's objectives and principles. Singh stated that while 'India may not be a party to the NPT, [its] conduct has always been consistent with the key provisions of the treaty as they apply to nuclear weapon states'.[4] This change in India's approach to the NPT was acknowledged again in 2005, during the NPT Review Conference, by then India's Minister of External Affairs, Natwar Singh. Explaining the significance of this change in India's position towards the NPT, Raja Mohan notes that '[e]ven as [India] recognized that the NPT system would not be able to confer the formal status of a nuclear-weapon state on India, New Delhi was confident enough to extend political support to the NPT and its objectives'.[5]

The India–US civil nuclear initiative announced in 2005 was premised on the political understanding that, while India remains outside the NPT, it will contribute to the global non-proliferation cause through other institutions and mechanisms. This was explicitly captured in the 18 July 2005 joint statement, wherein the US government, while acknowledging 'India's strong commitment to preventing WMD proliferation', further recognised India 'as a responsible state with advanced nuclear technology', which should receive 'the same benefits and advantages as other such states'.[6] The political premise of the India–US civil nuclear initiative has been largely accepted by the international community. For instance, the NSG in 2008 granted India the waiver from the requirement of implementing the International Atomic Energy Agency's (IAEA's) full-scope safeguards for engaging in international nuclear trade.[7] Subsequently, in 2008 following the separation of civilian and military nuclear facilities by India, the Board of Governors of the IAEA approved a safeguards agreement that placed India's civilian nuclear facilities under the IAEA's watch.[8] The Additional Protocol to the safeguards agreement was approved by the IAEA in March 2009[9] and it entered into force on 25 July 2014.[10]

Continuing the process of its integration into the global nuclear order, the Indian government, with support from the US and other like-minded governments, began working towards joining the four export control bodies – NSG, MTCR, WA and AG. In a joint statement issued by the Indian Prime Minister Manmohan Singh and US President Barack Obama on 8 November 2010, it was noted that:

> the United States intends to support India's full membership in the four multilateral export control regimes (Nuclear Suppliers Group, Missile Technology Control Regime, Australia Group, and Wassenaar Arrangement) in a phased manner, and to consult with regime members to encourage the evolution of regime membership criteria, consistent with maintaining the core principles of these regimes, as the Government of India takes steps towards the full adoption of the regimes' export control requirements to reflect its prospective membership, with both processes moving forward together.[11]

In its quest to join these export control bodies, India updated its list of Special Chemicals, Organisms, Materials, Equipment and Technology (SCOMET) several times over the last decade.[12] India's domestic controls over export of these items from the SCOMET list are enforced via legislations that meet the guidelines of these multilateral bodies.[13] For instance, India had met the guidelines of the NSG and the MTCR through its national export control framework by 2015. This was acknowledged by the US President Barack Obama in January 2015 during his visit to New Delhi. President Obama stated that 'India meets NSG and MTCR requirements … and that [the US] supports India's early application and eventual membership in all four regimes'.[14]

The US government's support for India's inclusion in the four export control bodies builds upon the political understanding established in 2005 that India will support the NPT from outside and contribute to the global non-proliferation efforts by joining other institutions and mechanisms of the order. Over the years, this understanding on the benefits of bringing India into the global nuclear order, established through memberships to the four export control regimes, was endorsed by other established powers as well. For instance, a 2010 joint statement by then Russian President Dmitry Medvedev and then Indian Prime Minister Manmohan Singh, during President Medvedev's visit to India, noted:

> India and the Russian Federation are interested in strengthening multilateral export control regimes as an important component of the global non-proliferation regime. In this regard, the Russian side expressed readiness to assist and promote a discussion and positive decision in the NSG on India's full membership in the NSG, and welcomed India's intention to seek full membership. India underscored its determination to actively contribute to international efforts aimed at strengthening nuclear non-proliferation regime. Russia also took into positive consideration India's interest in full membership in MTCR and the Wassenaar Arrangement.[15]

Similarly, the joint statement, issued during French President Mr. Francois Hollande's visit to India on 14–15 February 2013, noted that 'France also reiterates its support to India joining the Nuclear Suppliers Group and other export controls bodies'.[16] The joint statement issued during the India–United Kingdom summit of 2013, it was noted that 'the leaders agreed to work actively together to achieve India's ambitions to join the major export control regimes (Nuclear Suppliers Group, Missile Technology Control Group; Australia Group; Wassenaar Arrangement)'.[17] The joint statement issued after the second round of Indo–German inter-governmental consultations held in Berlin in April 2013 notes, 'Both sides agree to continue working together to prepare the ground for India to accede to the export control regimes and thereby strengthen the international non-proliferation regime'.[18] Finally, in the joint statement with Indian Prime Minister Manmohan Singh, dated 17 October 2012, 'Prime Minister Ms Julia Gillard noted India's sound non-proliferation record and expressed Australia's recognition of the importance of India's engagement with the four multilateral export control regimes with the objective of full membership'.[19]

Despite this critical support, India had difficulty in completing its integration into the global nuclear order. Consequently, New Delhi stepped up its efforts in reaching out to members of all four export control bodies to both expand and consolidate the political understanding for its integration into the global nuclear order. It is a result of the Modi government's proactive engagement policy that India was able to secure support from countries like Japan,[20] Canada[21] and South Korea,[22] which had traditionally held a strong position against India's nuclear programme.

India is now member to the MTCR, WA and AG. It applied for membership to the NSG in May 2016, a month before the Seoul plenary of the NSG, after over a decade of cooperation with the Group.[23] Its application to the NSG, however, has hit a block. Consensus is still to be reached in the NSG on whether India should be included and what implications that would have on the NPT due to the overlap between the Group's and the Treaty's nuclear non-proliferation objectives. Of the countries that have not yet joined the consensus over granting India the NSG membership, China has been the most vocal but not the only one. Thus, while, with the 2008 NSG waiver and with the memberships to the MTCR, WA and AG, India has been partially integrated into the global nuclear order, the completion of that integration process is contingent on India securing entry to the NSG as well.

Explaining India's partial integration

From being viewed as a pariah state by the global nuclear order, India has traversed a long way into being partially integrated into the order. India's case has indeed been an exception considering that other states that challenged the order did not meet the same fate. What explains India's exceptionalism?

The global nuclear order as it was created during the Cold War was in part a product of the power structure of the international system.[24] On the fronts the two superpowers shared interests, significant progress was made. Major arms control initiatives negotiated between the US and the Soviet Union were possible because of the stability induced by the bipolar system. Nuclear non-proliferation was another such front. The decision to accept 1 January 1967 as the cut-off date for a state to be a legitimate nuclear-have was acceptable because those nuclear-haves did not pose significant challenge to the bipolar structure of the international system, they were largely observed as status quo powers. Other machineries of nuclear and missile non-proliferation, as conceptualised and institutionalised, were designed to reinforce that structure.

Following the end of the Cold War, the US emerged as the sole superpower and it enjoyed what is referred to as the unipolar moment. The US supremacy in the international system remain unchallenged for the large parts of the two decades following the end of the Cold War. Developments pertaining to the global nuclear order in this period, including the indefinite extension of the NPT in 1995 and the negotiation of the Comprehensive Test Ban Treaty in 1996, reinforced the structure of the international system led by the US.

India challenged the global nuclear order in 1998 by conducting tests and proclaiming itself a de facto nuclear weapon state. Yet, within a decade of the tests, India signed a civil nuclear cooperation agreement with the US and acquired a waiver from the NSG on the condition of implementing full scope safeguards of the IAEA to engage in global nuclear commerce – a status previously enjoyed only by the five nuclear weapon states of the NPT.

Studies have attempted to examine if the structural framework explains India's partial integration into the global nuclear order. Ji Yeon-jung, for instance, argues that structuralism fails to explain India's rise in the global nuclear order since India's case does not reflect the typical elements of a classical revisionist state challenging the status quo, even if India, like all rising powers, has sought to revise the global nuclear order to better its relative position.[25] Yeon-jung assesses recent literature around the behaviour of rising powers that challenge the dominant structural theories of state behaviour. She studies the work of George Tsebelis, who postulates that rising powers seek to acquire the status of a 'veto player' – 'an individual or collective actor whose agreement is necessary for policy change' – by increasing their influence and political will in order to partly or entirely reconstruct the international political consensus.[26] Amrita Narlikar, in order to gauge how India has attempted to acquire the status of a veto player, develops a theory that presents several stages which a rising power operates on in changing the existing global order, including the acquisition of the agenda-setting power and selective and flexible coalition building.[27] Yeon-jung applies this model of veto-power strategy to explain India's rise in the global nuclear order by studying India's cooperation with members of the NSG. Yeon-jung correctly assesses how India has developed coalitions with the US and other like-minded members of the NSG to build consensus and how the veto-power strategy explains India's partial integration with the global nuclear order.

However, the veto-power strategy does not explain the challenges that remain to India's complete accommodation within the global nuclear order – why China, for instance, blocked India's membership to the NSG. Before attempting to explain those challenges, it might be interesting to re-examine India's case through the framework of realism and particularly the role of changing balance of power on international institutions, since that may explain both India's partial integration and the challenges that remain.

It is important to highlight here that the global nuclear order and the structure of the international system are two distinct entities and, as mentioned earlier, often the order in question can be viewed as a product of the structure of the international system. Even though India openly challenged the global nuclear order in 1998 and has sought to better its position in the order since, it has largely remained a status quo power insofar as the structure of the international system is concerned. That India's rise was not viewed as a threat to the structure of the international system by the sole superpower was evident from the efforts Washington undertook to facilitate India's rise. On the other hand, the rise of China is viewed in Washington DC with great anxiety because Beijing is considered to be a revisionist state. To restrain China's rise particularly in Asia and balancing its growing economic-military power, India is viewed as a natural partner especially when New Delhi is rising both economically and militarily. Accommodating India in the global nuclear order was therefore a part of US strategy to maintain its hegemony in Asia while simultaneously balancing China. Helping India's rise in the global order serves US national interests.

In the last two decades therefore, US and India have made significant strides in their bilateral relationship. US signed several other pacts of cooperation covering domains of civilian space, high-technology trade, military and missile defense, and terrorism and regional stability in the 2000s.[28] These agreements marked a dramatic shift in the US approach to India and captured the views in Washington on the role India could play in preserving the structure of the international system. Of these agreements, most critical was arguably the one on civil nuclear cooperation as that suggested 'a reversal of more than three decades of US nonproliferation policy', capturing how the sustenance of the structure of the international system took precedence over the sanctity of the global nuclear order.[29] This was also captured in Condoleezza Rice's testimonies before the House and Senate Committees as the US Secretary of State in 2006, wherein she identified India to be 'a rising global power that could be a pillar of stability in a rapidly changing Asia', arguing that a strong bilateral relationship with India, anchored around the civil nuclear deal, would allow the US to ensure sustenance of stability in Asia.[30]

While the Indian and the US governments dramatically increased their bilateral engagements to establish a strategic partnership, there were opponents to such partnership in both their capitals. Opponents in New Delhi, for instance, argued that the pact would constrain the expansion of India's nuclear arsenal in the future.[31] That the US was invested in Pakistan for its objectives of stabilising Afghanistan was another pitfall. There were also concerns raised on the nature of the military and high-technology trade being more of a donor–recipient kind than of a true partnership with joint investment, co-development and technology-sharing. Similarly, concerns were raised in Washington about the likely consequences of the US decision to challenge the global nuclear order, especially on the non-proliferation front, by virtually offering India the status of a nuclear weapon state, despite it being outside the NPT.[32] Another concern flagged was that India was unlikely to act as a 'balancer' against

China, especially on terms imposed by a foreign power – hinting at India's long-held policy of non-alignment that had its roots in the Cold War.[33] Despite these oppositions, significant developments made in the India–US relationship in the 2000s suggest that the two governments were inclined to serve their aligned interests.

A factor that to a large extent encouraged the US to promote India's rise in the international system and, in the process, challenge the global nuclear order has been the rise of China, the latter largely viewed as detrimental to the US interests in Asia and the world. For instance, President Bush's 2002 *National Security Strategy of the United States* stated that 'US interests require a strong relationship with India'.[34] Some key non-governmental experts in Washington explained that the rise of China and potential disturbance of the Asian stability was a key reason why the US sought to bolster relationship with India in order to create a hedge. In fact, some Pentagon officials from those years suggested that supplies of conventional weapons to India, worth up to $5 billion, would include platforms which could be 'useful for monitoring the Chinese military'.[35]

As a Congressional Research Service (CSR) report of 2005 sums it, 'A rising concern for US policymakers is China's growing global "reach" and the consequences that China's increasing international economic, military and political influence has for US interests'.[36] The report further adds that 'recent US moves to embrace New Delhi are widely seen in the context of Washington's search for friendly Asian powers that may offset Beijing's power, prevent future Chinese hegemony, and give Washington more nuanced opportunities for leveraging in Asia'.[37] As has been noted with regard to the 2008 NSG waiver to India, 'even in those countries that have been largely supportive of the deal, the perception was strong that the deal was part of the broader effort to reshape the Asian balance of power'.[38]

It is important to highlight here that China has been a mainstream actor in the global nuclear order, being one of the five nuclear weapon states recognised by the NPT and a member of the NSG since 2004. Thus, China has never been a revisionist power as far as the global nuclear order is concerned. However, China's rise, both economic and military, has been a classic case of a revisionist power challenging the US-led international system. Washington's embrace of India has thus been viewed as an attempt to ensure that Chinese hegemony does not ensue in Asia.

Indeed, in the 2000s, the competition between the US and China had begun materialising and it was visible in the global nuclear order as well. The US practiced its significant influence in securing consensus at the NSG for a waiver for India in 2008. Even though China did not wield significant influence in the 2000s over NSG members and chose to instead sit behind few members of the NSG that had initially held their reservations against granting India the waiver, it was visibly opposed to the idea.[39] In its response to India being granted the waiver by the NSG in 2008, China announced that it would build nuclear reactors at sites Chashma 3 and 4 in Pakistan, flouting NSG guidelines.[40] This was done without the implementation of the IAEA's full scope safeguards in Pakistan, and no waiver from the NSG was acquired for undertaking the supply. China explained that the export of the reactors is grandfathered by an agreement made between China and Pakistan in the 1980s, much before 2004 when China joined the Group.[41] However, China did not disclose its plans of exporting new reactors to the NSG in 2004 which it was required to notify.[42] On the contrary, it had assured the NSG that it will not export any reactors than Chashma 1 and 2.[43] Furthermore, in 2013, China signed an agreement to build an additional nuclear reactor in Karachi and offered no justification for the decision.

In essence, the US demonstrated its willingness to modify the global nuclear order by letting India rise in it in the attempt to preserve the structure of the international system and safeguards its interests in Asia. The US embraced and promoted India as a counter to the prospective Chinese quest for regional and eventual global hegemony.

Challenges to complete integration

A question that demands answer at the onset to establishing the challenges that remain to India's complete integration is as to what exactly entails India's complete integration into the global nuclear order. It is interesting to note here that India's attempt to rise up in the global nuclear order has not included reforming the NPT and signing the Treaty as a nuclear weapon state. Historically, India has called to establish a framework for comprehensive nuclear disarmament that eventually replaces the NPT. While the call has remained, India has expressed its willingness to make peace with the NPT-led global nuclear order since it conducted the nuclear tests in May 1998. New Delhi has been content with supporting the principles of the NPT even as it stayed outside the Treaty framework. None of its integration plans involved signing the NPT as a nuclear weapon state, a recognition of the argument that the NPT is too big an institutional framework to get influenced by a single or a group of rising and/or established powers. Even the US, as the sole superpower since the end of the Cold War and as the leader of the international system, never considered altering the NPT regime to further its structural interests of promoting India as a counter to China, even though it may have compromised the norms on which the NPT is built. Thus, institutional framework has defined the extent to which India's integration into the global nuclear order has been or would be possible.

It is a consequence of the same that India's complete integration into the global nuclear order has been envisioned to include New Delhi joining the four export control regimes, most importantly the NSG. Though the 2008 NSG waiver to India to engage in global nuclear commerce resulted almost in its acceptance as a nuclear weapon state, two factors still withheld such recognition.

First was that while the US and some other like-minded countries were on board to granting India the waiver, there were countries that had held their reservations. While these countries eventually joined the consensus, they did so reportedly under tremendous US pressure.[44] Even in agreeing to grant India the waiver, these countries viewed the decision to be a one-time exception rather than a principled acceptance of India as a nuclear weapon state.[45]

Second was that the 2008 waiver only bestowed upon India relatively limited agenda-setting power insofar as the global nuclear order is concerned. It still remained outside the tent and was not privy to internal deliberations of the NSG where members discussed emerging proliferation challenges and the best means to mitigate and address them. This led New Delhi to set the next and possibly the final step of its integration into the global nuclear order – membership to the NSG and other three export control bodies.

Even though the other three export control bodies have different mandates than the NSG, they are often viewed under the same category. This is perhaps because they collectively form the framework to prohibit transfers of means through which rogue and revisionist states could challenge the stability of the extant international system. Also, from the point of view of India's integration into the global nuclear order, the other three export control bodies become important because as of March 2017, 30 countries are members to all four of these bodies, representing a substantial majority. Argument was thus made that by joining the other, politically less sensitive, export control bodies, India could build a stronger impression of its unwavered commitment to non-proliferation of sensitive items.[46] This, in part, also forms the veto-power strategy which Yeon-jung discusses. This has and may help India bring more countries on board to accepting it as a like-minded partner and member to the NSG. However, one challenge which India has faced in its quest to securing membership to the NSG and which was absent in 2008 when it secured the waiver has been China's *vocal* opposition to India's inclusion in the Group.

Soon after India applied for the membership to the NSG in 2016, the Chinese government issued a public statement noting that it had concerns over India joining the NSG as that would have detrimental effects on the NPT. The spokesperson of China's foreign ministry, Lu Kang, added that 'All the multilateral non-proliferation export control regime including the NSG has regarded NPT as an important standard for the expansion of the NSG'.[47] This concern was also expressed by some other countries like Brazil, Switzerland, New Zealand, Ireland, South Africa and Turkey, during the Seoul plenary of the NSG held in June 2016.[48] It is interesting to note, however, that leaders of many of these countries have gone on record to express their support for India's accession to the NSG. Also, while these countries expressed their concern over the likely impact of India's entry to the NSG on the NPT, they were willing to have discussions over the same.

Nonetheless, when it comes to China's objection to India's entry to the NSG, several factors make the structural framework hold better explanatory power. Firstly, arguably the 2008 waiver had the same, if not greater, implications for the NPT as that bestowed on India the status previously enjoyed only by the five nuclear weapon states of the NPT.[49] If indeed China's opposition to India's NSG membership was principled, then why did it not block the 2008 waiver? A possible explanation is that the US wielded significant influence on all NSG members in 2008 and China did not want to stand alone in blocking that consensus. However, by 2016, China had amassed significant power and influence to take a more vocal position. Not only did Beijing express its willingness to lead the opposition to India's entry to the NSG, it reportedly also attempted to use its influence over certain members of the NSG, channelled through its economic power, to generate support for its opposition.[50]

Secondly, in response to the fury of writings coming out of New Delhi on China's opposition to India's entry to the NSG, especially after the Seoul plenary of June 2016, Beijing's official mouthpiece, the *Global Times*, expressed its frustration that partly captured China's apprehension to the US' intentions behind promoting India. For instance, an editorial piece in the *Global Times*, dated 28 June 2016, notes that:

> US backing adds the biggest impetus to India's ambition. By cozying up to India, Washington's India policy actually serves the purpose of containing China. The US is not the whole world. Its endorsement does not mean India has won the backing of the world. This basic fact, however, has been ignored by India.[51]

This captures the centrality of the structural framework in explaining the contours of the debate over India's bid to join the NSG. The perception that the US is promoting India to counter China's rise in the international system exists in Beijing as well. From that perspective, Beijing's vocal opposition to India's entry to the NSG is just a case in point to its larger strategy of blocking the US attempts of promoting India and India's rise in general.

Thirdly, China has played its own balance-of-power card by linking India's membership application to the NSG to that of its ally, Pakistan – this forms part of China's larger strategy of countering the US attempts at promoting India in the international system. Pakistan submitted its membership application to the NSG just a week after India and this came as a surprise to most. Advisor to Pakistan's Prime Minister on Foreign Affairs, Sartaz Aziz, explained Pakistan's membership application to the NSG on grounds that Pakistan's non-proliferation credentials were stronger than that of India.[52] This, coupled with the Chinese attempts to tag India's and Pakistan's NSG membership applications, appeared to New Delhi a mockery of its bid to join the NSG, given Pakistan's rather poor non-proliferation record, including the infamous proliferation network *allegedly* led by the father of Pakistan's nuclear programme, A. Q. Khan. In a more explicit reference, Aziz reportedly stated that China helped Pakistan in blocking India's quest to become a member of the NSG.[53] Aziz further claimed that Pakistan's Prime Minister in 2016, Nawaz Sharif wrote personal letters to 17 head of NSG member-states to prevent India from gaining entry to the NSG.[54] These instances suggest that both Chinese and Pakistani attempts were aimed more at denying India membership to the NSG rather than securing Pakistan's entry to the Group. Although, a counter-argument to that, however, would be that if India gains entry to the NSG first then it could block consensus on Pakistan's bid to join the Group in the future.

These factors make the challenges to India's membership to the NSG more structural than normative or institutional. As China continues its rise in the international system and bridge the relative power gap with the US, it is likely to exert more pressure against any US attempts at preserving the status quo including via promoting India. Even the mere perception that India's rise, irrespective of the US support, could be a counter to China's hegemonic ambitions is likely to motivate Beijing into ensuring that the same does not occur.

Conclusion

This study concludes that India's partial integration into the extant global nuclear order and the challenges that remain to its complete integration are better explained by the structural framework, though normative and institutional arguments fill in some explanatory gaps as well. It was India's recognition as a rising power which is not a revisionist state vis-à-vis the international system that allowed India to rise with relative peace. That the current structure of the international system faced a serious threat from a revisionist China led the US, as the founder and the guarantor of the system, to promote India as a counter. However, in the last decade, China has continued its rise in the international system, emboldening it to rigorously pursue its revisionist agenda, including by countering the US attempts to promote India.

The dominant structural framework captures the global nuclear order to be more a product of the structure of the international system. In essence, as the structure in question evolves, so would the global nuclear order and not necessarily in a systematic and organised manner. Washington's decision to promote India in the global nuclear order, while sacrificing some of its long-held non-proliferation norms, is a case in point. Similarly, Beijing's decision to flout the NSG guidelines to promote Pakistan in response further substantiates this argument. There are limitations to how much institutions like the NPT can be challenged, especially by the established powers in their respective pursuits of structural interests. But even those limited challenges would have significant consequences for the stability of the global nuclear order.

Disclosure statement

No potential conflict of interest was reported by the authors.

Notes

1.   Ministry of External Affairs, "Draft Indian Nuclear Doctrine"; Press Informational Bureau, "Operationalizing India's Nuclear Doctrine."
2.   For a liberal exposition on institutions, see Ruggie, "What Makes the World Hang Together?" For a constructivist understanding of institutions, see Finnemore and Sikkink, "International Norm Dynamics and Political Change"; Kowert and Legro, "Norms, Identity and their Limits."
3.   Mearsheimer, "False Promise of International Institutions."
4.   For analysis of Jaswant Singh's statement at the Parliament, during the 2000 NPT Review Conference, see Raja Mohan, "India's Nuclear Exceptionalism," 160.
5.   Raja Mohan, "India's Nuclear Exceptionalism," 160.
6.   US Department of State Archive, "Joint Statement by President George W. Bush and Prime Minister Manmohan Singh."
7.   IAEA, "Communication dated 10 September 2008 received from the Permanent Mission of Germany to the Agency regarding a 'Statement on Civil Nuclear Cooperation with India.'"
8.   IAEA, "IAEA Board Approves India-Safeguards Agreement."
9.   IAEA, "India Safeguards Agreement Signed."
10. IAEA, "India's Additional Protocol Enters into Force."
11. White House, "Joint Statement by President Obama and Prime Minister Singh of India, November 08, 2010."
12. See Directorate General of Foreign Trade, "Notification No. 116 (RE-2013)/2009-2014, March 13, 2015"; Directorate General of Foreign Trade, "Notification No._05 /(2015-2020), April 29, 2016."
13. Directorate General of Foreign Trade, "Guidelines for Exports of SCOMET Items."
14. White House, "US–India Joint Statement "साझा प्रयास - सबका विकास"'Shared Effort; Progress for All.'"
15. Ministry of External Affairs, "Joint Statement: Celebrating a Decade of the India–Russian Federation Strategic Partnership and Looking Ahead, December 21, 2010."
16. Ministry of External Affairs, "Joint Statement issued by India and France during the State Visit of President of France to India, February 14, 2013."
17. Ministry of External Affairs, "Joint Statement on the India–United Kingdom Summit 2013 – India and the UK: A stronger, wider, deeper partnership, February 19, 2013."
18. Federal Ministry of Education and Research (Germany), "Joint Statement on the Further Development of the Strategic and Global Partnership between Germany and India: Shaping the Future, April 11, 2013."
19. See Ministry of External Affairs, "Joint Press Statement on the State Visit of Prime Minister of Australia to India, October 17, 2012."

20. Ministry of External Affairs, "Tokyo Declaration for India–Japan Special Strategic and Global Partnership, September 01, 2014."
21. Ministry of External Affairs, "India–Canada Joint Statement: नया उत्साह, नए कदम New Vigour, New Steps, April 15, 2015."
22. Ministry of External Affairs, "India–Republic of Korea Joint Statement for Special Strategic Partnership, May 18, 2015."
23. Mitra, "India's 300-page Application for NSG."
24. For an overview of how major players of the international system colluded to establish the global nuclear order that served their mutual interests, see Trachtenberg, "Making Sense of the Nuclear Age," 261–86.
25. Yeon-jung, "A Path to NSG," 19–37; Raja Mohan, *Crossing the Rubicon*; Pardesi, "Is India a Great Power?" 1–30.
26. Tsebelis, *Veto Players*.
27. Narilkar, "Is India a Responsible Great Power?" 1607–21.
28. For an assessment of these agreements, see Kronstadt, "US–India Bilateral Agreements in 2005."
29. Kronstadt, "US–India Bilateral Agreements," 1; Pant, "US–India Nuclear Deal," 305–16.
30. O'Neil, "Rice Urges Congress on Deal."
31. Pant, "US–India Nuclear Deal," 308–10.
32. Bender, "US to Aid India on Nuclear Power"; Weisman, "US to Broaden India's Access." See also Robbins, "Bush's India Deal Bends Nuclear Rules"; "Green Light for Bomb Builders"; Holt, "US Shift on India Nuclear Policy."
33. Cohen, "South Asia"; Harding, "Evolution of the Strategic Triangle."
34. White House, "The National Security Strategy."
35. Linzer, "Bush Officials Defend India Deal."
36. Kronstadt, "US–India Bilateral Agreements," 16.
37. Ibid.
38. Pant, "US–India Nuclear Deal," 310.
39. This was noted by former Indian Foreign Secretary, Shyam Saran, in an interview. See, Chaudhury, "China to not be the Only Country Unhappy." Chinese official Xinhua news agency also published Beijing's opposition to the US–India civil nuclear deal. See "Chinese Media Sees Red."
40. Bokhari, "Pakistan in Talks to Buy Chinese Reactors."
41. Lodhi, "Nuclear Doublespeak." Quoted in Tellis, "China–Pakistan Nuclear 'Deal,'" 4. Also see Balachandran and Patil, "China's Reactor Sale to Pakistan."
42. Tellis, "China–Pakistan Nuclear 'Deal,'" 5.
43. Sibal, "NSG Stamp for Sino-Pak Pact."
44. Ganapathy, "India Powers its Way into Nuke Biz."
45. This was also affirmed by representatives of several members countries of the NSG during interviews with the authors.
46. Rajagopalan and Biswas, *Locating India within the Global Non-Proliferation Architecture*.
47. Chaudhury, "China to not be the Only Country Unhappy."
48. Rajagopalan and Biswas, "India within the Global Non-Proliferation Architecture," 21–30.
49. Biswas, "Explained: India, NSG."
50. Malik, "The Real Seoul Story."
51. "Delhi's NSG Bid Upset by Rules."
52. "Pakistan's Credentials Stronger than India."
53. Press Trust of India, "China Helped Pakistan Block India's NSG Membership."
54. Haider, "Indian Bid for NSG Foiled."

Bibliography

Balachandran, G. and Kapil Patil. "China's Reactor Sale to Pakistan: The Known Unknowns." *IDSA Issue Brief*, November 15, 2013.

Bender, Bryan. "US to Aid India on Nuclear Power." *Boston Globe*, July 19, 2005.

Biswas, Arka. "Explained: India, NSG, and the Chinese Roadblock." *Swarajya*, June 8, 2017. https://swarajyamag.com/world/explained-india-nsg-and-the-chinese-roadblock.

Bokhari, Farhan. "Pakistan in Talks to Buy Chinese Reactors." *Financial Times*, January 2, 2006.

Chaudhury, Dipanjan Roy. "China to not be the only country unhappy with India's candidature for Nuclear Suppliers Group: Shyam Saran." *Economic Times*, July 21, 2015.

"Chinese Media Sees Red." *Press Trust of India*, March 3, 2006.

Cohen, Stephen. "South Asia." In *America's Role in Asia*. Asia Foundation, 2004.

"Delhi's NSG bid upset by rules, not Beijing." *Global Times*, June 28, 2016. http://www.globaltimes.cn/content/990889.shtml

Directorate General of Foreign Trade. "Notification No. 116 (RE-2013)/2009-2014." Accessed March 1, 2018. http://dgft.gov.in/Exim/2000/NOT/NOT13/not11613.pdf

Directorate General of Foreign Trade. "Notification No._05 /(2015-2020)." Accessed March 1, 2018. http://dgft.gov.in/exim/2000/NOT/NOT16/noti0516.pdf

Directorate General of Foreign Trade. "Guidelines for Exports of SCOMET Items." Accessed March 1, 2018. http://dgft.gov.in

Federal Ministry of Education and Research (Germany). "Joint Statement on the Further Development of the Strategic and Global Partnership between Germany and India: Shaping the Future." Accessed March 1, 2018. http://www.bmbf.de/pubRD/Joint-Declaration_2013-03-14_en.pdf

Finnemore, Martha and Kathryn Sikkink. "International Norm Dynamics and Political Change." In *Exploration and Contestation in the Study of World Politics*, edited by Peter Katzenstein, Robert Keohane and Stephen Krasner. MIT Press: Cambridge, 1999.

Ganapathy, Nirmala. "India powers its way into nuke biz." *Economic Times*, September 7, 2008.

"Green Light for Bomb Builders" (editorial). *New York Times*, July 22, 2005.

Haider, Mateen. "Indian bid for NSG foiled due to Pakistan's diplomatic efforts: Sartaj Aziz." *Dawn*, June 27, 2016. https://www.dawn.com/news/1267590

Harding, Harry. "The Evolution of the Strategic Triangle: China, India, and the United States." In *The India-China Relationship: Rivalry and Engagement*, edited by Francine R. Frankel and Harry Harding. New Delhi: Oxford University Press, 2004.

Holt, Pat. "US Shift on India Nuclear Policy Tilts Regional Balance." *Christian Science Monitor*, August 4, 2005.

IAEA. "Communication dated 10 September 2008 received from the Permanent Mission of Germany to the Agency regarding a 'Statement on Civil Nuclear Cooperation with India'." Accessed March 1, 2018. https://www.iaea.org/sites/default/files/publications/documents/infcircs/2008/infcirc734c.pdf

IAEA. "IAEA Board Approves India-Safeguards Agreement." Accessed March 1, 2018. https://www.iaea.org/newscenter/news/iaea-board-approves-india-safeguards-agreement

IAEA. "India Safeguards Agreement Signed." Accessed March 1, 2018. https://www.iaea.org/newscenter/news/india-safeguards-agreement-signed

IAEA. "India's Additional Protocol Enters Into Force." Accessed March 1, 2018. https://www.iaea.org/newscenter/news/indias-additional-protocol-enters-force

Kowert, Paul and Legro, Jeffrey. "Norms, Identity and Their Limits: A Theoretical Reprise" in Peter Katzenstein (ed.) *The Culture of National Security: Norms and Identity in World Politics*, Columbia University Press: New York, 1996.

Kronstadt, K. Alan. "US-India Bilateral Agreements in 2005." *CRS Report*, August 2, 2006, http://www.au.af.mil/au/awc/awcgate/crs/rl33072.pdf

Linzer, Dafna. "Bush Officials Defend India Deal." *Washington Post*, July 20, 2005.

Lodhi, Maleeha. "Nuclear Doublespeak." *News*, July 6, 2010.

Malik, Ashok. "The real Seoul story: At the NSG plenary, China behaved not as an enlightened power but as a strategic small-timer." *Times of India*, June 27, 2016.

Mearsheimer, John J. "The False Promise of International Institutions", *International Security*, 19, no. 3 (1994): 5–49.

Ministry of External Affairs (Government of India). "Draft Report of National Security Advisory Board on Indian Nuclear Doctrine." Accessed March 1, 2018. http://mea.gov.in/in-focus-article.htm?18916/Draft+Report+of+National+Security+Advisory+Board+on+Indian+Nuclear+Doctrine

Ministry of External Affairs. "Joint Statement: Celebrating a Decade of the India- Russian Federation Strategic Partnership and Looking Ahead." Accessed March 1, 2018. http://mea.gov.in/outoging-visit-detail.htm?5118/Joint+Statement+Celebrating+a+Decade+of+the+India+Russian+Federation+Strategic+Partnership+and+Looking+Ahead

Ministry of External Affairs (Government of India). "Joint Statement issued by India and France during the State Visit of President of France to India." Accessed March 1, 2018. http://www.mea.gov.in/bilateral-documents.htm?dtl/21175/Joint+Statement+issued+by+India+and+France+during+the+State+Visit+of+President+of+France+to+India

Ministry of External Affairs (Government of India). "Joint Statement on the India-United Kingdom Summit 2013 - India and the UK: A stronger, wider, deeper partnership." Accessed March 1, 2018. http://www.mea.gov.in/bilateral-documents.htm?dtl/21197/Joint+Statement+on+the+IndiaUnited+Kingdom+Summit+2013++India+and+The+UK+A+stronger+wider+deeper+partnership

Ministry of External Affairs (Government of India). "Joint Press Statement on the State Visit of Prime Minister of Australia to India." Accessed March 1, 2018. http://www.mea.gov.in/bilateral-documents.htm?dtl/20713/Joint+Press+Statement+on+the+State+Visit+of+Prime+Minister+of+Australia+to+India

Ministry of External Affairs (Government of India). "Tokyo Declaration for India - Japan Special Strategic and Global Partnership." Accessed March 1, 2018. http://mea.gov.in/bilateral-documents.htm?dtl/23965/Tokyo_Declaration_for_India__Japan_Special_Strategic_and_Global_Partnership

Ministry of External Affairs (Government of India). "India-Canada Joint Statement: नया उत्साह, नए कदम: New Vigour, New Steps." Accessed March 1, 2018. http://mea.gov.in/bilateral-documents.htm?dtl/25073/IndiaCanada+Joint+Statement++++New+Vigour+New+Steps

Ministry of External Affairs (Government of India). "India - Republic of Korea Joint Statement for Special Strategic Partnership." Accessed March 1, 2018. http://www.mea.gov.in/bilateral-documents.htm?dtl/25261/India__Republic_of_Korea_Joint_Statement_for_Special_Strategic_Partnership_May_18_2015

Mitra, Devirupa. "Exclusive: India's 300-page Application for NSG Membership." *The Wire*, July 1, 2016, https://thewire.in/diplomacy/revealed-indias-300-page-application-for-nsg-membership

Narilkar, Amrita. "Is India a responsible great power?" *Third World Quarterly* 32, no. 9 (2011): 1607–21.

O'Neil, John. "Rice Urges Congress on Deal with India." *New York Times*, April 5, 2006.

"Pakistan's credentials stronger than India for NSG membership: Sartaj Aziz." *Dawn*, June 12, 2016. https://www.dawn.com/news/1264368

Pant, Harsh V. *The US-India Nuclear Pact: Policy, Process and Great Power Politics*. New York: Oxford University Press, 2011.

Pant, Harsh V. "The US-India nuclear deal: Great power politics versus non-proliferation." In *Handbook of Nuclear Proliferation*, edited by Harsh V. Pant, 305–316. London and New York: Routledge, 2012.

Pardesi, Manjeet S. "Is India a Great Power? Understanding Great Power Status in Contemporary International Relations." *Asian Security* 11, no. 1 (2015): 1–30.

Press Informational Bureau (Government of India). "Cabinet Committee on Security Reviews Progress in Operationalizing India's Nuclear Doctrine." Accessed March 1, 2018. http://pibarchive.nic.in/archive/releases98/lyr2003/rjan2003/04012003/r040120033.html

Press Trust of India. "China helped Pakistan block India's NSG membership bid: Aziz." *Hindu*, September 16, 2016.

Raja Mohan, C. "India's nuclear exceptionalism." In *Nuclear Proliferation and International Security*, edited by Morten Bremer Maerli and Sverre Lodgaard, 152–171. Oxon and New York: Routledge, 2007.

Rajagopalan, Rajeswari P. and Arka Biswas. *Locating India within the Global Non-Proliferation Architecture: Prospects, Challenges and Opportunities*. New Delhi: Observer Research Foundation, 2016.

Robbins, Carla Ann. "Bush's India Deal Bends Nuclear Rules." *Wall Street Journal*, July 20, 2005.

Ruggie, John Gerard. "What Makes the World Hang Together? Neo-Utilitarianisnm and the Social Constructivist Challenge." In *Exploration and Contestation in the Study of World Politics*, edited by Peter Katzenstein, Robert Keohane and Stephen Krasner. Cambridge, MA: MIT Press, 1999.

Sibal, Kanwal. "NSG stamp for Sino-Pak pact a blow to India." *India Today*, July 12, 2011.

Tellis, Ashley J. *The China-Pakistan Nuclear 'Deal': Separating Facts from Fiction*. Washington DC: Carnegie Endowment for International Peace, 2010.

Trachtenberg, Marc. "Making Sense of the Nuclear Age." In *History and Strategy*, 261–286. Princeton, NJ: Princeton University Press, 1991.

Tsebelis, George. *Veto Players: How Political Institutions Work*. Princeton, NJ: Princeton University Press, 2002.

US Department of State Archive. "Joint Statement by President George W. Bush and Prime Minister Manmohan Singh." Accessed March 1, 2018. http://2001-2009.state.gov/p/sca/rls/pr/2005/49763.htm

Weisman, Steven. "US to Broaden India's Access to Nuclear-Power Technology." *New York Times*, July 19, 2005.

White House. "Joint Statement by President Obama and Prime Minister Singh of India." Accessed March 1, 2018. https://www.whitehouse.gov/the-press-office/2010/11/08/joint-statement-president-obama-and-prime-minister-singh-india

White House. "US-India Joint Statement साँझा प्रयास - सबका विकास" – 'Shared Effort; Progress for All.'" Accessed March 1, 2018. https://www.whitehouse.gov/the-press-office/2015/01/25/us-india-joint-state-ment-shared-effort-progress-all

White House. "The National Security Strategy." Accessed March 1, 2018. https://georgewbush-white-house.archives.gov/nsc/nss/2002/

Yeon-jung, Ji. "A Path to NSG: India's Rise in the Global Nuclear Order." *Rising Powers Quarterly* 2, no. 3 (2017):19–37.

China's role in the regional and international management of Korean conflict: an arbiter or catalyst?

Hakan Mehmetcik and Ferit Belder

ABSTRACT
There are diverging assessments of China's role in resolving the nuclear crisis on the Korean Peninsula. China's role has been characterised variously as a bystander, arbiter, catalyst and mediator over the years. This paper aims to clarify where China stands on North Korea and assesses the different phases of the Chinese approach to conflict resolution during the North Korean nuclear crisis. The main argument is that China wishes to maintain the regional status quo while appearing to adjust its position in line with the international community. China's current duplicity stems from its different priorities and concerns to the remainder of the world, and can best be explained using a role theory analysis.

Introduction

Ever increasing nuclear proliferation threats from North Korea are reshaping the security policy of the entire North-east Asian region, and its effects extend well beyond the region to the rest of the world. North Korea has had several incentives and challenges while pursuing nuclearisation and in recent years its pace has accelerated.[1] Throughout the entire history of proliferation, there has not been a single country that has made 'the technically tough, and politically dangerous journey towards nuclear weapons alone'.[2] India has done so thanks to Canada, Pakistan managed with the help of China, and Israel used American technology. Even the United States could not have managed to develop the atomic bomb without the help of German nuclear scientists. Along the long march towards nuclear – and missile – proliferation, many countries, intentionally and unintentionally, have helped North Korea by offering different forms of technology, expertise and finance. Pakistan, Iran, and illicit networks are on that list.[3] According to some area experts, Chinese supports have also been important in maintaining the pace of the North Korean programme.[4] However, China has also been taking part in increasing countermeasures and sanctions against North Korea, to deter nuclear and missile proliferation. However, some argue that China's cooperation in sanctioning North Korea through the United Nations (UN) Security Council is merely the public face of Chinese diplomacy. Backstage, China maintains its de facto strategy of engagement with North Korea, which supports the North Korean nuclear programme overall.[5]

This article has been republished with minor changes. These changes do not impact the academic content of the article.

Others argue that even if China does not support North Korea intentionally, it has the responsibility to solve the issue since China is the only country that has significant economic and political leverage in that country.[6] Some argue that China's perceptions of North Korea have been changing slowly,[7] while further arguments state that it is no longer wedded to North Korea's survival[8] and others argue that China will not abandon its tacit support for North Korea anytime soon.[9] Thus, the key questions in need of exploration here are, How do we assess China's role in resolving the nuclear crisis on the Korean Peninsula? How can China's role be characterised? Is China a bystander, an arbiter, a catalyst or simply a mediator?

This paper aims to analyse the contending roles of China in the North Korean dispute and its effects on China's patterns of conflict resolution, using a role theory approach. Even though there are numerous contemporary studies using realist, constructivist, rationalist approaches, formal and informal theories and models on the China's foreign policy, there are very few works that take a role theoretical perspective on this.[10] When it comes to conflict on the Korean Peninsula, China's role, to the best of the authors' knowledge, has never been analysed with a role theoretical explanation. There are two important benefits to using role theory within this context. Firstly, it provides a theoretically rich and sound analysis, and, secondly, the key concepts of role theory explain spatial and temporal change. To this end, the paper begins with an explanation of the key concepts of role theory employed in this paper, before extending that discussion to an analysis of China's role in North Korean nuclearisation. The paper pays attention to changing Chinese attitudes towards the North Korean conflict to explore the possibility of a conflict resolution in Chinese terms. Finally, the paper will apply categories of conflict identification, namely framing and scoping, to analyse China's perception of conflict resolution.

Role theory

Role theory first emerged in foreign policy analysis during the 1970s with Holsti's seminal article 'National Role Conceptions in the Study of Foreign Policy'.[11] With the publication of Stephen G. Walker's edited book, *The Role Theory and Foreign Policy Analysis*, in 1987 a pivotal point has been reached.[12] Since then, an increasing interest in the potential of role theory to illuminate various foreign policy issues has emerged.[13] Providing rich vocabulary on its own, merging several levels of analysis into one and harnessing its concepts to other theories' conceptual vocabulary, role theory[14] deals with the intersection between state self-defined foreign policy roles and roles attributed to states by the dynamics of the system. Therefore, it offers an encouraging avenue for undertaking one of international relations theory's most intractable problems, the relationship between agent and structure.[15]

Roles explain how an actor's self-identity[16] is mediated by the external perceptions of the actor's function within a specific social group. Yet roles differ from status, which consists of several role sets.[17] In this sense, roles are either ascribed or achieved/assumed social positions. As achieved positions, roles are more self-assured or self-conscious, because they stem from self-identification. The actor has resolved who they are and the roles and functions they play in a given society or group. These types of roles generally derive from national identities or self-identification in the context of international relations. They are often termed ego-centric roles, as opposed to ascribed, alter-centric roles. The roles that are ascribed to the role holder by others stem from external perceptions or structural, systemic elements.

In this situation, there are three possibilities for the role holder: rejection/non-performance, performance or transposition. The role beholder can neglect an ascribed role, embrace and perform the role or perform the role by slightly changing its meaning as well as its function. If the role holder has few options to neglect others' expectations of their ascribed role, they will often try to transpose the role in accordance with their own desire. However, some roles are constitutive or regulatory to a specific group, eg the EU, and are thus ascribed on a permanent basis and offer limited options for transposition. That is, as a recognised member of that group, you have no other option than to accept the role ascribed, and perform it as it is. Some roles or role sets may also be functionally specific, eg balancer, initiator, buffer or ally; even if they derive from structural forces, they are often performed within prescribed patterns of behaviour.

At the conceptual level, there are several other important points to consider. Firstly, whether roles are ascribed or achieved, all are meaningful as long as they are formally or informally agreed upon. Yet the expectations of an actor's role in an organised group may vary noticeably, and sometimes there is a big social and material gap between the role a state pursues for itself and the expectations that the group has of a state's ascribed role.[18] That is, a conflict may exist between an ascribed role function and assumed role sets. Such a disagreement causes a conflict among group members. Furthermore, role performance requires the acceptance of the international community while role rejection or non-performance diminishes an actor's capacity for interaction with the international community.

Secondly, changes in roles and role sets are important determinants of both role enactment and identity formation. Role enactment refers to an actor's behaviour when performing a role. Roles are socially constructed by material and immaterial forces and they are remarkably durable; however, changes occur over time and space. Changes in roles and their enactment arise in two ways: adaptation and learning. Role adaptation refers to changes in the strategies and instruments used to perform a role. However, the underlying purpose of the role remains fixed. Learning describes changes in beliefs, or the development of new beliefs, skills or procedures, based upon the observation and interpretation of experience. Therefore, to apprehend changes in either assumed or ascribed roles, the learning and adaptation phases of an actor's socialisation into a role must be analysed.

Thirdly, international roles can also be defined along three dimensions: time, space and obligation. The temporal dimension stresses the 'historicity of roles' while the spatial dimension refers to the specific cultural and political settings that condition roles and role creation. Obligations are generally derived from the constitutive and regulative or normative positioning within a formal or informal institution.[19] While roles are either ascribed or achieved social positions, the constitutive and regulative impact of institutions, such as the EU, in stabilising national foreign policy roles is important to evaluate the role of the state in international relations.

Fourthly, roles are also often associated with the material and immaterial commitments of an actor. A low set of commitments permits agents to take up more roles than do a resource-draining high number of commitments. Similarly, roles come with low or high material and immaterial benefits and costs. The lower the costs, the higher the benefits, and the more space a role holder has to play. Finally, auxiliary roles, which are often characterised as leadership roles, include an initiator, an agenda-setter and a mediator component, as well as a representative function. In this sense, leadership entails partly achieved roles, yet mostly ascribed roles. Leadership roles are therefore not only more complex and prohibitive in terms of costs and benefits for the role holder, they are also less prone to change.

China's emerging process of self-identification involves the contestation of domestic roles, international/external role perceptions, and contested auxiliary roles with different levels of commitment. This demonstrates China's conflicting ascribed and achieved/assumed roles, not only within the North Korean context, but also in terms of its foreign policy conduct internationally.[20] To evaluate China's changing role in North Korea, this paper explores China's achieved roles as a function of (1) self-identification and conflict framing; (2) historical context and conflict scoping; and (3) cultural and political context and conflict communication. It then explores China's ascribed roles as a function of (1) the normative and constitutive context and (2) external expectations. China's international roles vary across each of these dimensions and often lead to the incompatibility of role perceptions and role enactment in the context of the international community.

China's role in the North Korean nuclear issue

Self-identification and conflict framing

Following more than three decades of high-level economic growth, social change and modernisation, China has moved to the centre stage of the new global order. Through shifting processes of positive and negative self-identification, the scope and function of China's international role covers a vast variety of areas. In general, China arrogates a role of a great power, which is an auxiliary role encompassing several functions such as initiator, balancer, mediator, etc. China claims to be a responsible great power in areas such as open trade and climate change, and the diminished perception of the US's capacity for leadership offers a gap for China to fill.[21] China is one of the most important actors to take the lead in Africa.[22] There are numbers of other examples of China's wholehearted embrace of the role of a great power.[23] Yet, at the same time, China is domestically bound to the international role of 'a developing country'[24] which is a limiting role in the context of international politics. However, Chinese role adaptation as self-identification is often derived from ego vs alter expectations. Thus, China has both ego-centric and alter-centric roles, and it is often easy-going with role contestation. Yet, although the Chinese mode of engagement is generally characterised by socialisation, learning and adaptation, China has been pursuing a recalibration of existing norms, values, and institutions on its own terms. That is, China transposes some of its ascribed roles, which has caused occasional disturbances in its relations with the rest of the world. Contradictions, incoherent actions and difficulties in the Chinese code of conduct over many issues, such as the South China Sea, the dispute with Japan about several islands, or the border clashes with India, are evidence of this. Yet one of the most appealing examples of 'China's role adaptation' is its North Korea policy. China's ascribed and assumed roles regarding the North Korea nuclear issue have changed significantly over the years. China has been trying to deal with the issue on its own terms during the current phase of the crisis, while cooperating with the international community to implement harsher sanctions against North Korea. As a member of the international community, China accepts its obligations to condemn North Korea and exert pressure through economic sanctions to deter the North Korean nuclear programme. The constitutive and regulative role of being a permanent member of the Security Council and a responsible member of a non-proliferation regime demonstrates the Chinese code of conduct. China's current role enactment derives from its participation in various international bodies where it has promoted learning and adaptation. China showed little to no cooperation with the international community during North Korea's first nuclear crisis of 1993–1994. Following a principle of non-interference, China was a de facto bystander, choosing to free-ride rather than cooperate with the international community. However, China's posture changed when North Korea's second nuclear crisis which began in 2002. China understood that it was in its own interests to cooperate with international sanctions against North Korea.[25]

Cooperating with the international community through international bodies and institutions has improved China's national image on the international stage. China has become a key stakeholder in upholding non-proliferation within the international community and has remained committed to safeguarding nuclear non-proliferation internationally. China has increased its status and influence by positioning itself as a responsible great power committed to non-proliferation.[26] Therefore, China's adaptation due to learning from its participation in international bodies has tamed China's position towards North Korea as it recognises the importance of externally ascribed roles. As such an actor, China has promoted the denuclearisation of the Korean Peninsula, maintaining peace and stability on the peninsula and in North-east Asia, and resolving the Democratic People's Republic of Korea (DPRK) nuclear issue peacefully through dialogue and negotiations.[27] However, China does not fulfil expectations of its ascribed role in North Korea that would require it to harass the regime with ever increasing pressure, as that would deviate from what China deems 'acceptable behaviour'.

Identifying China's role in the North Korean issue varies, due to its position as a neighbouring state with an ideologically and culturally bound sense of brotherhood. None of China's enacted roles satisfies the expectations and actions of external actors, including the USA, Japan and South Korea. Some of China's role enactment stems from shared ideological ground with North Korean concepts of 'ontological security', which motivates the expansion of its nuclear programme. The anticipation of a threat from North Korea is constitutive of Chinese rhetoric and practice in the peninsula, while meeting the expectations of its ascribed role internationally is not. Therefore, it makes sense that China proposes that the denuclearisation of the Korean Peninsula can only proceed following the desecuritisation of the relationship between North and South Korea, as well as between the US and North Korea, and not the other way around.[28]

In many cases, China (mis)perceives others' actions against North Korea, as a cover to divert attention from against its own actions. This is especially true for the USA and Japan. Although Chinese perception of international regimes has changed, it still identifies North Korean sanctions as features of a US global order. China is particularly wary of the USA using sanctions against North Korea as a means of expanding its influence in the region, and countering China's rise. In other words, resolving North Korea's nuclear issue could justify stronger military cooperation between the US alliance and the use of a missile defence system, while also consolidating its strategy to counter the rise of China.[29] China's considerable apprehension over the deployment of the Terminal High Altitude Area Defense (THAAD) system on the Korean Peninsula, soon after North Korea conducted its fourth nuclear test, indicates China's greater concern.[30] In a similar fashion, China suspects Japan of using North Korea to counter the rise of China, as Japan is China's biggest rival in the region. Negative memories of Japan and colonial western powers constitute important aspects of Chinese self-identification. The investment of historical memories into the contemporary era shapes the Chinese domestic process of self-identification, in addition to hampering Chinese role-taking and role-making commitments.

Framing this conflict is important to understand China's enactment of ascribed, assumed and auxiliary roles, both domestically and nationally. China frames the North Korean conflict in terms of positions rather than interests, which makes it rather difficult to bridge assumed and ascribed roles. Even though it is occasionally committed to a single position on the North Korean issue, which can be characterised as keeping North Korea floating, it often obscures win–win solutions on other fronts. Without understanding the value of North Korea to China's strategic interests and geopolitical world view, we cannot understand the position-based framing of the North Korean conflict from a Chinese perspective. For China, the North Korean nuclear conflict is first and foremost a conflict between the USA and North Korea,[31] stemming from mutual distrust and securitisation. For China, the North Korean issue is mainly about maintaining stability in the peninsula.[32] This frame is incompatible with the perspective of the USA and its allies, who define the conflict in terms of their own positions and interests, which makes conflict resolution more difficult.

China's emphasis on regional stability creates another type of 'threat', which reflects the dangers that are likely to occur should the Pyongyang regime fall, even by non-military means. In such a scenario, South Korea would be the first country adversely affected by refugees, and even from an assault. Even in the absence of a direct nuclear threat to China, nuclear fallout and the refugee problem emerge as priority concerns for China.[33] Every year significant numbers of people are caught on the China–North Korea border and sent back to North Korea.

Historical context and conflict scoping

The international community's non-proliferation policy towards North Korea has seen significant changes over the years. The Chinese approach to the North Korean nuclear issue has seen some continuities and changes as well. China's role in the North Korean nuclear issue has evolved significantly from that of a passive onlooker to a reticent host, and, finally, to chief mediator.[34] After a years-long crisis followed by North Korea's declaration of its intention to withdraw from the Treaty on the Non-Proliferation of Nuclear Weapons (NPT), the USA and North Korea signed an agreement named the 'Agreed Framework' on 21 October 1994. That agreement was inked due to Pyongyang's promise to freeze the operation and construction of nuclear reactors suspected of being part of a covert nuclear weapons programme, in exchange for two proliferation-resistant nuclear power reactors, and US-supplied nuclear fuel. An international consortium called the Korean Peninsula Energy Development Organization (KEDO) was formed to implement the agreement. The Agreed Framework succeeded in temporarily freezing North Korea's nuclear programme. Yet as the Bush administration took over from Clinton, the crisis evolved once again. Harnish underlines that: 'Analytically, the crisis was caused by the United States attempt to altercast North Korea into a role similar to that of "Iraq", another defiant member state of the US-dominated non-proliferation regime'.[35]

During North Korea's first nuclear crisis in 1993–1994, China showed little interest and no cooperation.[36] The key actor was the US-led international non-proliferation community, and China never asked for any special role. It was a bystander at most. As the crisis worsened in 2003, North Korea declared its withdrawal from the NPT, and China changed its position in the crisis. China tried to reach out to both parties as an intermediary actor, which was China's first major non-proliferation initiative.[37] Due to this Chinese initiative, North Korea agreed to Six-Party Talks with the US, North Korea, China, Russia, Japan and South Korea, which were aimed at eliminating the North Korean nuclear programme and at the complete de-nuclearisation of the Korean Peninsula. The talks failed eventually, although they were maintained over several years and provided a promising breakthrough. Facing stiffened US sanctions and the refusal to provide economic aid in exchange for a freeze, North Korea escalated the conflict throughout 2006 when it conducted its first nuclear test. China only changed its strategy following North Korea's withdrawal from the Six-Party Talks in 2009, which led to stiffer sanctions from China.[38]

China's changing position and role was a reflection of broader systemic changes. Following a series of nuclear missile tests, the international non-proliferation regime and the UN Security Council became the primary forum for conflict resolution.[39] By galvanising both the UN Security Council and the NPT, China rebranded itself as an influential and responsible power in that club. Although China has expanded its role, it remains limited to re-establishing diplomatic channels. China has never imposed unilateral sanctions on North Korea, but has instead chosen to support international sanctions.[40] Nonetheless, the scope and severity of international sanctions has gradually increased due to North Korea's continuing nuclear missile tests. China's policy towards North Korea could thus be explained as a function of US military intervention in the North Korean state of affairs. If US military intervention is unlikely and North Korea is stable, China can press North Korea for denuclearisation free of concern about the peninsula situation. However, if US military intervention remains unlikely and North Korea becomes unstable, China will focus on stabilising North Korea, because pressuring North Korea to resolve the nuclear issue could further undermine its stability. China promotes a soft engagement strategy that reinforces its influence over North Korea by avoiding negative sanctions and increasing contacts with Pyongyang. Should US military intervention become likely while North Korea is stable, China must discourage US military intervention by pressing North Korea for denuclearisation.[41] Therefore, China retrospectively becomes a bystander, facilitator, mediator and partner in response to the North Korean nuclear crisis, yet many of these changes in Chinese role enactment derive from changes in external affairs, not changes in Chinese perceptions. However, scoping the conflict is an important variable when trying to understand China's position. When a conflict-resolution strategy overlooks issues which are important to parties involved it is generally destined to fail. Conflicts do not stand alone; they are a product of history, deriving from a social, cultural, political and economic context, in which even justice and fairness may have different meanings for the parties involved. The Chinese scoping of the North Korean conflict sees denuclearisation of the Korean Peninsula as the core responsibility of the USA, not themselves. The official Chinese view is that China may only help firstly the US and North Korea, but also South Korea and Japan, by inviting them for talks about a possible way out. Six-Party Talks or other Chinese initiatives such as the Dual Suspension proposal[42] have departed from this core understanding. In this sense, there is a big positional gap between China's assumed and ascribed role in solving the North Korean nuclear crisis.

Cultural and political context and communicating the conflict

Since the Korean War left the country divided, China's Korean policy has been influenced by ideology and domestic politics. China has become the largest trading partner for all Koreans.

Chinese perceptions of South Korea remain positive, despite its position as one of the most important US allies in the region. Asian identity, a similar Confucian heritage, shared anti-Japanese sentiments, and increasing cultural ties and trade relations have strengthened Chinese–Korean relations. In this sense, the region's cultural and political context forces China to take a different role than that assumed by external expectations.

Moreover, the fact that China chose to resume aid when North Korea was at its most vulnerable in 1999 shows that China prefers a stable communist regime to uncertain transition. China fears the proliferation of a North Korean nuclear arsenal and also fears a falling North Korea, which would destabilise the entire region threaten the security of Chinese borders. As a buffer state, North Korea is a geopolitical asset to China. Therefore, preventing economic collapse while restraining its nuclear programme is China's core mission in North Korea. Moreover, China has offered its economic and political model to North Korea to promote the country's development. Thus, China perceives that its basic policy of keeping diplomatic and economic channels open, interspersed with moderate sanctions in response to nuclear violations, represents the best policy mix for transforming North Korea into a more benign nation state.[43]

Several principles guide China's political position on North Korea. Firstly, China sees resolution within a multilateral framework that includes China as the only way to prevent this crisis smearing the Korean Peninsula. Nevertheless, China believes the North Korean nuclear issue should be addressed between the US and North Korea, first and foremost.[44] China also pursues a balanced relationship with both Koreas to protect its political and economic leverage on the peninsula. Finally, China strongly supports the preservation of the status quo on the peninsula and strongly opposes any unilateral military action against North Korea. China has also empowered multilateral forums and non-proliferation communities by stressing that sanctions must be implemented through the UN, not unilaterally by any single country.[45]

For China, ensuring that the North Korean regime succeeds in making a soft landing by adopting China's reform and open-door model is more important than simply solving the North Korea nuclear issue alone.[46] Currently, the national goal of the Chinese leadership is to make China a global power, which is represented in the expression of its vision of the 'Revival of Middle Kingdom China'. To achieve this goal, China's diplomatic policy is focused on creating an internationally stable environment in its peripheral regions. Such an environment would allow it to concentrate on reinforcing its strength, through which it could peacefully achieve the position of a global power in the international community. Thus, China is simultaneously applying the good neighbour policy and its 'Major Power Diplomacy' policy to the peninsula. Therefore, China's policy objectives in the Korean Peninsula involve maintaining peace and stability in the region to support China's rise.

Moreover, China attaches great importance to social coherence and regime survival. Thus, it prioritises a domestic-politics-driven mechanism of role taking and role making in its international relations, which is not in permanent opposition to the outside world. The contestation between domestic politics and the international positioning of a state[47] is a clear hurdle in the Chinese context.

Some of the important mantras for twenty-first century China are the 'peaceful rise' and 'responsible power'. However, North Korea directly impacts upon China's pursuit of the peaceful rise and responsible power rhetoric.[48] Moreover, China's commitment to economic development remains high on the agenda. It won't be distracted and wishes to see the external environment remain peaceful to enable China to grow.[49] Thus, despite China's conflict with

North Korea over the nuclear issue, China maintains its exchanges and cooperation with North Korea and is even attempting to systematise the relationship. As the scope and severity of sanctions has gradually increased, North Korea's relationship with China has become strained. Additionally, China sees North Korea's nuclear proliferation as an obstacle to its rise due to the issue's impact internationally. Therefore, China's is limited to playing a diplomatic role by facilitating and guiding the Six-Party Talks on the North Korea nuclear issue.[50]

The international community often has a high opinion of China's influence on North Korea. The reasons behind such an evaluation are twofold. The first stems from North Korea's high level of economic dependence on China. The second is related to the special character of China–North Korea relations. In the former case, China is indeed the biggest trading partner and largest provider of food and oil to North Korea. Over the course of the increasing sanctions against the North Korean economy and finance, North Korea's dependency on China has deepened. China is intending to secure a structural political advantage over Pyongyang in the form of its economic exchange with the DPRK. In short, China's trading activities and donation of aid to North Korea are being conducted as part of China's peripheral diplomacy. Since 2003, China has doubled its overseas investment in its so-called 'peripheral nations', including Myanmar, Cambodia, Bangladesh and North Korea. This indicates that China's increased investment in North Korea forms part of its overall strategy to stabilise its peripheral regions.[51]

In the latter case, even though China has a special relation with North Korea, its influence is very limited. China–DPRK relations have recently worsened due to North Korea's two nuclear tests and China's consent to UN sanctions against North Korea. Although North Korea and China have a mutual defence treaty, Chinese officials have emphasised that the relationship between China and North Korea is no different than any relationship between normal neighbouring countries.[52] It is also true that China has more cordial relations with South Korea than it does with the North. China cheers on both Koreas to denuclearise the peninsula by respecting each other's security concerns. In 2018 just before the Winter Olympics in Seoul, North Korea decided to send a group, and the two teams walked together during the opening session. Soon after this rapprochement, Kim Jong Un held his first direct talks with a South Korean delegation. Due to the interdependent character of the issue, this relatively positive environment encouraged dialogue and opened a path for direct talks with the US, and Trump and Kim Jong Un decided to meet in May.

Meanwhile, the North Korean leader Kim Jong Un made a secret trip to Beijing, which demonstrates that he values obtaining China's support and advice before meeting Trump.[53] The inclusion of North Korea in direct talks instead of unilateral sanctions increases the chances of success in resolving the crisis. However, previous experiences indicate the limitations of multilateral talks which resulted in North Korea's escalation of conflict and eventual withdrawal from talks in 2009. Moreover, North Korea's lack of experience in navigating such initiatives with other countries also threatens a comprehensive method of conflict resolution, and further complicates the scoping issue.

Normative and constitutive context

North Korea has not only managed to successfully transition to become a de facto nuclear-weapon state, yet to be recognised, but it has also substantially transformed the roles played by the United States, China, the International Atomic Energy Agency (IAEA), and the UN Security Council in the non-proliferation regime. In effect, Pyongyang's behaviour has resulted in the creation of a newly supplemented non-proliferation regime, based on Security Council resolutions and multilateral agreements which no longer prohibit North Korean nuclear weapons, but try to control their growth.[54] As a member of the UN Security Council, China was ascribed the role of a responsible actor in implementing the sanctions that are designed to disincentivise North Korean nuclear ambitions. However, China has supported sanctions conditionally, stressing 'that the measures are not intended to produce negative humanitarian consequences in the DPRK, nor affect normal economic and trade activities'. Indeed, China has offered its political and economic support to North Korea since the Korean War in the 1950s. China remains North Korea's most important trading partner. North Korea has employed many dual-use components coming from China to develop its illicit nuclear missile programme. China also offers the offshore financing from Chinese banks that Pyongyang needs to finance its activities.[55] China's province of Dandong is a critical hub for trade and investment.[56] China provides aid directly to North Korea, primarily in the form of food and energy assistance. Yet this Chinese engagement-oriented strategy not only keeps the North Korean people afloat, but also keeps North Korea open to Chinese-led initiatives. China's engagement-oriented strategic approach is informed by the previous failure of strong coercive pressure or siding with the US, which only reinforced North Korea's inflexibility.[57] According to Chinese thinking, North Korea resorts to extortion to compensate for its economic failings and regime vulnerabilities. The basic Chinese assumption is that an economically and politically secure North Korea would be more willing to engage with the outside world. In other words, China thinks pressuring North Korea will lead only to negative results.[58] Therefore, China promotes engagement strategies over coercion. The important point here is that even if China's engagement strategy inadvertently enables North Korea to pursue a nuclear programme economically, the political motivation of that very same programme arises as a response to US coercion. The history of nuclear proliferation clearly demonstrates that a politically motivated country will get the bomb sooner or later, even when subjected to the most strident sanctions. Therefore, China favours the existing status quo in a stable environment and tries to accommodate conflicting frames, to prevent the transformation of the issue into a zero-sum game. However, the negative image of North Korea's leader and surrounding uncertainties constitute the two main challenges to reaching this goal.

Firstly, the media representation of the North Korean leader Kim Jong Un as an 'irrational' dictator, or in Trump's words a 'madman', erodes China's capacity to reframe the North Korean issue in a more moderate context or establish reliable channels of communication characterised by mutual trust. Secondly, two types of uncertainties surround the North Korean nuclear issue: first, North Korea refused to release any information about the size, character, readiness or potential impacts of the weapons in its possession.[59] Another uncertainty emerges in line with China's wishes for regional stability, because regime instability in North Korea would create a flow of refugees across Chinese borders in addition to an undesired US base at its doorstep.[60] The latter evokes China's greatest nightmare of US military intervention – or worse, a nuclear war in its own backyard.

External expectations

Over the years, some have accused China of supporting the North Korean nuclear programme directly; others argue that China indirectly supports North Korea by supplying the needed materials and finance. Still others underline how China is the only country that has both the influence and the capacity to pressure North Korea to halt its nuclear programme.[61] Therefore, critics accuse China of refusing to capitalise on its political and economic weight in North Korea to stop its nuclear weapons programme. China has been under enormous pressure from the international community, especially from the US, to play an active role in responding to North Korea's bellicose acts. External perceptions impose a specific set of expectations on China to resolve the issue. However, China strongly rejects both the catalyst and arbiter roles, and maintains its traditional position of engagement. Thus, China has not reconciled its role with external expectations, despite altering its role to a certain degree.

Many suspect that China has less leverage than is generally perceived. The bilateral relationship between North Korea and China was once described as 'close as lips and teeth'.[62] They share a similar culture, a similar ideology. They fought shoulder to shoulder during the Korean War, and they have extensive trade relations. Yet the relationship has changed significantly since the 1970s and 1980s, when China resumed wide-ranging interactions with the United States, began doing business with South Korea, and recognised South Korea diplomatically in 1992, all of which alarmed North Korea. Since Chinese troops left North Korea in 1958, Beijing has had limited leverage over the country's policy direction.[63] Overall, as examined and reviewed above, the history of the relationship between China and North Korea has been characterised by feelings of disparity, anxiety, uneasiness and betrayal, rather than cordiality.[64]

Roles are relational, intersubjective concepts and cannot be sustained unilaterally. They must be recognised and reified through complementary roles and respective behaviour to support their constitutive and causal meaning.[65] The external actors in this conflict, including the USA, South Korea and Japan, expect China to take a specific role in solving the North Korea nuclear crisis which is more coercive than China's current intentions. Yet, should China embrace the ascribed coercive role and try to intervene rather heavy handedly, North Korea would be unlikely to acknowledge China's role. Despite the fact that Chinese aid is significant for North Korea's survival, it is dissatisfied with the scale of China's aid, and has openly expressed such dissatisfaction. North Korea thinks it plays a significant role as a buffer zone for China and as the protector of China's security by investing its limited resources in national defence.[66] Thus, North Korea actually tests its relationship with China every time it conducts another nuclear test. China, however, has not responded in the way that North Korea's brinkmanship strategy would expect; rather, it has responded in the way that the United States and the international community expect.

China defines its role on this issue with reference to several principles, yet it strongly emphasises sovereignty and non-interference in its foreign policy conduct, and these principles are significantly embedded in Chinese foreign policy rhetoric and practice. If China intervened it would be softly, with little formal action being taken. Indeed, China has altered its foreign policy behaviour over the course of the North Korean nuclear development through adaptation and social learning. However, this does not indicate that China has reconciled the expectations of the international community with its own perceptions.

China's approach towards the North Korean nuclear dispute pays special attention to North Korea's security needs. The search for security motivated North Korea to nuclearise; therefore, the pathway to de-nuclearisation should aim to fulfil the country's security needs. According to the Chinese perspective, subordinating North Korean security concerns undermines the effectiveness of international sanctions and disables Chinese leverage in North

Korea. Furthermore, the US approach drives North Korea to flex its military muscles, which escalates the risk of conflict.

Conclusion

Roles are relational social positions which are constituted by the ego and alter expectations of an actor in an organised group. The function of a role is limited in time and scope, and dependent on the group's structure and purpose. Some roles are constitutive of the group, eg a recognised member of the international community. Other international roles or role sets are functionally specific. China's changing role during the development of the crisis basically derives from the fact that both China and related actors have been learning and adapting.

As North Korea races towards the nuclear finishing line, if it has not already crossed that line, many analysts, experts, area specialists, politicians and diplomats see China's role as crucial in persuading North Korea to halt its nuclear programme. However, this is an immature assessment. When we analyse the current situation and China's role in the crisis from a role theory point of view, China has limited capacity and interest in fulfilling these external expectations. Many argue that China has refrained from actively engaging in sanctioning North Korea due to its geopolitical value as a buffer zone, as well as the costs associated with a neighbouring regime collapse. However, this fails to fully explain China's role-taking and role-making patterns within this conflict. Unless China changes its strategic goals to maintain peace and stability in the Korean Peninsula, China must simultaneously pursue regime stability alongside the denuclearisation of North Korea.

Finally, China is particularly wary of the US applying sanctions against North Korea as a means of expanding its influence in the region and countering China's rise. China is also concerned that the isolationist, provocative behaviour of North Korea may cause the collapse of the North Korean regime, which would strengthen the alliance between South Korea, the United States and Japan, thereby causing further tension on the Korean peninsula. China will therefore concentrate its diplomatic efforts on preventing the following dilemma: having to choose between the denuclearisation of North Korea and the stable maintenance of a China-friendly North Korean regime. Considering China's Korean Peninsula policy goals, however, if it cannot avoid choosing between the two, it is possible that it will choose the latter.

Disclosure statement

No potential conflict of interest was reported by the authors.

Notes

1. Fifield, "North Korea Is 'Racing towards the Nuclear Finish Line.'"
2. Sagan, "Nuclear Latency and Nuclear Proliferation," 81.
3. Pande, "North Korea's Pakistan Connection."
4. Manyin, *Foreign Assistance to North Korea*.
5. Corr, "Chinese Involvement in North Korea's Nuclear Missile Program."
6. Eleanor, "China–North Korea Relationship."
7. "How the China–North Korea Equation Is Changing."
8. Mastro, "Why China Won't Rescue North Korea."
9. S.-H. Lee, "Why China Won't Abandon North Korea Anytime Soon."
10. Harnisch, Bersick, and Gottwald, *China's International Roles*; He and Walker, "Role Bargaining Strategies for China's Peaceful Rise"; Michalski and Pan, "Role Dynamics in a Structured Relationship"; Uemura, "Understanding Chinese Foreign Relations."
11. Holsti, "National Role Conceptions in the Study of Foreign Policy."
12. Walker, *Role Theory And Foreign Policy Analysis*; see also Walker, "Role Theory and the Origins of Foreign Policy"; Walker, "Role Theory as an Empirical Theory."
13. Frankel, "Role Theory and Foreign Policy Analysis"; Harnisch, Frank, and Maull, *Role Theory in International Relations*; Cantir and Kaarbo, "Contested Roles and Domestic Politics"; Harnisch, "Conceptualizing in the Minefield"; Thies, "Role Theory and Foreign Policy"; Thies and Breuning, "Integrating Foreign Policy Analysis and International Relations"; Walker, "Role Theory as an Empirical Theory."
14. Thies, "Role Theory and Foreign Policy."
15. Harnisch, Frank, and Maull, *Role Theory in International Relations*, 2.
16. See for an innovative theoretical explanation of how past self-esteem effects foreign policy: Clunan, *Social Construction of Russia's Resurgence*.
17. Merton, "On Sociological Theories of the Middle Range [1949]."
18. Harnisch, Frank, and Maull, *Role Theory in International Relations*, 8.
19. Ibid., 12.
20. Harnisch, Bersick, and Gottwald, *China's International Roles*, 3.
21. Oualaalou, "US Era of Dominance Is Dwindling."
22. Poplak, "New Scramble for Africa."
23. Phillips, "Xi Jinping Heralds 'New Era.'"
24. Harnisch, Bersick, and Gottwald, *China's International Roles*, 7.
25. K. Lee and Kim, "Cooperation and Limitations of China's Sanctions."
26. Osnos, "Biggest Winner in Singapore."
27. D. R. Lee, "China's Policy and Influence."
28. Osnos, "Biggest Winner in Singapore."
29. Kim, "Endangering Alliance or Risking Proliferation?"
30. K. Lee and Kim, "Cooperation and Limitations of China's Sanctions."
31. Page, "Unexpected Winner from the Trump–Kim Summit."
32. "Foreign Minister Wang Yi Meets the Press."
33. Eleanor, "China–North Korea Relationship."
34. Taylor, "Why China Is So Mad about THAAD."
35. Harnisch, "Role Theory, Organizational Actors and Regime Stability."
36. K. Lee and Kim, "Cooperation and Limitations of China's Sanctions."
37. Harnisch, "Role Theory, Organizational Actors and Regime Stability."

38.   "China Imposes Import Bans on North Korean Iron."
39.   Harnisch, "Role Theory, Organizational Actors and Regime Stability."
40.   K. Lee and Kim, "Cooperation and Limitations of China's Sanctions."
41.   Song and Lee, "China's Engagement Patterns towards North Korea."
42.   "China Says 'Dual Suspension' Proposal Still Best."
43.   Kong, "China's Engagement-Oriented Strategy towards North Korea."
44.   "China Hits Back at Trump Criticism."
45.   K. Lee and Kim, "Cooperation and Limitations of China's Sanctions."
46.   D. R. Lee, "China's Policy and Influence."
47.   Cantir and Kaarbo, "Contested Roles and Domestic Politics."
48.   Kong, "China's Engagement-Oriented Strategy towards North Korea."
49.   "Speech by Fu Ying – Munich Security Conference."
50.   D. R. Lee, "China's Policy and Influence."
51.   Lee, "Why China Won't Abandon North Korea Anytime Soon."
52.   Song and Lee, "China's Engagement Patterns towards North Korea."
53.   Myers and Perlez, "Kim Jong-Un Met with Xi Jinping."
54.   Harnisch, "Role Theory, Organizational Actors and Regime Stability."
55.   Blanco, "Is Trump Willing to Anger China."
56.   Eleanor, "China Has the Most Leverage."
57.   Kong, "China's Engagement-Oriented Strategy towards North Korea."
58.   D. R. Lee, "China's Policy and Influence."
59.   Bennett, *Uncertainties in the North Korean Nuclear Threat*.
60.   Weley, "Why China Won't Help US."
61.   Lockie, "China Could Stop North Korea's Nuclear Threat."
62.   Xiaohe, "Evolution of the Lips and Teeth Relationship."
63.   Cathcart, "North Korea Doesn't Trust China."
64.   Choo, "A Question of Leverage."
65.   Harnisch, "Role Theory, Organizational Actors and Regime Stability."
66.   D. R. Lee, "China's Policy and Influence."

Bibliography

Bennett, Bruce W. *Uncertainties in the North Korean Nuclear Threat*. Documented Briefing, DB-589-NDU. Santa Monica, CA: RAND, National Defense Research Institute, 2010.

Blanco, Rici. "Is Trump Willing to Anger China and Go after the Companies Supplying North Korea's Nuclear Program?" *Newsweek*, July 13, 2017. http://www.newsweek.com/2017/07/21/trump-stop-chinese-companies-supplying-north-koreas-nuclear-weapons-635538.html

Cantir, Cristian, and Juliet Kaarbo. "Contested Roles and Domestic Politics: Reflections on Role Theory in Foreign Policy Analysis and IR Theory: Contested Roles and Domestic Politics." *Foreign Policy Analysis* 8, no. 1 (January 2012): 5–24. https://doi.org/10.1111/j.1743-8594.2011.00156.x.

Cathcart. "North Korea Doesn't Trust China an Inch." *Foreign Policy* (blog), March 8, 2017. https://foreignpolicy.com/2017/03/08/north-korea-doesnt-trust-china-an-inch/

"China Hits Back at Trump Criticism over North Korea." *Reuters*, August 1, 2017. https://www.reuters.com/article/us-northkorea-missiles-idUSKBN1AG04F

"China Imposes Import Bans on North Korean Iron, Coal and Seafood." *BBC News*, August 15, 2017, sec. Business. http://www.bbc.com/news/business-40932427

"China Says 'Dual Suspension' Proposal Still Best for North Korea." *Reuters*, November 16, 2017. https://www.reuters.com/article/us-northkorea-missiles-china-usa/china-says-dual-suspension-proposal-still-best-for-north-korea-idUSKBN1DG10Y

Choo, Jaewoo. "A Question of Leverage: China's Role in the Korea Crisis." *Asia Times*, February 8, 2003. http://www.atimes.com/atimes/Korea/EB28Dg01.html

Clunan, Anne L. *The Social Construction of Russia's Resurgence: Aspirations, Identity, and Security Interests*. Baltimore, MD: Johns Hopkins Press, 2009.

Corr, Anders. "Chinese Involvement in North Korea's Nuclear Missile Program: From Trucks to Warheads." *Forbes*, July 5, 2017. https://www.forbes.com/sites/anderscorr/2017/07/05/chinese-involvement-in-north-koreas-nuclear-missile-program-from-warheads-to-trucks/

Eleanor, Albert. "China Has the Most Leverage on Kim Jong-Un's Regime. Will It Use It?" *Council on Foreign Relations*, March 28, 2018. https://www.cfr.org/backgrounder/china-north-korea-relationship

Eleanor, Albert. "The China–North Korea Relationship." *Council on Foreign Relations*, March 28, 2018. https://www.cfr.org/backgrounder/china-north-korea-relationship

Fifield, Anna. "North Korea Is 'Racing towards the Nuclear Finish Line.'" *Washington Post*, October 8, 2016, sec. World. https://www.washingtonpost.com/world/north-korea-is-racing-towards-the-nuclear-finish-line/2016/10/07/c4288d30-84c5-11e6-b57d-dd49277af02f_story.html

"Foreign Minister Wang Yi Meets the Press." Ministry of Foreign Affairs of People's Republic of China, March 8, 2017. http://www.fmprc.gov.cn/mfa_eng/zxxx_662805/t1444204.shtml

Frankel, Joseph. "Role Theory and Foreign Policy Analysis." *International Affairs* 64, no. 1 (1987): 106–107. https://doi.org/10.2307/2621503.

Harnisch, Sebastian. "Conceptualizing in the Minefield: Role Theory and Foreign Policy Learning: Role Theory and Foreign Policy Learning." *Foreign Policy Analysis* 8, no. 1 (2012): 47–69. https://doi.org/10.1111/j.1743-8594.2011.00155.x.

Harnisch, Sebastian. "Role Theory, Organizational Actors and Regime Stability." Paper presented at the Integrating Foreign Policy Analysis and International Relations through Role Theory, Annual ISA-Conference, Montreal, March 19, 2011.

Harnisch, Sebastian, Sebastian Bersick, and Jörn-Carsten Gottwald, eds. *China's International Roles: Challenging or Supporting International Order?* 1st ed. New York, NY: Routledge, 2015.

Harnisch, Sebastian, Cornelia Frank, and Hanns W. Maull, eds. *Role Theory in International Relations*. 1st ed. London, UK: Routledge, 2012.

He, Kai, and Stephen Walker. "Role Bargaining Strategies for China's Peaceful Rise." *The Chinese Journal of International Politics*, 8, no. 4 (2015): 371–388. https://doi.org/10.1093/cjip/pov009.

Holsti, K. J. "National Role Conceptions in the Study of Foreign Policy." *International Studies Quarterly* 14, no. 3 (1970): 233. https://doi.org/10.2307/3013584.

"How the China–North Korea Equation Is Changing." *The Economist*, June 2017. https://www.economist.com/news/united-states/21723118-america-strives-respond-clear-and-present-danger-how-china-north-korea-equation

Kim, Sung Chull. "Endangering Alliance or Risking Proliferation? US–Japan and US–Korea Nuclear Energy Cooperation Agreements." *The Pacific Review* 30, no. 5 (2017): 692–709. https://doi.org/10.1080/09512748.2017.1293715.

Kong, Tat Yan. "China's Engagement-Oriented Strategy towards North Korea: Achievements and Limitations." *The Pacific Review*, 31, no. 1 (2018): 76–95. https://doi.org/10.1080/09512748.2017.1316301.

Lee, Dong Ryul. "China's Policy and Influence on the North Korea Nuclear Issue: Denuclearization and/or Stabilization of the Korean Peninsula?" *Korean Journal of Defense Analysis* 22, no. 2 (2010): 163–181. https://doi.org/10.1080/10163271003744421.

Lee, Kihyun, and Jangho Kim. "Cooperation and Limitations of China's Sanctions on North Korea: Perception, Interest and Institutional Environment." *North Korean Review* 13, no. 1 (2017): 28.

Lee, Seong-Hyon. "Why China Won't Abandon North Korea Anytime Soon." *Huffington Post* (blog), August 18, 2017. http://www.huffingtonpost.com/entry/china-north-korea-trump_us_5995b-f3ae4b0acc593e5ff38

Lockie, Alex. "China Could Stop North Korea's Nuclear Threat in a Heartbeat without Firing a Shot." *Business Insider*, June 9, 2017. http://www.businessinsider.com/china-disarm-north-korea-trump-2017-6

Manyin, Mark E. *Foreign Assistance to North Korea*. Washington, DC: Library of Congress Congressional Research Service, 2005.

Mastro, Oriana Skylar. "Why China Won't Rescue North Korea." *Foreign Affairs*, December 12, 2017. https://www.foreignaffairs.com/articles/asia/2017-12-12/why-china-wont-rescue-north-korea

Merton, Robert King. "On Sociological Theories of the Middle Range [1949]." In Social Theory and Social Structure, 39–53. New York: Simon & Schuster, The Free Press, 1949.

Michalski, Anna, and Zhongqi Pan. "Role Dynamics in a Structured Relationship: The EU–China Strategic Partnership." JCMS: Journal of Common Market Studies 55, no. 3 (2017): 611–627. https://doi.org/10.1111/jcms.12505.

Myers, Steven Lee, and Jane Perlez. "Kim Jong-Un Met with Xi Jinping in Secret Beijing Visit." The New York Times, March 27, 2018, sec. Asia Pacific. https://www.nytimes.com/2018/03/27/world/asia/kim-jong-un-china-north-korea.html

Osnos, Evan. "The Biggest Winner in Singapore: China." The New Yorker, June 12, 2018. https://www.newyorker.com/news/daily-comment/the-biggest-winner-at-the-us-north-korea-summit-china

Oualaalou, David. "US Era of Dominance Is Dwindling as China Takes over the World Economy." Huffington Post (blog), December 15, 2014. http://www.huffingtonpost.com/david-oualaalou/us-era-of-dominance-is-dw_b_6299040.html

Page, Jeremy. "The Unexpected Winner from the Trump–Kim Summit: China." Wall Street Journal, June 13, 2018, sec. World. https://www.wsj.com/articles/the-unexpected-winner-from-the-trump-kim-summit-china-1528882206

Pande, Aparna. "North Korea's Pakistan Connection." Huffington Post (blog), January 8, 2016. http://www.huffingtonpost.com/aparna-pande/north-koreas-pakistan-con_b_8938516.html

Phillips, Tom. "Xi Jinping Heralds 'New Era' of Chinese Power at Communist Party Congress." The Guardian, October 18, 2017, sec. World News. http://www.theguardian.com/world/2017/oct/18/xi-jinping-speech-new-era-chinese-power-party-congress

Poplak, Richard. "The New Scramble for Africa: How China Became the Partner of Choice." The Guardian, December 22, 2016, sec. Global Development Professionals Network. http://www.theguardian.com/global-development-professionals-network/2016/dec/22/the-new-scramble-for-africa-how-china-became-the-partner-of-choice

Sagan, Scott D. "Nuclear Latency and Nuclear Proliferation." In Forecasting Nuclear Proliferation in the 21st Century, edited by William C. Potter and Gaukhar Mukhatzhanova, vol. 2, 80–101. Palo Alto, CA: Stanford Security Studies, 2010.

Song, Wenzhi, and Sangkeun Lee. "China's Engagement Patterns towards North Korea: China's Engagement with North Korea." Pacific Focus 31, no. 1 (2016): 5–30. https://doi.org/10.1111/pafo.12063.

"Speech by Fu Ying – Munich Security Conference." Accessed August 27, 2017. https://www.security-conference.de/en/activities/munich-security-conference/msc-2016/speeches/speech-by-fu-ying/

Taylor, Adam. "Why China Is So Mad about THAAD, a Missile Defense System Aimed at Deterring North Korea." Washington Post, March 7, 2017. https://www.washingtonpost.com/news/worldviews/wp/2017/03/07/why-china-is-so-mad-about-thaad-a-missile-defense-system-aimed-at-deterring-north-korea/

Thies, Cameron. "Role Theory and Foreign Policy." In International Studies Association Compendium Project, Foreign Policy Analysis Section, 1–44, 2009. http://myweb.uiowa.edu/bhlai/workshop/role.Pdf

Thies, Cameron, and Marijke Breuning. "Integrating Foreign Policy Analysis and International Relations through Role Theory: Integrating FPA and IR." Foreign Policy Analysis 8, no. 1 (2012): 1–4. https://doi.org/10.1111/j.1743-8594.2011.00169.x.

Uemura, Takeshi. "Understanding Chinese Foreign Relations: A Cultural Constructivist Approach." International Studies Perspectives 16, no. 3 (2015): 345–365. https://doi.org/10.1111/insp.12038.

Walker, Stephen G. Role Theory and Foreign Policy Analysis. Durham, NC: Duke University Press, 1987.

Walker, Stephen G. "Role Theory and the Origins of Foreign Policy." In New Directions in the Study of Foreign Policy, edited by Charles F. Hermann, Charles W. Kegley, and James N. Rosenau 269–284. London, UK: Routledge, 1987.

Walker, Stephen G. "Role Theory as an Empirical Theory of International Relations: From Metaphor to Formal Model." January 25, 2017. https://doi.org/10.1093/acrefore/9780190228637.013.286

Weley, Rahn. "Why China Won't Help US against North Korea | DW | 15.09.2017." *DW.COM*, September 9,2017. http://www.dw.com/en/why-china-wont-help-us-against-north-korea/a-40525522

Xiaohe, Cheng. "The Evolution of the Lips and Teeth Relationship: China–North Korea Relations in the 1960s." In *China and North Korea: International Relations and Comparisons in Northeast Asia*, edited by C. P. Freeman, 119–137. New York, NY: Palgrave Macmillan, 2015. https://doi.org/10.1057/9781137455666_8.

Interests or ideas? Explaining Brazil's surge in peacekeeping and peacebuilding

Charles T. Call

ABSTRACT

Brazil is one of several rising powers that assumed greater protagonism in advancing peace on the global stage and in the Global South beginning in the early 2000s. In places like Haiti, East Timor, Guinea-Bissau, Angola and Mozambique, it expanded its peacekeeping deployments and exercised leadership on peacebuilding issues. What explains this notably increased activity on peace-related issues? In this article, I test four core theories of international relations – realism, liberalism, constructivism and post-colonial theory – to explain the rise and content of these policies in that country. Brazil has been vocal in its non-traditional approaches to peacekeeping and peacebuilding, and this study examines its rhetorical claims through theoretical lenses. It aspires to bring systematic theoretical thinking to a case whose empirics have been used to support each of the four main theoretical approaches. I argue that interest-based theories such as realism and liberalism best account for the emergence of Brazil's increased peacekeeping and peacebuilding initiatives in the early 2000s. However, idea-based constructivist and post-colonial approaches are necessary to account for the content of these approaches that reflect national identity and social and culturally historic experiences.

Rising powers have attracted much attention in the past decade, as scholars wrestled with whether the postwar liberal order was undergoing a fundamental transformation. Prompted in part by economic crisis in the late 1990s, the Group of Twenty (G20) arose to rival the Group of Eight (G8). Further shifts away from unipolarity were sounded by the rise of the BRICS (Brazil, Russia, India, China and South Africa) and the MINT (Mexico, Indonesia, Nigeria and Turkey) and the dramatic growth of these countries' middle classes and trade levels. The foreign security policies of these countries received less notice than their economic policies. Many 'rising powers' launched new initiatives of development cooperation, mediation efforts, peacekeeping commitments and post-conflict peacebuilding programmes in the early 2000s. China increased its deployment of peacekeeping troops substantially, and Turkey initiated high-profile 'humanitarian diplomacy' in Somalia and other places.

Brazil was among the most explicit and vocal about its enhanced support for peace on the global stage and in conflict-affected countries. The country became a high-profile

Article for special issue on 'Rising Powers and International Conflict Management', of *Third World Quarterly*
This article has been republished with minor changes. These changes do not impact the academic content of the article.

advocate of non-Western approaches to development cooperation, peace operations and other initiatives related to peacebuilding. Under President Luiz Inácio Lula da Silva (2003–2010), Brazil vastly expanded its technical cooperation with post-conflict countries such as Angola, Mozambique, Guinea-Bissau and East Timor, tripling its total aid to $923 million.[1] It also sponsored and executed peace-related development projects to support the United Nations (UN) Stabilization Mission in Haiti (MINUSTAH), deploying troops there and holding its military command continuously for 13 years starting in 2004. Both in its home region and beyond this vicinity, Brazil engaged in conflict mediation efforts, whether through regional organisations like the Union of South American States (UNASUR) or via ad hoc efforts as with Turkey on Iran's nuclear development.[2] This activism formed part of a broader pattern, as then-Foreign Minister Celso Amorim described in 2005:

> Brazilian diplomacy is presently going through a period of great dynamism, in accordance with priorities established by President Lula's Government: to expand the geographical reach of Brazil's foreign relations, … and to adopt a firm and active position in multilateral as well as regional negotiations, with a view to securing an international regulatory area that is fair and balanced.[3]

At the UN, Brazil was instrumental in the creation of the UN peacebuilding architecture in 2005 and assumed a leadership role of the Peacebuilding Commission, leading its efforts on Guinea-Bissau. In UN normative debates, Brazil promoted peacebuilding as a complement and sometimes as an alternative to militarised approaches to peacekeeping, arguing that investing in political processes and socioeconomic development was essential to the promotion of peace. It proposed 'Responsibility while Protecting' as a less interventionist alternative to the 'Responsibility to Protect' (R2P).

Brazil is just one example of rising powers that assumed greater protagonism in advancing peace on the global stage and in the Global South beginning in the early 2000s. What explains this new trend? Is it classic realist behaviour of middle powers seeking to rise in the global pecking order? Does it reflect a new liberal commitment to enhanced integrated approaches to global trade and order? Or do post-colonial theories find support from Brazil's proclaimed attempt to try to transform the Western-dominated overly militarised approach to global peace and security? Does Brazil's identity as a developmental, non-interventionist middle power expressing solidarity with other former colonies help explain these new policies? Why would a middle-income nation with developmental challenges of its own invest precious resources in foreign ventures?

In this article, I use the case of Brazil to explore these questions. Specifically, I test four core theories of international relations – realism, liberalism, constructivism and post-colonial theory – to explain the rise and content of these policies in that country. The treatment of these theoretical approaches is necessarily telegraphic for reasons of space and deriving testable hypotheses (see Table 1). Brazil is a case that has been vocal in its non-traditional approaches to peacekeeping and peacebuilding, and this study should help understand whether those claims rest on interest or ideas, on the influence of outside powers or on Brazil's own multilateral commitments. I undertook this study to try to bring greater theoretical thinking to a case whose empirics have been used to support each of the four main theoretical approaches. Based on secondary literature on Brazil's operations and on personal interviews with senior Brazilian diplomats, I here argue that interest-based theories such as realism and liberalism best account for the *emergence* of Brazil's increased peacekeeping and peacebuilding initiatives in the early 2000s. However, idea-based constructivist and

Table 1. Predicted behavior of rising powers in peacebuilding.

By this theory:	We expect the motives and content of peacebuilding policies to …
REALISM	Enhance the power and status of the state Enhance the country's economic power Enhance the regional power and status of the country
LIBERALISM	Expand investment and trade opportunities Enhance liberal order, including multilateral organisations Reflect the country's own domestic politics and processes
CONSTRUCTIVISM	Reflect socially generated traits, even when not in the state's interest Reflect state identities, as historically developed in relation to others
CRITICAL THEORY	
-Structural variant	Reflect elite action that benefits colonial or great powers Reflect the patterns and desires of dominant states, including stability in the periphery
-Agency variant	Reflect more emancipatory outcomes, but only where local peoples mobilise or are given voice

post-colonial approaches are necessary to account for the *content* of these approaches that reflect national identity and social and culturally historic experiences.

I. International relations theories and rising powers' peace promotion

Realism and rising powers

Among theories of international relations, realism 'offers the bleakest view of middle power's capacities'.[4] Structural realists draw a direct link between material capabilities and international standing and influence, generally dismissing the potential for the middle powers to engage in the realm of power politics dominated by the great powers.[5] Middle powers are generally seen as secondary partners in global alliances or, once they rise enough to knock on the door of the great powers club, potential swing states in power transitions that reconfigure the status quo.

In contrast with neorealists, classical or contemporary realists see a state's perceptions of its place in the world as shaping state behaviour. For contemporary realists, as the economies of rising powers grow, their foreign policy orientations should become 'more aggressive and status-seeking over time to match the growth in power'.[6] And multilateral organisations are peripheral to the pursuit of interests, a sideshow to bilateral exercise of power.[7] As Cooper and Flemes say, 'traditionally the image of emerging powers has not been a multilateral one'.[8]

For neoclassical realists, as the material capabilities of the middle powers grow, they may begin to challenge the hegemon or exercise power in a region.[9] Economic strength is seen as both secondary to and derivative of military strength. Since the military might of most rising powers is meagre relative to that of the United States, realist thinkers only widely recognised the emerging economic strength of middle powers after the global crisis of 2008, when the middle power economies seemed to be impervious to the crisis that encumbered the traditional global powers.[10]

Despite their eschewing multilateralism, realists may accept the utility of peacekeeping to manage stability in the periphery but not post-conflict peacebuilding.[11] In this view, deploying troops in peacekeeping operations can be rational as it serves security interests.[12] In contrast, investments in development aspects of peacebuilding fall outside the conceived logic of interstate competition for realists. Largely ignoring much of the literature on rising powers' South–South cooperation, realists emphasise how strategic interests seem to be the main factor guiding UN and rising powers' activities, supposed proof of the limited autonomous role of the UN. For instance, Gegout's study of the Democratic Republic of the Congo argues that Western interests, specifically France's attempt to maintain its post-colonial sphere of influence, guided external conflict prevention, peacekeeping and peacebuilding.[13]

According to realist theory, one should expect rising powers to engage in peacekeeping with a view to enhance their own status and military gains, through either alliance positioning or the concrete benefits of military experience and training. Rather than attempting to engage meaningfully with peacebuilding, rising powers should rationally act bilaterally and rarely if ever support efforts beyond the attempt to quell conflict. And in a realist view, emerging regional powers can be expected to focus especially on their regional sphere of influence, where their interests are most at stake.

Liberalism and rising powers

As with realism, there is important variation in liberalism, especially between its structural and classical variants. By adopting several realist assumptions, the neoliberal literature since the 1980s tends to allow for more expansive cooperation than earlier 'classical' liberals who focused more on domestic sources of policy and institutional incentives. Generally, neoliberals see the involvement of rising powers in peacebuilding and peacekeeping as deriving from strategic approaches to the world order and its liberal foundations.[14] Ikenberry,[15] for instance, argues that rising powers will be coopted into the dominant order because of its benefits and its self-reinforcing nature. Discussing China, he argues that economically, the benefits of economic openness as well as the possibility of a leadership role are significantly more promising than an attempt to create a new order from scratch. Due to middle powers' place within the global economy, as well as the benefits that they gain from this involvement, any attempt by rising powers to reform the system could destabilise the global economy. Thus, long-terms goals such as UN Security Council reform 'are evolutionary rather than revolutionary in scope and pace'.[16] Emerging powers calculate that they may lose status and position if they press too hard for transforming the order.

For neoliberals, the benefits of cooperation drive state involvement. These benefits rest in the liberal order. Like Chinese engagement with the World Trade Organization (WTO), involvement with the UN peace operations is a part of a wider system which has, as a whole, been greatly beneficial. In the understanding of Richmond and Tellidis, these rising powers should therefore be understood as status quo, rather than critical, states. They generally seek to expand trade and investment and to enhance their position in the international trade regime rather than challenging that regime. While they may not agree with the totality of the 'liberal/neoliberal peace system', they will find benefits to working within, rather than seeking to overturn, the system.[17] And that system is conceived primarily as a multilateral one, and interests are served by strengthening the multilateral system itself and their own role within it.

Strains of liberalism that draw on domestic sources, and especially a focus on the democratic peace, have different explanations of middle powers' role in peacemaking and peacebuilding. Some liberal theorists emphasise the norms that emerge among states that embrace peaceful resolution of conflicts,[18] and others the institutional structures that prevent disputes from becoming violent.[19] According to the latter argument, leaders have to mobilise public opinion and interest groups, as well as a variety of institutions, making it harder for democracies to mobilise for warfare. How these proclivities translate to foreign policy decisions of rising powers is not clear. Although liberals postulate that domestic regime types and electoral politics shape foreign policy, liberalism is not the only theory that 'sees' domestic factors, as we will see below. Constructivism and post-colonial theories also allow for such influence, although less explicitly and with less notoriety.

Constructivism and rising powers

By questioning the fixed, given nature of state preferences and analysing additional actors, constructivist research has challenged the realist focus on great powers. Finnemore argues that international organisations serve as one part of the social structure of the international system, one of many elements guiding the preferences and values of states: 'We cannot understand what states want without understanding the international social structure of which they are a part'.[20] Examining norm entrepreneurs, Finnemore and Sikkink[21] analyse how multilateral organisations can be used as a platform for actors in the emergence of new norms. In this process, secondary actors, including emerging powers, can generate and help institutionalise norms that reconstitute the great power club.[22]

For constructivists, the increase in rising powers' involvement in peacekeeping and peace-building is not difficult to explain. Rather than a focus on material capabilities and given interests postulated by realists or neoliberals, constructivists point to identities constructed mutually and historically within international society as shaping the foreign policy of rising powers. Instead of seeing the move towards the status of regional or 'great power' as related to, say, a country's nuclear status or military might, constructivists emphasise the social element of this position.[23] Multilateral institutions like the UN and civil society, global discourse and evolving norms all play a role in state identities, which in turn reconstitute the former.

The distinctive identities of middle powers shape rising powers' foreign policies and their degree of coherence with the dominant liberal order. While it would be foolish to attempt to identify a clear set of norms and identities held by these powers, Capie[24] highlights that they, 'share a common experience of being outside the core group of states who shaped the post-World War II international order'. One can identify a series of characteristics that roughly align with rising states' identities, specifically their post-colonial status and history of non-alignment. This does not necessarily mean that these states will contest the international order. Rather than attempting to overthrow this system, their foreign policy may revolve around reshaping established norms *and* the introduction of new norms.

Peacebuilding and peacekeeping can therefore fit neatly into the proposed actions of rising powers according to constructivist theory. Peace actions through the UN can be seen as linked to the formation and reinforcement of new norms, an example of constructivism in action. Bearing in mind the role of states' interests, it is possible to see how these norms influence the nature of peacekeeping undertaken by states. As rising powers increasingly contribute both troops and funds towards peace operations, their interaction with the UN and other states will shape the conceptualisation and operations of these missions. This can reshape peacebuilding to reflect non-Western ideas: 'Peace missions entail the dissemination (read construction) of new norms'.[25] In this way rising powers shape both the concrete mission and the business of peacebuilding in accordance with their own identities.

One should not aggregate middle powers around a single set of interests or identity characteristics. As Richmond and Tellidis[26] claim, 'Variations in interests, ideology, capacity, and experience' serve to shape the form peacebuilding and peacekeeping take, as well as their wider development agenda. Yet we can here see some commonalities, such as the Westphalian emphasis on sovereignty,[27] and an emphasis on rapid and inclusive economic development as the precursor to, rather than the outcome of, security.[28] In addition, while these states vary in their embrace of democracy and globalisation, they tend to reject intervention. One would thus expect that rising powers will shape peacebuilding in ways that reflect their shared and particular identities, and that their actions may not reflect rational pursuit of material and power interests.

Critical theory and rising powers

Although constructivist work presented a critical challenge to the dominance of neorealism and neoliberalism, for critical theorists constructivism still maintains an orthodox view of global governance. While there are elements of crossover between the two schools of thought, for critical theorists the mainstream of international relations is unwilling to engage with the structures underlying the role and functions of the various elements in the international system. With their focus on the questioning the purpose of global governance, as well as the elite-focused nature of multilateral organisations, critical theorists discussing multilateral organisations often emphasise the limitations of taking their behaviour and roles at face value. Instead, according to Gill these organisations are part of the contemporary system of global governance that mediates 'relations of the ruled and the rulers'.[29]

A significant amount of critical literature specifically discusses international organisations and peace operations. Much of this has a structural tenor, emphasising the overweening power of the Western-dominated capitalist system. Drawing on the work of Cox, Pugh argues that peacekeeping can be seen as being dictated by 'problem-solving imperatives'.[30] In this way, for Pugh peacekeeping is a form of 'riot control', directed against states unwilling to accept the dominant neoliberal values. Looking more directly at the national involvement in the operations themselves, another key focus is the burden taken on by developing countries in regards to troop contribution. Even as rising powers such as India and Brazil dedicate more troops to peace operations, they and other middle powers lament that their risk and sacrifice are not matched by decision-making power over the mandates and resources of such operations, which remains largely in the hands of the UN Security Council.[31] Beyond these critiques of representation and governance of peace operations, rising powers and others of the Global South also criticise liberal models as deepening marginalisation and exclusion in ways that serve Western interests.[32] Even where peace operations have sought to allay criticism, the shift to bottom-up approaches has only imbued the liberal peace with a sheen of 'local legitimacy' while doing nothing to address the hierarchies of exclusion reinforced by peace operations.[33]

This structural variant of critical theory, in which peacebuilding seems highly determined by former colonial powers and the dominant liberal order, is accompanied by another that allows for more agency. Some critical theorists advocate 'emancipatory' peacebuilding that can transform these patterns towards empowerment of local peoples.[34] In this view, local peoples and their allies, implicitly even powerful and less powerful states, can transform dominant approaches to post-conflict countries. Rising powers have received little attention in this literature.[35] Although as a group the rising powers are hardly revolutionary in their engagement with liberal institutions, Richmond and Tellidis argue that they have been critical in peacebuilding policies and the R2P, and that these positions can be influential.[36] In this agent-centric critical view, one can expect rising powers to exhibit some liberating impulses that can undermine or transform liberal peacebuilding.

II. Explaining Brazilian peacebuilding

Having examined how four major theories of international relations speak to the role and policies of rising powers surrounding their efforts to advance peace in other countries and globally, I now turn to examining how these theories apply to the case of Brazil. Brazil has long sought to expand its economic and political position in the world, and to play a role befitting its status as the world's eighth-largest economy and fifth-most populous country. It is one of few countries that spans a continent, a regional hegemon.

In the early 2000s, Brazil launched an open campaign for greater prominence on the international stage. At the 2003 WTO meeting in Cancún, Brazil adopted firmer positions for fairer terms of trade and also 'emerged as a catalyst and organizer' of developing countries that brought negotiations over North–South trade to a standstill.[37] Especially under the leadership of President Luiz Inácio Lula da Silva, it pressed for transformations in the multi-lateral system, including helping create and then exercise leadership in fora such as the BRICS coalition and the IBSA (India, Brazil, and South Africa) Dialogue Forum. It also worked to gain greater influence within the multilateral system, but one that contested militarised approaches and pressed for stronger development content during UN engagements in con-flictive countries. Under Lula, Brazil almost tripled its development cooperation to $1.6 billion reais (USD $923 million at the time). Some 66.3% of this total was channeled through mul-tilateral cooperation, and the remainder through bilateral efforts focusing on Latin America and Africa.[38] This represented a significant surge and diversification in Brazil's role in devel-opment, including in many conflict-affected countries. Lula visited 27 countries in Africa and opened 19 new embassies there.[39] This activity continued with less intensity under presidents Rousseff and Temer, and its future is unclear under President Bolsonaro.

Brazil's greater efforts to advance peace and development in other countries coincided with this expanded global leadership. Its assumption of the leadership and largest military contingent within MINUSTAH and its earlier contribution to the UN mission in East Timor (UNTAET) show its commitment to a greater role in the world's highest profile multilateral security mechanism: peacekeeping. It sought more prominence in peacebuilding and medi-ation, as seen by Brazil's leadership role in the UN Peacebuilding Commission and its country grouping on Guinea-Bissau, as well as its effort to broker a deal with Iran on nuclear issues. Its development cooperation increased dramatically, as did its humanitarian aid. In the sec-tion that follows, I apply the theories described earlier to argue that interest-based accounts – specifically realism and liberalism – best account for the origins of this new peacebuilding profile. The subsequent section will argue that other, idea-centric theories best account for the content of those policies.

A. Interests and the origins of Brazil's new peace-advocacy role

Realism. In considering the predictions of competing international relations theories for Brazil's new peacebuilding role, realism certainly holds relevance. Several pieces of evidence support realist tenets that Brazil's behaviour is no different from classic middle power behaviour as they seek power, status and economic might in an anarchic system of states. Chief among these is the country's open campaign for a permanent seat on the UN Security Council that coincided with its new peacebuilding role. Other new policies point towards the state's aspirations for enhanced status and power: disrupting a Western-designed reform at the 2003 Cancun meeting of the WTO; the decision to develop a nuclear-powered submarine, the successful campaign to host the Olympics and the World Cup; and the eventually successful effort to place a Brazilian national at the helm of the WTO.[40] Brazil mobilised a new bloc of rising powers – UNASUR, the Community of Latin American and Caribbean States (CELAC) the BRICS and IBSA – with the express intent of rivaling great powers' control of the global liberal order. This represents realist second-tier powers bandwagoning against the dominant powers.

Brazil's projection of military power is exemplified by its offer to take the military leadership of the UN Mission in Haiti in 2004. Although Brazil had a long history of participating in UN peacekeeping missions,[41] the 2004 offer was surprising to some on the Brazilian right and left as it seemed to ratify and support only the most recent of a litany of US-led interventions in a desperately poor country. Brazil's eagerness to lead the UN mission that would administer the country on the heels of the UN-authorised, US-led deployment puzzled many observers. It seemed to legitimise an intervention that, unlike the US-led intervention that restored democracy in 1994, was decried by the left across Latin America when it forced out a popular leftist elected president. As such, Brazil's cooperation with the post-intervention peace operation seemed to tacitly approve an intervention that defied the country's principles of foreign policy endorsing force only as a last resort.

Ultimately, Brazil would hold the Force Commander position that oversaw all military troops of MINUSTAH for an unprecedented 13 years (2004–2017). That deployment was described by Brazilian defence officials as providing valuable training and real-world experience confronting armed challengers, especially as the military took on violent militias in shantytowns surrounding Port-au-Prince. The events surrounding an expanded role in peace operations support the thesis that Brazil was motivated mainly by a desire for greater power and status in the international system. In explaining Brazil's peacekeeping deployments, Sánchez Nieto dismisses arguments about military training, national development and of 'Good Samaritan' national pride; instead 'it is more motivated by global power-level goals'.[42]

Liberalism. If Brazil's behaviour reflects the acquisitive behaviour predicted by realists, three aspects of Brazil's peacebuilding policies epitomise liberal precepts. First is the country's emphasis on multilateralism. The vast majority of Brazil's engagements – not just peacekeeping and peacebuilding, but even its development – occur through multilateral institutions. As Lula stated in 2007, 'Our foreign policy, which is the cause of some pride due to the excellent results it has brought to the Nation, was defined by a clear choice for multilateralism, required for the establishment of a world of peace and solidarity'.[43]

Its highest profile endeavours of the past 20 years revolve around UN peacekeeping. This reflects the foreign policy establishment's widely held view that the core precept of the UN Charter regarding justified warfare is sound – that the only legitimate mechanisms for instigating interstate war are in self-defence or by authorisation of the Security Council. Despite the preparation of the Brazilian military for possible wars against its neighbours, such combat last occurred in the 1870s and is highly unlikely. Furthermore, the country's constitution, its commitment to sovereignty as a central precept of foreign policy, and its non-interventionist tradition generally militate against joining multinational interventions.[44] Peacekeeping operations are the principal manner in which Brazilian armed forces are likely to actually see combat. This has empirically been the case for the past six decades. Brazil's recent deployments into Haiti and the UN Interim Force in Lebanon (UNIFIL) reflect that multilateralist, liberal approach and defy realism's emphasis on material power. Another key indicator of multilateralism is that the majority of development cooperation is channeled through multilateral organisations, principally various UN agencies. This trait stands in contrast to rising powers like Turkey, India and China, whose development cooperation principally occurs bilaterally.

Second, Brazil's more expansive interests in foreign economic activities, especially direct investment abroad, seem to support liberal theories. Brazil began to change its foreign policy orientation in the late 1990s under President Cardoso. The financial crisis in 1998, and the subsequent economic stagnation, led to a re-evaluation of Brazil's relationship to donors and what Cardoso viewed as an 'asymmetrical globalization process'[45] unfavourable to Brazil. During this period Brazil began to forge stronger relationships with other emerging powers and look for new markets and opportunities for South–South trade, rather than depending on traditional partners of the North.[46] These shifts point to commitments to a liberal economic order, reflecting interests in financial and economic interdependence driving policies towards Global Southern partners.

President Lula's 2006 remarks in Algiers reflect both pursuit of enhanced economic exchange and leveraging its role to encourage other Southern countries to operate within the prevailing international order, supporting a liberal vision:

> Together we [the countries of the South] can become stronger, not only through the growth of our trade, but also by participating more actively in economic and political forums, such as the World Trade Organization and the United Nations, where questions of great interest to humanity are discussed.[47]

Third, the influence of domestic sources of foreign policy supports liberal theories. The presidency of Lula da Silva represented a new foreign policy positioning on the global stage. Lula explicitly sought to apply the principles of his domestic socialist platform, rooted in his decade-long struggle as a once-jailed union leader against Brazil's military authoritarianism, to his emphasis on fairer trade policies abroad, lifting the world's poor, attacking world hunger and institutionalising a more democratic global order.[48] He drew on his domestic programmes for foreign initiatives. In 2005 the Ministry of Social Development began disseminating the principles of its 'Bolsa Familia', with conditional cash transfers at its heart, to Nigeria and South Africa, and to other donors.[49] He partnered with the Food and Agriculture Organization (FAO) to extend its Zero Hunger initiative to Africa. Lula's speeches in Africa drew on his personal biography of suffering and struggling to elevate marginalised and working peoples into his domestic and foreign policies.[50]

On the one hand, liberalism may not best explain these traits as they predated Lula's presidency and simply received greater attention under his leadership. In addition, domestic-level explanations are not the sole purview of liberalism, but also reflect constructivist and post-colonial theories to some degree. On the other hand, even when Lula's handpicked successor Dilma Rousseff, also a left-of-centre politician who opposed the military regime, assumed the presidency, the emphasis on foreign policy dropped dramatically, as did development cooperation levels. Brazil's internal political crisis took most of the wind from Brazil's peacebuilding sails. President Temer's 2018 decision not to proceed with deploying peacekeepers to the Central African Republic was a sign of the post-Lula lessening of the country's global peace profile, especially after the UN mission in Haiti closed the year before.

To sum up, Brazil's surge in pro-peace activities seems rooted in a number of factors. Some of these reflect realist worldviews: a crisis of legitimacy of global order sparked partly by the US's defiant invasion of Iraq; resultant efforts by middle powers to strengthen and reform the global order; and Brazil's own geopolitical aspirations. Others reflect liberal interest-based views: full-throated multilateralism; eager expansion of agribusiness and other commercial interests abroad; and the correspondence of foreign policy swings to domestic changes. It is hard to deny that interest-based factors and theories best account for the surge in peace support efforts by Brazil.

B. Ideas and the content of Brazil's peacebuilding policies

Having addressed the rise of Brazil's peacebuilding policies, what theories best explain the content of those policies? While the content of these policies may partly reflect the global power positioning of Brazil and other rising powers, I argue here that constructivism and even critical post-colonial theories best account for the content of the policies that underlie the surge in pro-peace activity. Explaining Brazil's policies requires understanding a global identity reflecting specific social, cultural and historical developments, including its experience of colonialism, its role as the largest slave-importer in history, its multiracial population, and even its democratisation experience following military authoritarianism. Critical theories that see both the capitalist and Northern exploitation behind policies that stabilise the Global South also see agency in emancipatory policies that liberate the Global South from imposed policies that sacrifice Southern well-being in favour of Western security and economic interests. Brazil's policies seem to cohere with these theories.

Although critical theory more often critiques extant theories than offering hypotheses that can be tested empirically, it suggests that states and peoples can organise against the dominant forms of peacebuilding. Despite its structural proclivity, critical theory allows for agents that can modify dominant models and content. Post-colonial theories emphasise the historical legacies of foreign policies of former colonies. Brazil's positions reflect content that is not simply posturing for advancing in the existing order, but whose content challenges that very order, drawing explicitly on its colonial experience and its more recent history of democratisation reacting against military authoritarianism.

Brazil's proposals for reforming the international system reflect demands for more equality, democracy and peaceful approaches to conflict in the global order. Its demands to reform the UN Security Council are aimed not just at gaining its own seat, but at opening up this body of global security to more Global Southern representation. Yet its efforts to strengthen the power of Southern states – through the BRICS, IBSA and UNASUR – bypass the UN System and the G20 and contest the West from without. For instance, once the High-Level Panel on UN reform in 2004 failed to gain broader Security Council membership, Brazil turned further towards outside mechanisms of global governance that did not reflect the status quo. To quote one Brazilian diplomat in Brasília, 'This failure to reform added to the palpable sense of frustration among [us], thus strengthening the resolve to launch alternative routes outside the UN architecture, especially through the loose coalitions of rising powers'.[51]

The content of Brazil's official speeches and policies challenges top-down and securitised approaches of peacebuilding. At the UN, Brazil argued that the UN has neglected its original focus on conflict prevention and post-conflict reconstruction in favour of heavy-handed military interventionism, often led by the North Atlantic Treaty Organization (NATO) or a multinational force led by a former colonial power (like the French in Mali). As two Brazilian diplomats state,

> In general terms the UN has focused too much on the pillar of peace and security versus development. Decisions have been toward militarized solutions .... In our view, peacekeeping and peacebuilding shouldn't be sequenced, but should be dealt with together, in tandem. When dealing with a post-conflict situation, one must deal with the causes of the conflict – institutional, political, social and environmental.[52]

These positions reflect longstanding positions and principles enshrined in the 1988 constitution (Art. 4), some dating from far earlier constitutions: 'non-intervention', 'peaceful settlement of conflicts', 'self-determination of peoples', and 'defence of peace'. Earlier constitutions barred Brazil from engaging in any war of conquest and rejected the use of military force until arbitration has been exhausted. The emphasis on pacific resolution of disputes is common to many other states, but is explicitly articulated by Brazilian diplomats and appears frequently in diplomatic speeches.[53] In the early 1990s, Brazil proposed that the UN Secretariat produce an 'Agenda for Development' to complement the influential 1992 report 'Agenda for Peace' of Boutros Boutros-Ghali.[54]

Under Lula, Brazil placed greater emphasis on a transformative agenda. Reversing the realist logic that interests define value-based positions, President Lula stated in 2006. 'Brazil wants the Security Council to be expanded so that we can encourage greater attention to security based on the connection between peace, development and social justice'.[55] Similarly the director of the Brazilian Cooperation Agency stated in 2013:

> The policy of Brazilian cooperation is based on international solidarity ... we react to demands (we don't have previously prepared projects to be presented to partners). ... The principle of South–South cooperation that we follow is that of no conditionality, which is the non-linkage between technical cooperation and pursuit of economic and commercial goals and benefits or concessions in areas of services in exchange for cooperation. [Another principle Brazil respects is the] non-interference or non-intromission in internal affairs.[56]

When chairing the Security Council in 2011, Brazil convened a debate on 'security and development' precisely to inject more development thinking and resources and actors into the decision-making around peacekeeping and peacebuilding. Brazil emphasised the interconnectedness of these aims as reflected in its presidential statement adopted by the Council: 'The Security Council underlines that security and development are closely interlinked and mutually reinforcing and key to attaining sustainable peace'.[57] The statement also recognised and called for strengthening the links between peacekeeping and early peacebuilding, reflecting Brazil's approach in Haiti.

Brazil seems to emblemise the notion that peacekeeping itself might be considered an emerging 'norm' that regulates the use of force through this multilateral mechanism. In its view, except for self-defence, UN or regionally led peacekeeping operations – rather than multinational forces led by former colonial powers – are legitimate means of using force abroad. This approach, adhered to in Brazil's force deployments, rejects UN operations that replicate patterns of colonising states exercising outsized control over military actions in former colonies.

Haiti served as an instance of Brazil's attempt to reshape peacekeeping in ways that reflected its longstanding world view and the values it sees as crucial to peacebuilding. Thus,

Brazil repeatedly tried to strengthen the long-term development element of MINUSTAH's mandate.[58] It drew on its own bilateral resources to enhance the construction of roads and other infrastructure around Port-au-Prince. It used an expansive definition of what was necessary for UN peacekeeper operations to draw on the peacekeeping budget to construct roads as well. It deployed its own agriculture and health specialists as technical advisers for rural development. Crucially, Brazil saw the Haitian context as similar to its own, drawing explicitly on its experiences of addressing criminal gangs in Rio de Janeiro to devise outreach programmes to communities.[59] It arranged for Viva Rio, a well-known non-governmental organisation (NGO), to design and carry out programmes built on their success in that city.

The most identity-driven element of Brazil's peacekeeping approach is the cultural affinity and open, friendly manner it adopted in dealing with the Haitian population – what some Brazilian diplomats and analysts have catalogued as the 'Brazilian way'[60] Many Brazilian peacekeepers came from poor favelas that share traits with the most difficult communities in Haiti, and many are similarly dark-skinned, reflecting Brazil's complicated race relations.[61] The Brazilian contingent drew explicitly on the nation's reputed culture of warm conviviality. Brazil made an early decision to use force to drive out or kill leaders of politicised criminal gangs in shantytowns like Bel-air and Cité Soleil. However, it also decided to have its forces in greater contact and proximity to the populations.[62] One analyst described a decision that when Brazil's troops entered Bel-air in 2006, they would remove their sunglasses, look into the eyes of the people, and – in contrast to the Jordanian units – get out of their Armored Personnel Carriers and walk in the streets and converse with the population.[63]

Numerous analysts have evaluated and documented the more positive reaction of the inhabitants of these communities to the Brazilian units over earlier troops. Brazil trumpeted this different approach of how peacekeeping should be more development oriented. By committing to the mission leadership for 13 years, it expressed its longstanding policies in favour of multilaterally led UN operations but advocated one that looked much more like 'emancipatory' peacebuilding that embraces the interests and views of local peoples and their long-term well-being. Moreno et al. describe a 'post-colonial' approach that reshaped Western interests in favour of the subaltern in Haiti:

> By recognizing their internal (post-colonial) 'Others', bringing into the field their shared memories of suffering, Latin American components are able to establish a more empathetic relation with the host society and, simultaneously, to speak from an ambiguous site, potentially destabilizing the civilizational imaginary reproduced by the liberal peace model.[64]

The paternalistic tenor of Western intervention is thus seen to be displaced by the shared history of Latin American intervenors and Haiti. They found that Brazil's use of more robust force in confronting Haitian criminal gangs still was less than desired by the United States, France and Canada, who 'actively and intensively pressed for more aggressive and robust military action' in Haiti.[65] One Brazilian diplomat reflected on Brazil's efforts:

> I see that [UN Security Council presidential statement] statement as the culmination and heyday of a process of thinking about peacekeeping and peacebuilding in Brazil. From 2002 to 2011, we were learning how to be norm-setters in the international community. Haiti was formative in conceptual development but also in the coalition-building element. We learned how to twist arms to have our concepts included in the Council's resolutions.[66]

Similarly, Brazil's 2012 attempt to temper the principle of R2P by proposing the concept of Responsibility while Protecting (RWP) demonstrates its willingness to make a high-profile proposal for alternatives to Western approaches. RWP was a reaction against the perception that R2P was used as a fig leaf for regime change against Libya's Qaddafi. RWP proposed criteria – such as proportionality, balance of consequences and last resort – before authorisation of military intervention for humanitarian purposes.[67] The concept did not gain traction, partly because Brazil did not elaborate on or position the concept very strategically, having received a tepid international reaction. Nevertheless, the proposal is an example of how Brazil sees itself as a norm shaper on the global stage that pushes back against unchecked Western dominance but by bolstering multilateral norms rather than opposing them. It also showed that Brazil's primary normative venue for addressing the global order remains the UN.

Cultural and historical factors are heavily emphasised by the Brazilian public and diplomats. In framing its development and peacebuilding in Africa, the country emphasises that West African music and cultural traditions have heavily influenced Brazilian culture, and many Brazilians identify strongly with the continent.[68] A significant African diaspora in Brazil is linked to communities in West Africa that repatriated from Brazil in the nineteenth century. These cultural ties also play into Brazil's narrative of South–South cooperation and its ties with Africa.[69]

Some may argue that liberal theories – which emphasise how interests lead to cooperative multilateral foreign policies – better account for the content of Brazil's peacebuilding policies. Brazil's embrace of multilateralism, which is clearly not explained by a strict reading of neorealist theory, can be interpreted to reflect a power-seeking liberal approach. Here greater emphasis on a strengthened and reformed United Nations and more representative global trade are the best way for middle powers to gain in rank and curb the influence exercised by great powers. The emphasis on multilateralism and 'democratic' global order in this view reflects strategic 'bandwagoning' against the great powers rather than genuine values or commitments. Similarly, a critique of military power and military solutions, especially against unilateral use of force, reflects the comparative advantage of less militarily powerful states, rather than a prior, socially determined, values-based commitment to non-aggression or dialogue. In this view, values don't shape policies; instead, power capabilities determine policies that are justified by value statements.

The strongest evidence in support of this view is the common set of values articulated by similarly situated rising powers. Countries such as South Africa, India and Indonesia all claim solidarity with their former colonial brothers, sovereignty and non-interference in the affairs of other states, and stated commitment to peaceful resolutions to conflict with armed action only as a last resort.[70] These values are expressed through policies – an emphasis on South–South technical cooperation, more use of their own technical experts than providing money, non-conditionality and deference to the wishes of the sovereign government in determining the content of projects. These shared values that emphasise pacific resolution of conflict before resort to military force, and solidarity amongst the Global South, might reflect calculation and interests.

It may be that power position shapes common values among rising powers to some degree. However, interest-based explanations are limited in their ability to explain Brazil's apparently irrational behaviour. If Brazil were acting out of its economic and political interests, it would be very unlikely to focus its peacebuilding efforts on the least strategically important countries in the world. Guinea-Bissau, East Timor and Haiti are the least likely markets for generating profitable trade opportunities or return on investment. It stretches credulity that Brazil's behaviour in engaging these tiny poor countries reflects a power-based calculus to gain relative position, status and economic power on the global stage. They are emblematic of symbolic positions based on long-held values that define a Brazilian identity on the world stage – solidarity with former slave colonies, helping fellow former Portuguese colonies to follow a path to peaceful development, deference to sovereign wishes even in countries where Brazil could impose some of its own views, and emphasis on development over militarised approaches.

Constructivism and critical post-colonial theory have difficulty generating hypotheses for empirical work. However, constructivism's emphasis on how identity-generated positions and values cohere is necessary for explaining the content of Brazil's peacebuilding policies. Similarly, Brazil's positions on the global stage correspond to the predictions offered by post-colonial theory of challenges to the Western-dominated liberal order. It is difficult to sort them out from interest-based explanations that have some sway, but identity and culturally specific colonial history are necessary to account for the content of Brazil's reformist peace policies focused on unstrategic, weak post-conflict states.

III. Conclusions

It is hard to sort out the motives behind foreign policy. In some ways, determining whether commitments are 'genuine' or not is not a satisfying exercise. The Brazilian case shows that there are good reasons to see new pro-peace activities and policies as realist or liberal – essentially interest based. These policies are explained largely by the aspirations to play a greater role on the global stage, and they play to the strengths of Brazil. Brazil is not a great military power, although it has significant assets. Its interests are thus served by a policy of dialogue before force, and of multilateral concurrence on the use of force rather than unilateral wars. Brazil could offer a foreign policy that more directly challenges the great powers and the dominant European–American order, but calculates that it is better to seek a place within that order – precisely because it is strong enough and big enough to make such a claim (unlike Cuba or Venezuela).

The strongest evidence for status-based interest accounts lies in the emergence of similar pro-peace, multilateral efforts by several rising powers to challenge the closed structure of the UN Security Council, and to engage in new efforts to help bring peace to neighbours in the early 2000s. These policies would seem to reflect rising economies' calculation that their growing economic power and trade position can be leveraged to greater impact and influence on the global stage – and that their greater peace-promoting activity will help bolster their prestige and power in multilateral fora.

However, the content of Brazilian peace policies reflects context-specific, historically rooted factors that cannot be reduced to interests and ranking within the global pecking order of states. Constructivist non-rational theories are necessary to explain the content of Brazil's peacebuilding policies. Brazil's identity reflects a non-aggressive, non-military power, a former colony with a substantial number of Afro-descendants that emphasises solidarity with the Global South, especially in Africa. All of these traits constitute part of Brazil's identity on the global stage, and they are not shared by all rising powers. They reflect the specific history of Brazil as it evolved in relation to other states, in contraposition to some other states, and reflecting its postcolonial trajectory. It is inconceivable that the decision to focus most of the country's peace initiatives on East Timor, Haiti, Guinea-Bissau, Mozambique and Angola reflects geopolitical calculation or even economic interest. These are among the poorest, least populous and least powerful countries on Earth. Brazil had the resources to engage other, more wealthy and powerful countries in peace initiatives; however, it did not do so. The embrace of South–South solidarity and the historical ties to former Portuguese colonies and the fellow slave colony Haiti reflect concrete specific values and identities. Ideational theories, including agent-centred critical accounts, best account for the content of these policy choices.

The Brazilian case suggests that greater attention to the content of peace-promoting policies of all rising powers – their values, motives, assumptions, emphases and geographic focus – would provide a fuller understanding of global debates over peace and security, and of their trajectory. Some will object that critical theory and constructivism do not readily lend themselves to empirical testing based on positivist hypotheses. I have sought to bring those theories into dialogue with interest-based realist and liberal theories of international relations because they can contribute to better causal explanations of the origins and substance of peacebuilding policies and their effect on global power. Future research could usefully examine theoretical explanations as they apply to rising powers and their discourse, especially the comparative advantages and disadvantages of constructivism and critical theory.

Disclosure statement

No potential conflict of interest was reported by the authors.

Acknowledgements

I am grateful to Matthew Hartwell and Chris Brandt for research assistance. I am also grateful for feedback from two anonymous reviewers and Matt Taylor, and for the collaboration with Adriana Abdenur and Cedric de Coning, whose ideas in our 2017 co-authored pieces are drawn on in this article.

Notes

1. Abdenur and Neto, Brazil's Growing Relevance; Call and de Coning, *Rising Powers and Peacebuilding*.
2. This paragraph draws on Abdenur and Call, "A 'Brazilian Way'?"
3. Quoted in Ministry of External Relations, *Brazilian Foreign Policy Handbook*, 23.
4. Manicom and Reeves, "Locating Middle Powers in International Relations Theory," 24.
5. Waltz, *Theory of International Politics*, 72.
6. Thies and Nieman, *Rising Powers and Foreign Policy Revisionism*, 160.
7. Mearsheimer, "False Promise of International Institutions." Waltz has a slightly more expansive view of multilateral institutions, but still sees them as created and maintained in line with interests of the dominant states. Waltz, "Structural Realism after the Cold War," 21.

8.   Cooper and Flemes, "Foreign Policy Stategies of Emerging Powers," 947.
9.   Rose, "Neoclassical Realism and Theories of Foreign Policy"; Schweller and Pu, "After Unipolarity."
10.   Carranza, "Rising Regional Powers and International Relations Theories," 258.
11.   David, "Alice in Wonderland Meets Frankenstein."
12.   Velázquez, "Why Some States Participate," 168.
13.   Gegout, "The West, Realism and Intervention."
14.   Keohane, "International Institutions"; Keohane "Lilliputians' Dilemma."
15.   Ikenberry, *Liberal Leviathan*.
16.   B. de Carvalho and de Coning, *Rising Powers and the Future of Peacekeeping*, 4. Kahler focuses as well on the domestic dilemmas: Kahler, "Rising Powers and Global Governance," 712.
17.   Richmond and Tellidis, "Emerging Actors in International Peacebuilding."
18.   eg Moaz and Russett, "Normative and Structural Causes of Democratic Peace."
19.   eg Bueno de Mesquita et al., "An Institutional Explanation of the Democratic Peace."
20.   Finnemore, *National Interests in International Society*, 2.
21.   Finnemore and Sikkink 1998.
22.   Finnemore and Jurkovic, "Getting a Seat at the Table."
23.   Carranza, "Rising Regional Powers and International Relations Theories"; Brysk, *Global Good Samaritans*.
24.   Capie, "Indonesia as an Emerging Peacekeeping Power," 4.
25.   David, "Alice in Wonderland Meets Frankenstein," 3.
26.   Richmond and Tellidis, "Emerging Actors in International Peacebuilding," 566.
27.   Bellamy and Williams, *Understanding Peacekeeping*.
28.   Cooper and Flemes, "Foreign Policy Stategies of Emerging Powers," 952.
29.   Gill, "Reimagining the Future," 8.
30.   Pugh, "Peacekeeping and Critical Theory"; Cox, "Social Forces, States and World Orders."
31.   Personal interviews with senior Brazilian and Indian officials, New York and Brasilia, 2015.
32.   Pugh, "Peacekeeping and Critical Theory"; Pugh, "Political Economy of Peacebuilding."
33.   Nadarajaha and Rampton, "Limits of Hybridity," 70.
34.   Richmond, "Genealogy of Peace and Conflict Theory"; Richmond and Mac Ginty, "Where Now for the Critique of the Liberal Peace?"
35.   Richmond and Mac Ginty, "Where Now for the Critique of the Liberal Peace?"
36.   Richmond and Tellidis, "Emerging Actors in International Peacebuilding."
37.   Hernández, "Collapse in Cancún."
38.   IPEA, "Cooperação Brasileira."
39.   Abdenur and Call, "A 'Brazilian Way'?"
40.   Mares and Trinkunas, *Aspirational Power*; Valença and Carvalho, "Soft Power, Hard Aspirations"; Stuenkel and Taylor, *Brazil on the Global Stage*.
41.   It deployed troops to UN missions in the Sinai in 1956, to El Salvador and Angola in the early 1990s, and to East Timor in 1999, where the chief of mission was Brazilian Sergio Vieira de Mello. Sánchez Nieto, "Brazil's Grand Design," 164.
42.   Ibid., 174.
43.   Ministry of External Relations, "Brazilian Foreign Policy Handbook," 25.
44.   Stuenkel and Taylor, *Brazil on the Global Stage*.
45.   Cardoso, "Globalization vs Democracy."
46.   Christensen, "Brazil's Foreign Policy Priorities"; Nel and Taylor, "Bugger thy Neighbour."
47.   Cited in Ministry of External Relations, *Brazilian Foreign Policy Handbook*, 24–5.
48.   Pickup, "Foreign Policy of the New Left."
49.   Amanor, "South–South Cooperation in Africa," 26.
50.   Mawdsley, Kim and Marcondes, "Political Leadership and 'Non-tranditional' Development Cooperation." See extracts of Lula's speeches in Ministry of External Relations, *Brazilian Foreign Policy Handbook*.
51.   Adriana Abdenur, personal interview with a Brazilian diplomat who requested anonymity, Brasília, November 2015, quoted in Abdenur and Call, "A 'Brazilian Way'?"
52.   Patriota and Timerman, "Brasil e Argentina."

53.   Author interviews with diplomats in Itamaraty, August 2015; and see Ministry of External Relations, *Brazilian Foreign Policy Handbook*.
54.   Vigevani and Cepaluni, *Brazilian Foreign Policy in Changing Times*.
55.   Ministry of External Relations, "Brazilian Foreign Policy Handbook," 208.
56.   Abreu quoted in Steiner, "'Blending' of Aid and Private Flows," 14.
57.   United Nations, "Statement by the President of the Security Council."
58.   Kenkel, "South America's Emerging Power," 656.
59.   Ibid.
60.   Abdenur and Call, "A 'Brazilian Way'?"
61.   Abdenur and Call, "A 'Brazilian Way'?"
62.   Novaes Miranda, "The Pacification of Bel Air."
63.   Author's personal interview with Leopoldo Paz, August 2015, Brasilia.
64.   Moreno, Braga, and Gomes, "Trapped between Many Worlds," 383.
65.   Ibid.
66.   Author's personal interview with a Brazilian diplomat who had worked at the mission to the United Nations and who requested anonymity, August 2015, Brasilia.
67.   Spektor, "Humanitarian Intervention Brazilian Style?," 58.
68.   V. M. de Carvalho, "Brazilian Music at MINUSTAH."
69.   Amanor, "South–South Cooperation in Africa"; Leite et al., *Brazil's Engagement in International Development Cooperation*.
70.   Call and de Coning, *Rising Powers and Peacebuilding*.

Bibliography

Abdenur, Adriana, and D. Neto. *Brazil's Growing Relevance to Peace and Security in Africa*. Oslo: NOREF Report, 2014. doi:10.1080/15423166.2014.950118.

Abdenur, Adriana and Charles T. Call, "A 'Brazilian Way'?: Brazil's Approach to Peacebuilding." In *Rising Powers and Peacebuilding*, edited by Charles T. Call and Cedric de Coning, 15–38. Cham: Palgrave Macmillan, 2017.

Amanor, Kojo. "South–South Cooperation in Africa: Historical, Geopolitical and Political Economy Dimensions of International Development." *Pretoria: IDS Bulletin* 44, no. 4 (2013): 20–30. doi:10.1111/1759-5436.12039.

Bellamy, Alex J. and Paul D. Williams. *Understanding Peacekeeping*. Cambridge: Polity, 2010.

Brysk, Alison. *Global Good Samaritans: Human Rights as Foreign Policy*. New York: Oxford University Press, 2009.

Bueno de Mesquita, Bruce, James D. Morrow, Randolph M. Siverson, and Alastair Smith. "An Institutional Explanation of the Democratic Peace." *American Political Science Review* 93, no. 4 (1999): 791–807. doi:10.2307/2586113.

Call, Charles T. and Cedric de Coning. *Rising Powers and Peacebuilding: Breaking the Mold?* Cham: Palgrave Macmillan, 2017.

Capie, David. "Indonesia as an Emerging Peacekeeping Power: Norm Revisionist or Pragmatic Provider?" *Contemporary Southeast Asia* 39, no. 1 (2016): 1–27. doi:10.1353/csa.2016.0012.

Cardoso, Fernando Henrique. "Globalization vs Democracy." *New Perspectives Quarterly* 31, no. 2 (2014): 2–54.

Carranza, Mario E. "Rising Regional Powers and International Relations Theories: Comparing Brazil and India's Foreign Security Policies and Their Search for Great-Power Status." *Foreign Policy Analysis* 13 (2017): 255–277.

Christensen, Steen. "Brazil's Foreign Policy Priorities." *Third World Quarterly*. 34, no. 2, (2013): 271–286. doi:10.1080/01436597.2013.775785.

Cooper, Andrew, and D. Flemes. "Foreign Policy Strategies of Emerging Powers in a Multipolar World: An Introductory Review." *Third World Quarterly* 34, no. 6 (2013): 943–962. doi:10.1080/01436597.2013.802501.

Cox, Robert. "Social Forces, States and World Orders: Beyond International Relations Theory." *Millennium: Journal of International Relations* 10, no. 2 (1981): 126–155.

David, Charles-Philippe. "Alice in Wonderland Meets Frankenstein: Constructivism, Realism and Peacebuilding in Bosnia." *Contemporary Security Policy* 22, no. 1 (2001): 1–30. doi:10.1080/1352326 0512331391046.

de Carvalho, Benjamin and Cedric de Coning. *Rising Powers and the Future of Peacekeeping and Peacebuilding.* Oslo: NOREF, 2013. https://www.files.ethz.ch/isn/175234/f194e6326ee12f80c-3705117b151ef78.pdf

de Carvalho, Vinicius Mariano. "Brazilian Music at MINUSTAH – Music as a Diplomatic Weapon." In *Brazil's Participation in MINUSTAH (2004–2017),* edited by Eduarda Passarreli Hamann and Carlos Augusto Ramires Teixeira, 44–50. Rio de Janeiro: Igarapé Institute and CCOPAB, 2017, 44–50.

Finnemore, Martha. *National Interests in International Society.* Ithaca, NY: Cornell University Press, 1996.

Finnemore, Martha and Kathryn Sikkink. "International Norm Dynamics and Political Change." *International Organization.* 52, no. 4 (1998): 887–917.

Finnemore, Martha and Michelle Jurkovic. "Getting a Seat at the Table: The Origins of Universal Participation and Modern Multilateral Conferences." *Global Governance.* 20, no. 1 (2014): 361–373.

Gegout, Catherine. "The West, Realism and Intervention in the Democratic Republic of Congo (1996–2006)." *International Peacekeeping.* 16, no. 2, (2009): 231–244. doi:10.1080/13533310802685802.

Gill, Stephen. "Reimagining the Future: Some Critical Reflections 1. In *Critical Perspectives on the Crisis of Global Governance,* edited by Stephen Gill, 1–23. Basingstoke: Palgrave Macmillan, 2015.

Hernández, Andreas. "The Collapse in Cancún and the Transformation of the Global System," www.countercurrents.org, blog entry posted September 14, 2003.

Ikenberry, G. John. *Liberal Leviathan: The Origins, Crisis, and Transformation of the American World Order.* Princeton: Princeton University Press, 2011.

IPEA (Instituto de Pesquisa Econômica Aplicada). Cooperação Brasileira para o Desenvolvimento Internacional 2010. Brasília, 2011.

Kahler, Miles. "Rising Powers and Global Governance: Negotiating Change in a Resilient Status Quo." *International Affairs* 89, no. 3 (2013): 711–729.

Kenkel, Kai Michael. "South America's Emerging Power: Brazil as Peacekeeper." *International Peacekeeping.* 17, no. 5 (2010): 644–661. doi:10.1080/13533312.2010.516958.

Keohane, Robert. "International Institutions: Two Approaches." *International Studies Quarterly* 32 (1988): 379–396. doi:10.2307/2600589.

Keohane, Robert. "Lilliputians' Dilemma: Small States in International Politics." *International Organization,* 23, no. 2 (1969): 291–310. doi:10.1017/S002081830003160X.

Leite, I., B. Suyama, L. Waisbich, and M. Pomeroy. *Brazil's Engagement in International Development Cooperation: The State of the Debate.* Brighton, UK: Institute of Development Studies, 2014.

Manicom, James and Jeffrey Reeves. "Locating Middle Powers in International Relations Theory and Power Transitions". In *Middle Powers and the Rise of China,* edited by Bruce Gilley and Andrew O'Neil, 23–44. Washington DC: Georgetown University Press, 2014.

Mares, David R., and Harold A. Trinkunas. *Aspirational Power: Brazil on the Long Road to Global Influence.* Washington, DC: Brookings Institution, 2016.

Mawdsley, Emma, Sung-Mi Kim and Danilo Marcondes. "Political Leadership and 'Non-traditional' Development Cooperation." *Third World Quarterly* 38, no. 10 (2017): 2171–2186. doi:10.1080/01436 597.2017.1333416.

Mearsheimer, John J. "The False Promise of International Institutions." *International Security* 19, no. 3, (1995): 5–49 doi:10.2307/2539078.

Ministry of External Relations. *Brazilian Foreign Policy Handbook.* Brasilia: Fundação Alexandre de Gusmão, 2008.

Moaz, Zeev and Bruce Russett. "Normative and Structural Causes of Democratic Peace." *American Political Science Review* 87, no. 3 (1993): 624–638. doi:10.2307/2938740.

Moreno, Marta Fernández, Carlos Chagas Vianna Braga and Maíra Siman Gomes. "Trapped between Many Worlds: A Post-colonial Perspective on the UN Mission in Haiti (MINUSTAH)." *International Peacekeeping.* 19, no. 3 (2012): 377–392. doi:10.1080/13533312.2012.696389.

Nadarajah, Suthaharan and David Rampton. "The Limits of Hybridity and the Crisis of Liberal Peace." *Review of International Studies* 41, no. 1 (2015): 49–72. doi:10.1017/S0260210514000060.

Nel, Philip and Ian Taylor. "Bugger thy Neighbour? IBSA and South–South Solidarity." *Third World Quarterly* 34, no. 6 (2013): 1091–1110. doi:10.1080/01436597.2013.802507.

Novaes Miranda, André Luis. "The Pacification of Bel Air." In *Brazil's Participation in MINUSTAH (2004-2017): Perceptions, Lessons and Practices for Future Missions*, edited by Eduarda Passarreli Hamann and Carlos Augusto Ramires Teixeira. Rio: Igarapé and CCOPAB, 2017.

Patriota, Antonio Aguiar and Héctor Marcos Timerman. "Brasil e Argentina, Cooperação Nuclear." O Estado de São Paulo, 2011. http://www.itamaraty.gov.br/discursos-artigos-e-entrevistas-categoria/ministro-das-relacoes-exteriores-artigos/4598-brasil-e-argentina-cooperacao-nuclear-o-estado-de-s-paulo-06-7-2011.

Pickup, Megan. "Foreign Policy of the New Left: Explaining Brazil's Southern Partnerships." *Contexto Internacional. Rio de Janeiro* 38, no 1 (2016): 55–93. doi:10.1590/S0102-8529.2016380100002.

Pugh, Michael. "Peacekeeping and Critical Theory." In *The Politics of Peacekeeping*, edited by A. Bellamy and P. Williams, 39–58. London: Routledge, 2004. doi:10.1080/1353331042000228445.

Pugh, Michael. "The Political Economy of Peacebuilding: A Critical Theory Perspective." *International Journal of Peace Studies*. 10, no. 2 (2005): 23–42.

Richmond, Oliver. "A Genealogy of Peace and Conflict Theory," In *Palgrave Advances in Peacebuilding*, 14–38, London, UK: Palgrave Macmillan, 2010.

Richmond, Oliver and Mac Ginty, R. "Where Now for the Critique of the Liberal Peace?" *Cooperation and Conflict* 50, no. 2 (2015): 171–189. doi:10.1177/0010836714545691.

Richmond, Oliver and Tellidis, I. "Emerging Actors in International Peacebuilding and Statebuilding: Status Quo or Critical States?" *Global Governance* 20, no. 1 (2014): 563–584.

Rose, Gideon. "Neoclassical Realism and Theories of Foreign Policy." *World Politics* 51, no, (1) (1998): 144–172. doi:10.1017/S0043887100007814.

Sánchez Nieto, Alejandro. "Brazil's Grand Design for Combining Global South Solidarity and National Interests: A Discussion of Peacekeeping Operations in Haiti and Timor." *Globalizations*, 9, no. 1 (2012): 161–178. doi:10.1080/14747731.2012.627719.

Schweller, Randall L. and Xiaoyu Pu. "After Unipolarity: China's Visions of International Order in an Era of US Decline." *International Security* 36, no. 1 (2011): 41–72. doi:10.1162/ISEC_a_00044.

Spektor, Matias. "Humanitarian Intervention Brazilian Style?" *Americas Quarterly* 6, no. 3 (2012): 54–60.

Steiner, Priscilla. "'Blending' of Aid and Private Flows in South-South Cooperation." MA thesis in socio-economics, University of Geneva, 2014.

Stuenkel, Oliver and Matthew Taylor. *Brazil on the Global Stage: Power, Ideas and the Liberal Order.* London: Palgrave, 2014.

Thies, Cameron G. and Mark Nieman. *Rising Powers and Foreign Policy Revisionism.* Ann Arbor: University of Michigan Press, 2017.

United Nations. "Statement by the President of the Security Council." S/PRST/2011/4, February 2011.

Valença, Marcelo M. and Gustavo Carvalho. "Soft Power, Hard Aspirations: The Shifting Role of Power in Brazilian Foreign Policy." *Brazilian Foreign Policy Journal.* 8, no. 3 (2014): 66–94. doi:10.1590/1981-38212014000100021.

Velázquez, Arturo. "Why Some States Participate in UN Peace Missions While Others Do Not: An Analysis of Civil–Military Relations and Its Effects on Latin America's Contributions to Peacekeeping Operations." *Security Studies* 19, no. 1 (2010): 160–195. doi:10.1080/09636410903546822.

Vigevani, Tullo and Gabriel Cepaluni. *Brazilian Foreign Policy in Changing Times: The Quest for Autonomy from Sarney to Lula.* Lanham, MD: Lexington Books, 2012.

Waltz, Kenneth N. "Structural Realism after the Cold War." *International Security.* 25, no. 1 (2000): 5–41. doi:10.1162/016228800560372.

Waltz, Kenneth N. *Theory of International Politics.* New York, NY: McGraw Hill, 1979.

Assessing Turkey's changing conflict management role after the Cold War: actorness, approaches and tools

Emel Parlar Dal

ABSTRACT

This paper aims to shed light on Turkey's conflict management role after the Cold War using a three-layered framework consisting of the layers of actorness, approaches and tools. In doing so, it seeks to profile Turkey's international conflict management since the Cold War years with a special focus on the nature of its participation in conflict management as an active or passive actor, the perspectives from which it approaches conflict management, and the conflict management instruments it utilises. First, the paper will provide a conceptual framework of international conflict management based on the above-mentioned triad of actorness, approaches and tools as derived from the existing literature. Second, it will apply the selected three-layered analytical framework to Turkey to decipher its strengths and limitations in managing international conflicts.

Introduction

In recent years the world has witnessed significant systemic and regional changes influencing the nature and form of organised violence and wars as well as the ways in which states attempt to encounter these challenges. Despite the decrease in the frequency of international wars in the post-Cold War era, the number of ethnic and religious conflicts in the form of civil war have increased considerably. This shift in the type of warfare continues with the diversification of actors involved. A revolutionary change in conflicts has occurred with the emergence of new violent non-state actors threatening the sovereignty and territorial integrity of states as well as international peace and security. These shifts in the nature and structure of conflicts have made it clear that there is a need to reassess conflict management and its actors, as well as its transforming approaches and instruments over time. The transformation of conflict has also reflected the conflicting interests of states and non-state actors in terms of geopolitics, economics and security. As contemporary world politics are marked by several intermingled economic, political and security challenges, conflict management is no longer restricted only to major powers. Rising powers, as status seekers and new poles of attraction aspiring to be internationally acknowledged by major powers, in particular and other states also aim for greater involvement in crisis management, especially in the field of conflict prevention and peacekeeping.

Given this background, it is of paramount importance to grasp the actorness characteristics and the approaches and instruments engaged in by rising powers in managing contemporary conflicts. This paper analyses Turkey as a rising power with its own conflict management understanding and practices. Turkey's geographical proximity to the conflict zones in the Middle East, the Balkans and the Caucasus and its historical and cultural ties with the majority of states currently or presently under conflict also necessitate a multidimensional approach and policy towards conflicts. Added to this, Turkey has transformed into an important actor in the Syrian conflict with the diffusion of the civil war across its borders.

Despite the existence of a robust literature on conflict management, a very limited number of studies have attempted to locate states in international conflict management from a wider perspective covering their actorness, conflict approaches and tools. This study aims to fill this lacuna by offering a holistic framework for the assessment of Turkey as an international conflict management actor using different approaches and instruments depending on its changing interests and priorities. Another novelty of this paper is to scrutinise and profile Turkey as a conflict management actor in the changing post-Cold War international system. The third novelty of this paper is its use of a three-layered embedded framework built on conflict management *actorness*, *approaches* and *tools*. The first framework, actorness, looks at the historical trajectories and the ways in which the third parties adopt *active*, *passive*, or *a mix of active and passive conflict management* approaches vis-à-vis international disputes. The second framework, approaches, employs Bercovitch and Regan's four categories of approaches to conflict management, which are *threat-based, deterrence-based, adjudicatory and accommodationist*. The third framework of conflict management tools is drawn from Michael J. Butler's four-layered international conflict management applications of *peacebuilding, mediation, peace enforcement* and *adjudication*.

With these aims in mind, this study seeks to first assess the changing dynamics of international conflict management on the basis of a three-layered embedded analytical framework based on *actorness, approaches* and *tools*. Second, it aims to locate Turkey in international conflict management by applying the above-mentioned conceptual triad at conceptual and empirical levels. In doing so, it tries to understand Turkey's strengths and limitations in international conflict management depending on the changing international conjuncture and its regional priorities.

Making sense of conflict management and its tools

International conflict can be distinguished from other social conflicts only by the involvement of third parties and is manifested under many forms such as diplomatic or economic sanctions, verbal threats, violence or displays of force.[1] Conflict management can be best described as any effort made by third parties to control and contain the harmful effects of an enduring conflict between political actors at the state level and non-state actors on both the actors involved and uninvolved parties.[2] Conflict management also seeks to control the aggravation of a conflict and the acceleration of violence and thus departs from the assumption that conflicts, once triggered, will escalate and spill over to neighbouring regions.[3] At the conceptual level, there are differences between conflict management and conflict resolution. While conflict management is limited to attempts to control and diminish the damaging effects of a conflict, conflict resolution aims for deeper, long-term mutual understanding to meet the basic needs, requirements and values of all parties. Compared to conflict management, conflict resolution necessitates the existence of a more developed institutional, diplomatic and political willingness of the third parties and requires the use of both coercive and soft-power instruments. Additionally, conflict management differs from crisis management, in which conflicts can be managed by the disputants themselves through methods such as peacekeeping, mediation, peacebuilding, etc.[4]

The robust literature on conflict management is both diverse and confusing and thus needs to be reviewed and reassessed in a comprehensive manner based on a framework including three determining factors of *actorness*, *approaches* and *tools*, which explain respectively the role of the agency, its conflict conception and understanding, and the instruments used by the latter in management of the conflicts.

Actorness in conflict management

The actorness of a third party in a conflict can be best understood by placing special focus on the type of behaviour adopted and the role played in its management of a conflict. In this regard, the existing literature offers a very modest distinction based on two broad types of conflict management: *active conflict management* and *passive conflict management*. This distinction between 'active' and 'passive' conflict management behaviour attributes third parties' specific actorness role and behaviour. Here, actorness differs from approach by its focus on the agency rather than the position and methods adopted by the latter in an international conflict. As stated by Guy Burton in *Rising Powers and the Arab–Israeli Conflict since 1947*, when a third party seeks to adopt an active conflict management behaviour, it deals with the root causes of the conflict. Active conflict management corresponds to some extent with the term 'provention', invented by John Burton. a pioneer in the studies of conflict and conflict resolution. Provention as defined by Burton is the taking of steps to end the sources of conflict and creating favourable conditions for a peaceful settlement.[5] Here, the active stance of the third party in managing the conflict signifies an open-ended adaptation and a change by destroying the root causes of the conflict.[6]

On the other hand, passive conflict management behaviours aim to diminish the negative impacts of the conflict by employing tools including limited diplomacy, peacekeeping, mediation and negotiation. In contrast to active conflict management, passive conflict management is similar to conflict prevention, which aims to hold, contain or control a conflict. While active conflict management places the finding of a resolution to a conflict (rather than the settlement or management of a conflict) to the fore, passive conflict management prioritises non-coercive methods such as diplomacy and mediation over coercive methods. Compared to the more substantive active conflict management, which requires a more direct engagement in a conflict with the aim of finding a peaceful solution, passive conflict management has a less expanded scope in building peace. Active conflict management uses more wide-ranging conflict management tools such as expanded diplomacy, constructive mediation, negotiation and peacekeeping, as well as foreign and development aid.

Bercovitch and Gartner identified three types of actorness of third parties in conflict management.[7] In the first, the third party attempts to prevent the physical outcomes of the conflict. In the second, it engages in managing or containing the conflict, and in the third it attempts to resolve the root causes of the conflict. The first two types of actorness in conflict management refer to the efforts of the third party to minimise violence, which may be related to negative or conservative peace or passive conflict management. The third type of actorness is concerned with the causes of the conflict and aims to end it, and can thus be associated with positive or liberal peace, or, in other terms, active conflict management.[8] Here it must be underlined that in adopting either conservative or liberal peace the same tools of conflict management are used but to varying degrees in terms of impact and intensity, and for different ends.

Whether third parties would act as active or passive conflict management actors depends on their self-perceptions of the role they have been playing in international conflicts, the shifting domestic, regional and global conditions affecting their foreign and security policy, and their varying national interests in each conflict case. In some cases, third parties may adopt both active and passive behaviours over time in managing conflicts. Their attitudes towards conflicts and the tools they use may fluctuate depending on the prospect for a peaceful resolution of the conflict. In contemporary international politics, states have a much greater tendency to pursue passive conflict management approaches rather than directly becoming involved in conflicts and taking initiative in the resolution of the conflict.

Approaches to conflict management

Conflict management approaches refer to the perspectives adopted by third parties in conflicts in which a resolution seems to be a distant possibility and there is an absolute need to contain and limit its damaging consequences.[9] In the face of an escalating conflict, third parties may assume certain positions depending on their security perceptions, interests and means. According to two prominent scholars of international conflict management, Bercovitch and Regan, third parties use four main approaches representing their objectives and means: (1) threat-based, (2) deterrence-based, (3) adjudicatory, and (4) accommodationist approaches.[10]

The threat-based approach can be defined by the use and/or threat of force and other tools to force the conflicting parties to find a resolution. The deterrence-based approach refers to the employment of a passive threat aimed at keeping an adversary from acting, the use and/or threat of force, or the use of coercive diplomacy means with the aim of squeezing the parties concerned. Here, the objective of the third party is to maintain military power for the purpose of discouraging attack and the employment of coercive diplomacy aims to influence an adversary's decision-making through the threat of future military force.[11] The adjudicatory approach utilises the recognition of and appeal to a legal or an extra-legal system and a system of norms and approaches to construct a legal settlement for a dispute with the participation of all conflicting parties. It is designed to contain and control conflict, not resolve or transform it. Admitting that all conflict has a normative dimension and may be resolved thanks to obeisance to morally responsible rules,[12] adjudication aims to bring accountability and common good in the context of conflict management. The adjudicatory approach may also be used as an alternative method of dispute resolution and to make the law more related to the management of conflict. Finally, the accommodationist approach to conflict management refers to the use of traditional and non-traditional diplomatic means. Here, greater emphasis is placed on the use of persuasion and soft power by the third parties in managing the conflicts. In managing ethnic conflicts, the accommodationist approach refers to the recognition of ethnic differences and the promotion of dual or multiple public identities and equality, in contrast to the integrationist approach which aims at weakening differences through the promotion of a common (civic) public identity.[13]

Tools of conflict management

States adopt various wide-ranging tools of conflict management covering the different dimensions of strategy, military, economy, humanitarian-development aid, and judicial/legal-based measures, with ends ranging from coercion/hard power to non-coercive/soft power.[14] Michael Butler distinguished four types of conflict management tools: peacekeeping, mediation, peace enforcement and adjudication.[15] Joseph Lepgold, on the other hand, mentioned three main tools of conflict management: prevention, peacekeeping and enforcement.[16] William Dixon proposed seven types of tools: public appeals, communication, observation, intervention (peacekeeping and sanctions), humanitarian aid, adjudication and mediation.[17] Bercovitch and Fletter[18] noted three broad types of conflict management tools: state-based (diplomatic), legal (international law) and political (international and regional organisations). Finally, Diehl[19] pointed to the existence of four types of tools: alliances, regional collective security, peace-making and diplomacy. This study will make use of Michael Butler's four-layered conflict management tools: peacekeeping, mediation, peace enforcement and adjudication.

Peacekeeping

Peacekeeping is a generally misused and confusing term due to the existence of numerous connotations. It has been used, for instance, to refer to operations such as the US invasion of Granada in 1983, Operation Desert Storm in 1991, and the multifaceted deployments in Kosovo and East Timor in 1999. In 1992 the former United Nations (UN) Secretary-General Boutros Boutros-Ghali added the concept of post-conflict peacebuilding to the Agenda for Peace which introduced four areas of action for securing peace: (1) preventive diplomacy aims to prevent disputes between the parties, to prevent the ongoing disputes from transforming into conflicts and to limit their contagion towards other regions; (2) peacemaking seeks to bring the conflicting parties to the table to reach an agreement by the use of peaceful means indicated in Chapter VI of the UN Charter (3) peacekeeping refers to the sending of troops and civilian staff by the UN with the aim of preventing the conflict and assuring peace; and (4) peacebuilding aims to determine and support structures seeking to reinforce peace and prevent conflict.[20]

Peacekeeping represents the systematic efforts of third parties to support the cessation of conflict where the cost of continuing an armed conflict is higher than any potential gains. In fact, peacekeeping does not necessarily impose the cessation of the conflict or a peace settlement. Rather, it must be conceived as a facilitator providing the necessary conditions for an eventual peace between conflicting parties. A peacekeeping mission may be appealed to the United Nations Security Council (UNSC) by any UN member state, regional group, or the UN Secretariat. According to international law, a peacekeeping mission may take place only if the UN gives the order. When the necessary conditions exist to launch a peacekeeping mission, a draft resolution is sent to the UNSC for a vote. After the resolution is approved by the UNSC, the latter asks the UN Secretary General to prepare a more detailed plan.

Although most peacekeeping operations during and after the Cold War occurred under the control of the UN, peacekeeping may also be carried out jointly by the UN and non-UN actors such as other international organisations or pivotal states. For instance, parallel efforts by the UN and North Atlantic Treaty Organization (NATO) in Afghanistan United Nations Assistance Mission in Afghanistan/ International Security Assistance Force (UNAMA/ISAF) and Kosovo United Nations Mission in Kosovo/ Kosovo Force (UNMIK/KFOR) and their joint efforts in Darfur as the UN–AU Hybrid Operation United Nations-African Union hybrid operation in Darfur (UNAMID) are good examples. The UN's collaboration with Australia in East Timor United Nations Integrated Mission in East Timor/ International Stabilization Force ((UNMIT/ISF) and the UN's collaboration with Russia in Georgia United Nations Observer Mission in Georgia (UNOMIG) can be cited as examples of the UN's collaborative peacekeeping operations with pivotal states. Examples of peacekeeping missions realised by non-UN actors include the EU's European Union Force (EUFOR) in Bosnia and Herzegovina or the Commonwealth of Independent States (CIS) border force led by Russia in Tajikistan.

Peacekeeping has some commonalities with other peace and collective security-related operations, mainly due to their use of military forces attributed by states. However, peacekeeping operations may be clearly distinguished from other military operations of states by the mandated responsibilities attributed by multilateral agreements, peace agreements, UN resolutions, or the resolutions of regional organisations with the aim of creating buffer or security zones, monitoring ceasefires and assisting in the transition to a post-conflict settlement. In short, the majority of peacekeeping operations have been carried out by the UN or with its authorisation. UN member states, as the main voluntary contributors to the UN peacekeeping troops and police, also provide logistical support, coordination, transportation and equipment for the UN force.

Mediation

For William Zartman and Saadia Touval, two prominent scholars on conflict mediation, mediation can be described as a third-party intervention in a conflict that does not employ the direct use of force and acknowledges neutrality as one of the central parameters of mediation. The authors see mediation as a method of negotiation in which third parties not concerned with the original dispute help the conflicting parties find a reasonable solution.[21] For Wilkenfeld et al.,[22] mediation can be seen as an important step in making the conflicting parties overcome their disagreements and mistrust. Michael Butler identified three main mediation strategies generally followed by mediators in inter-state conflicts: communication-facilitation strategies, procedural strategies and directive strategies. Butler notes three main factors leading to successful mediation: (1) mediation must include two or more mediators/actors aiming to reflect their own interests and agendas to the resolution of the conflict; (2) mediators do not apply any violence or physical force; (3) mediators are technically impartial and this impartiality is characterised by three features: (a) the resolution must be acceptable by all conflicting parties; (b) the resolution must not lead to bringing victory to one party; and (c) the mediator must have strong interests in managing and solving the conflict which are more important than its self-interests regarding gaining status and security-related strategic interests.[23] Regarding the neutrality of mediators, scholars such as and Bercovitch[24] have noted that third parties aren't always independent and become mediators as a result of their own interests. Gent and Shannon, for instance, underline that having a bias might help a third party influence the conflict antagonists.[25]

Violent conflicts such as those in Somalia, Haiti, Bosnia and East Timor showcase the difficulty of mediation in practice. Mediators must facilitate communication between all parties to develop new options for a possible resolution that addresses their needs. Due to the complexity of some disputes, mediation does not always appear to be efficient. However, this ignores that there has been a remarkable increase in intra- and inter-state conflict management. In addition, another new trend in mediation can be observed in the proliferation of new mediation actors such as non-governmental organisations (NGOs), regional organisations and private individuals.

Peace enforcement

Peace enforcement is a form of third-party intervention carried out under international auspices with the aim of forcing conditions of a peace settlement on the parties and preventing the rise of violent conflict. The idea of peace enforcement emerged as a result of the existing limitations of some peace operations organised in the context of peacekeeping. The UNSC gives authorisation to launch such peace enforcement operations. Peace enforcement can be conceptualised as a complement to peacekeeping and peacebuilding and involves the imposition of a cessation of violent conflict and the creation of conditions necessary for the signature of a possible peace agreement or cease fire. Peace enforcement is often a misused concept, and thus needs to be distinguished from other peace operation concepts such as peacekeeping, peacebuilding and peace-making. However, it is not easy, at least academically, to delineate a clear line between these terms as peace operations often begin in one format, in legal and operational terms, and quickly transform into another. Peace enforcement is a secondary stage in peace operations, and the number of peace enforcement operations has increased since the end of the Cold War. The US Army Field Manual 100-23 of 1994 defined peace enforcement as 'the application of military force or the threat of its use, normally pursuant to international authorization, to compel compliance with generally accepted resolutions or sanctions'.[26] What divides peacekeeping from peace enforcement is not the level of violence, but simply the consent of the parties concerned. Peace enforcement occurs when peacekeeping goes wrong.

Peace enforcement, or the enforcement of a ceasefire by the threat of use or the actual use of armed force to seek peace, can be performed in various ways. Such operations can include international sanctions against parties actively involved in the armed conflict or those driving it; isolation of the conflict zone to prevent movement of arms or armed formations into the area; air or missile strikes targeting active belligerent actors; or deployment of armed forces to the conflict zone, aiming to contain the conflict by disarming or eliminating armed actors who continue fighting.[27]

In short, peace enforcement operations are generally designed to enforce terms, which are often heralded in the UN mandate. Departing from this definition, peace enforcement operations are those in which force size and capabilities are often limited to sustain compliance with UN resolutions. In this sense, many of the UN-led peace operations' stages can be classified as peace enforcement operations (for instance, Somalia and Bosnia missions in the 1990s and the first Gulf War in 1991 were examples of such peace enforcement operations.)

On the other hand, some peace enforcements are not UN-led peace operations, such as those launched by pivotal states or by ad hoc coalitions. Peace enforcement operations organised and led by individual states are generally rare and may be distinguished from other peace enforcements by the contribution of the lead state(s) and the degree of its operational command and control. Pivotal states participating in peace enforcement generally have higher material (military and economic) power compared to the other actors involved in the conflict. Another important point is the fact that pivotal states undertaking such peace enforcement also consider that peace conditions comply with their own material and ideological interests. In general, the geopolitical ambitions of pivotal states and their geographical proximity play a determinant role in their launch of such peace enforcement in order to prevent the spillover effects of the conflict.

International adjudication

International adjudication means the use of international tribunals to adjudicate international conflicts. After the Second World War, the use of arbitrators and more independent standing courts made international adjudication a much more frequently utilised method of conflict management. The decade following the end of the Cold War has seen the opening of more international tribunes than any other decade.[28] Currently, approximately 20 distinct international legal bodies make binding decisions relevant to trade disputes, strengthen rules in the law of the sea, and give judgements aiming to develop human rights and the rights of refugees and civilians during war. International adjudication is also a tool of international conflict management since it requires sending an ongoing dispute to an impartial third-party tribunal to obtain a binding decision. In international conflict management, adjudication refers to the attempt of an impartial third party to use legal, extra-legal or normative approaches and institutions to create legal settlements between conflicting parties.[29] As a tool of international conflict management, adjudication also aims to diminish the devastating effects of international disputes and to eliminate the use of coercive methods. However, it may be distinguished from the other tools of conflict management by both its reliance on legal systems, processes, standing and ad hoc legal institutions, and the involvement of an impartial third party engaged in finding an intermediary solution to the conflict. In this regard, adjudication may be used together with other conflict management methods such as negotiation between parties and mediation.[30]

Locating Turkey in international conflict management

Between the Republican era and the 2000s, Turkey was a generally cautious and passive actor in international conflict management and distanced itself from regional and global crisis, with a few exceptions such as in Cyprus and Kosovo. Turkey's close attachment to the Western alliance in general and the US specifically during the Cold War years also pushed successive Turkish governments to adopt a parallel line of conflict management strategies in most cases. With the end of the Cold War, the successive Yugoslavian crisis became a breaking point for Turkey's longstanding passive conflict management strategies. Since the 1990s, conflict management has gradually become an important policy field in Turkish politics, with the use of an increasing number of tools and practices. As the country's economic and political clout increased in the early 2000s thanks to political stability and economic growth, Turkey began to pursue a proactive foreign policy, which has had repercussions on the country's conflict management. Overall, during the first decade of the 2000s, Turkey gradually increased its profile and status by investing in its resources and capacities in development cooperation and peaceful resolution of conflicts in its region.[31]

Characterising the actorness of Turkey in conflict management since the Cold War: a retrospective analysis

Historically, Turkish conflict management activities can be divided into four distinct phases. In the first era, up until the end of the Cold War, Turkey was largely passive in international conflict management. Between the 1990s and early 2000s, Turkey was both an active and passive conflict management actor. In the 2000s to 2011, Turkey was active in international conflict management, with an increasing profile in international affairs, and its conflict management practices transitioned from military to civilian dominated. Since 2011, Turkey has followed a mix of active and passive conflict management, with increasing attention to its hard-power instruments.

Turkey during the Cold War: a passive conflict management actorness

Turkey first participated in a peacekeeping mission with its contribution of troops to the Korean War in 1950. From the mid-1960s to the late 1970s, the Cyprus issue was an important agenda for Turkey. In 1974, Turkey intervened militarily in the island, seeking a coercive solution to the long-standing intercommunal conflict and to guarantee the legitimate rights of the Turkish Cypriot community. Since 1974, Cyprus has become one of Turkey's most important conflict management problems. Nevertheless, during the Cold War, Turkey did not take part in any significant international conflict management missions, with the exception of the fiasco of the Baghdad Pact and brief mediation efforts between Iran and Iraq during the 1980s war. However, it would be false to claim that Turkey successfully pursued an active conflict management policy aiming to eliminate the root causes of the Cyprus problem. Despite Turkish leaders' strong willingness to solve the Cyprus crisis since 1974, Turkey has not always been proactive in managing this crisis. During the Cold War Turkey generally avoided any potentially long-term entanglements in its immediate environment, and it was focused on protecting its territorial integrity, domestic peace and societal security in the 1980s, especially after the launch of violent attacks in the South Eastern part of the country by the Partiya Karkerên Kurdistanê or Kurdistan Workers Party (PKK).

Turkey in the 1990s and early 2000s: a mix of passive and active conflict management actorness

Turkey's first significant foray into international conflict management experience came with the eruption of violent ethno-national conflicts in the Balkans and Caucasus. The war in

Bosnia waged by Serbia in particular radically altered Turkey's foreign policy environment.[32] Conflicts in Eastern Europe and historical and cultural bonds with the newly independent states of Central Asia created opportunities for Turkey to expand its role. However, because of both limited capacities at the time and worsening domestic politics due to the increasing Kurdish insurgency in the Eastern part of the country, Turkey played a very limited role in conflict management in the Balkans during the 1990s. Turkey's conflict management efforts were typically part of international organisations at the time as Turkey contributed to multilateral peacebuilding and peace enforcement missions within the UN and NATO missions. Since then, Turkey has participated in eight UN peacekeeping missions in various part of the world, in addition to NATO and EU peacekeeping operations in countries such as Afghanistan, Bosnia and Herzegovina, and Kosovo. However, in the 1990s and early 2000s, while Turkey began to feel responsible for other peoples in different countries,[33] its economic, political and military capacities were insufficient for projecting effective conflict management operations.

Turkey in the 2000s to 2011: towards an active conflict management actorness

The 16 years of the Justice and Development Party (JDP) government era can be roughly divided into two significant periods. Between 2002 and 2011 when the Arab Spring broke out, the JDP aimed to increase political, economic and cultural contacts with neighbouring regions, with the mantra 'zero problems with neighbours'. This era was marked by structural reforms and rapid economic development, and the EU was accepted as an important priority in Turkey's foreign policy agenda.[34] Democratisation and political reforms, in tandem with economic growth during this period, enabled Turkey to pursue a proactive foreign policy. Turkish foreign policy in the new millennium had been defined by policymakers, scholars and Turkish experts as, variously, total performance,[35] multi-track diplomacy, rhythmic diplomacy, humanitarian diplomacy and virtuous power.[36] During this proactive period, Turkey pursued multidimensional and ambitious conflict management operations. This era also witnessed a shift in Turkey's conflict management understanding from a hard security-based peacebuilding to a more civilian peacebuilding approach.[37] Along the way, Turkish NGOs, charities, semi-autonomous state institutions and business have become the primary drivers of Turkish efforts in intervening humanitarian crisis and peace missions. The Turkish Cooperation and Coordination Agency (TIKA), Disaster and Emergency Supreme Board (AFAD), Turkish Red Crescent, Presidency of Religious Affairs (Diyanet), Turkish Airlines (THY) and numbers of Turkish NGOs, charity organisations and businessmen made significant contributions to Turkish conflict management activities in distant regions, especially in Africa. Turkey effectively addressed both the humanitarian and security aspects of entrenched conflicts in the Caucasus, Balkans, Central Asia, Middle East and Africa. This diversification of tools and geographies in foreign policy was one of the most effective factors paving the way for the success of Turkish conflict management.

Although Turkey's new dynamism in international conflict management focused on the Balkans, the Middle East, the Caucasus and Africa, Turkey was also proactive in addressing decades-old conflicts such as the Cyprus issues,[38] Kurdish openings[39] and relations with Armenia.[40] In short, Turkey's active foreign policy during the first decade of the twenty-first century positively reflected on Turkey's active conflict management in the making. During this era, Turkey pursued a more expanded conflict management strategy, also aiming to find responses to root causes of certain conflicts.[41]

Turkey since 2011: towards a mix of passive and active conflict management actorness

Turkey's soft-power-laden foreign policy was significantly entrenched in the post Arab Spring era. Turkey seized the Arab Spring as an opportunity to expand and deepen its influence in the Middle East. Initially, Turkey had indeed managed to consolidate its position by capitalising on improved relations with the Arab nations. Yet, beginning with the counter-revolutionary coup in Egypt in 2013, Turkey entered a new environment marked by cycles of violent revolutions and counter-revolutions. Until mid-2012, it seemed that Turkey was up to the task of asserting itself in the region as a mediator and model of stable democratic transition. It deployed a range of soft-power instruments such as financial assistance, technical expertise and civil society support to Tunisia, Egypt, Libya, Syria and Yemen. Additionally, already-expanding trade relations within the region intensified even more after the protests. However, as Syria's uprising evolved into civil war, Turkey's policies became increasingly erratic, confrontational and interventionist.[42]

In addition to the existing systemic challenges with its own domestic and foreign policy problems, Turkey has plunged into a new era of instability which necessitated more active use of hard and coercive power. This is especially true for Syria and Iraq, as these terrains become toxic for Turkey's own security and stability. Diplomatic supports to political transition in Syria were soon overshadowed by large-scale security concerns with overarching regional and international ramifications in terms of Turkish foreign policy. The nearly five million refugees, existential and emanating military threats from Islamic State of Iraq and Syria (ISIS) and the People's Protection Unit (YPG), stark policy differences with traditional allies, and un-abating geopolitical rivalries among regional and great powers in Syria have made Turkey's security and stability more vulnerable. Thus, Turkey's decades-old soft-power-laden conflict management evolved into a hard-power-laden one. In this sense, Turkey's ability to be a political model or a neutral mediator, cultural arbiter or peace provider has eroded as it was forced to become embroiled in the unfolding regional conflicts. Moreover, Turkey's rhetorical stands against the West have further isolated the country and significantly diminished its active conflict management capacities.

However, since 2011, Turkey has increased its conflict management role in the African context, especially in Somalia, where it has organised a number of peace talk initiatives as an independent third party respected by almost all conflicting sides.[43] Turkish civil society, NGOs, charities and businessmen also actively participated in this endeavour.[44] In this sense, as a result of its identity and strategic-based interests in Africa, Somalia has become the epicenter of Turkey's active conflict management strategy since 2011.

Assessing Turkey's approaches to conflict management since the Cold War

As Turkey's conflict management actorness was dependent on its NATO alliance and special relationship with the US during the Cold War, the country generally adopted an accommodationist approach to conflict management. The lone exception was the Cyprus crisis, during which Turkey followed the threat-based, deterrence-based and adjudicatory approaches. As the only example of Turkey's coercive interventionist approach to conflict management, the Cyprus crisis reflected the limits of Turkey's conflict management capacity during the Cold War years. During the first decade following the end of the Cold War, Turkey's passive conflict management became more visible and significant through its role in an important number of the peacekeeping operations in the Balkans and the Middle East. Turkey used traditional and non-traditional methods in managing conflicts from both accommodationist and adjudicatory perspectives. The first decade of the twenty-first century was marked by a gradual shift in Turkey's conflict management approach, from passive to active, through its engagement as an international mediator in regional and global conflicts such as those between Israel and Palestine, Israel and Syria, Somalia and Somaliland, and Serbia and Bosnia and Herzegovina. During this period, Turkey also started to pursue a more expanded diplomacy than in the past, with the aim of finding an intermediary solution between the conflicting parties. With the Arab revolts and the Syrian War most specifically, Turkey began to pursue a mix of active and passive conflict management actorness based mostly on the threat-based and deterrence-based approach. Turkey's two recent military operations in Syria, Euphrates Shield and Olive Branch, clearly illustrate the shift towards threat- and deterrence-based approaches compared to the non-coercive accommodationist approach in its Syrian conflict management policy.

Turkey's change in its conflict management approach from accommodationist to threat and deterrence based in Syria seems to have increased Turkey's ability to manoeuvre in managing and solving the Syrian conflict. In the Syrian case in particular, Turkey also pursues a limited adjudicatory approach as evidenced by its assertion that the January 2018 Olive Branch military operation in Afrin complies with international law, particularly UNSC resolutions 1624 (2005), 2170 (2014) and 2178 (2014), Article 51 on the Right of Self Defence of the UN Charter, and respect for Syria's territorial integrity. In line with this adjudicatory approach, Turkey has argued that Operation Olive Branch is not subject to the UNSC ceasefire resolution in Syria's Eastern Ghouta as the resolution excludes counter-terrorism activities, and that Turkey's aim in Afrin is the elimination of the PKK-affiliated People's Protection Units (YPG).

In conclusion, since the Cold War years, Turkey has pursued a conflict management approach heavily weighted on accommodationist approach. With the Syrian War, Turkey's threat and deterrence-based approach has become bolder as a result of its use of a mix of active and passive conflict management actorness.

Decrypting Turkey's conflict management tools in practice

Peacekeeping

Turkey's contribution to peacekeeping missions under the command of the UN began in 1988 with its 10-man contribution to the UN Iran–Iraq Military Observer Group (UNIIMOG) and was followed by participation in the UN Iraq–Kuwait Military Observer Group (UNIKOM), between 1991 and 2003, with 75 personnel. Between 1992 and 1996, Turkey participated in Operation 'Sharp Guard' which sought to monitor the embargo of Bosnia and Herzegovina with naval assets. Turkey contributed 1450 troops to the UN Protection Force (UNPROFOR) in Bosnia and Herzegovina between 1993 and 1995, at the peak of the operation. Similarly,

Turkey was active in the UN Operation in Somalia (UNOSOM-II) with over 300 troops in 1993 and 1994. As shown in Figure 1 and Table 1, Turkey's contribution to United Nations peace-keeping operations (UNPKOs) entered an active phase during the first decade of the

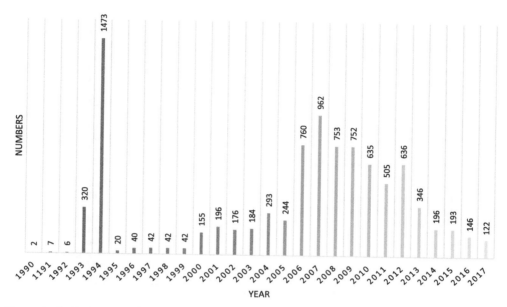

Figure 1. Turkey's personal contributions to United Nations peacekeeping. Source: UN Peacekeeping Data, https://peacekeeping.un.org/en/data.[45]

Table 1. A list of United Nations- or regional organisation-led peacekeeping operations with contribution of troops from Turkey.

Past operations	Past international observer missions to which Turkey contributed	Operations in which Turkish armed forces currently participate
• UN Operation in Somalia (UNOSOM)	• UN Iran–Iraq Military Observer Group (UNIIMOG)	• EU Operation ALTHEA
• UN Protection Force (UNPROFOR) and NATO Implementation/Stabilization Force (IFOR/SFOR)	• UN Iraq–Kuwait Military Observation Mission (UNIKOM)	• NATO Kosovo Force (KFOR)
• Operation Sharp Guard	• UN Observer Mission in Georgia (UNOMIG)	• United Nations Interim Administration Mission in Kosovo (UNMIK)
• Operations Deny Flight/Deliberate Forge/Joint Guardian	• Temporary International Presence in Hebron (TIPH)	• International Security Assistance Force (ISAF) and Resolute Support Mission (RSM)
• Operation ALBA	• OSCE Kosovo Verification Mission (OSCE KVM)	• UN Interim Force in Lebanon (UNIFIL)
• Operations Essential Harvest, Amber Fox, Allied Harmony, Concordia and Proxima	• OSCE Border Monitoring Operation in Georgia (OSCE BMO)	• United Nations Assistance Mission in Somalia (UNSOM)
• UN Mission in the Democratic Republic of the Congo (MONUC)	• UN Mission of Support in East Timor (UNMISET)	• Combined Task Force 151 (CTF 151)
• UN Mission in Sudan (UNMIS)	• UN Mission in Bosnia and Herzegovina (UNMIBH)	• Operation Sea Guardian (OSG)
• NATO Training Mission Iraq (NTM-I)	• EUPOL Mission in the Democratic Republic of Congo (EUPOL KINSHASA)	• Defence Capacity Building (DCB) Initiative
• Operation Unified Protector (OUP)		• Forward Operating Base Konya support to NATO Airborne Early Warning & Control NAEW & C Force
• UN-African Union Mission in Darfur (UNAMID)		
• Operation Ocean Shield (OOS)		• SEDM including South Eastern Europe Brigade (SEEBRIG)
• United Nations Assistance Mission in Afghanistan (UNAMA)		• The BLACKSEAFOR
• Operation Active Endeavour		

Source: TSK database. www.kkk.tsk.tr (Turkish Armed Forces).

Table 2. Contribution of Turkey to United Nations (UN) peacekeeping missions (police, UN military experts on mission, staff officers and troops, on 31 March 2018).

UN peacekeeping mission	Contributions of Turkey to UN peacekeeping	All contributions to UN peacekeeping
MINUJUSTH (Haiti)	12	1211
MINURSO (Western Sahara)	–	227
MINUSCA (Central African Republic)	–	12720
MINUSMA (Mali)	1	13644
MONUSCO (D.R. Of the Congo)	2	17219
UNAMA (Afghanistan)	–	3
UNAMI (Iraq)	–	241
UNAMID (Darfur)	20	12327
UNDOF (Golan)	–	1017
UNFICYP (Cyprus)	–	863
UNIFIL (Lebanon)	84	10472
UNIOGBIS (Guinea-Bissau)	–	13
UNISFA (Abyei-Sudan-South Sudan)	–	4522
UNMIK (Kosova)	2	17
UNMISS (South Sudan)	16	15367
UNMOGIP (India and Pakistan)	–	42
UNOWAS (West Africa and the Sahel)	–	3
UNSMIL (Libya)	–	238
UNSOM (Somalia)	1	601
UNSOS (Somalia)	–	46
UNTSO (Middle East)	–	152
UNVMC (Colombia)	–	113
Total	138	91058

Source: UN Peacekeeping, https://peacekeeping.un.org.

twenty-first century (particularly between 2006 and 2014). Here it must be remembered that Turkey's contribution to UN peacekeeping started to increase in October 1996 with the expansion of United Nations Interim Force in Lebanon (UNIFIL) in Lebanon. Currently, Turkey has around 800 Turkish troops serving in Bosnia and Herzegovina, Kosovo, Macedonia, and Albania. In addition, 101 Turkish police officers took part in the International Police Task Force (IPTF) in Bosnia and Herzegovina and the UN Mission in Kosovo. From 2014 onward there has been a remarkable decrease in the number of the troops, police, and staff attributed by Turkey to UNPKOs. Paradoxically, Turkey's decreasing involvement in UNPKOs is in contrast with the increasing trend observed in recent years in other rising powers' participation in UN peacekeeping (eg China, Brazil, etc). Turkey's reluctance to contribute to UNPKOs may be explained by a combination of structural and domestic reasons. First of all, Turkey lacks a global commitment to becoming a major actor in international peace and security and does not consider the contribution to UNPKOs as a way to increase its global status and international recognition. It seems clear that UN peacekeeping does not constitute a niche diplomacy area for Turkey as it does for some rising states such as India, Brazil, and very recently China. Second, Turkey gives the impression of prioritising contributions to peacekeeping operations mandated by regional organisations, most specifically NATO. As of 2007, Turkey had an average of 2910 personnel in operations, 1717 of which were sustained in NATO operations, in addition to an average of 1415 personnel contributing to the NATO Response Force. On the other hand, it must be underlined that Turkey's participation in EU-mandated peacekeeping operations is generally provided in the form of police and military experts and thus remains at a very symbolic level.

The vicissitudes in Turkey's involvement in UN peacekeeping, as shown clearly in Figure 1, have proven that Turkey lacks a coherent peacekeeping strategy as an integral part of its global governance strategy. As of 2017, Turkey was 62nd among 125 countries in terms of contributions to UNPKOs. Turkey contributes the most personnel to the Balkans, Middle East and African (most specifically Somalia) regions, respectively. Compared to other countries contributing troops, police and experts to Africa, Turkey does not have an expanded geographic peacekeeping reach in Africa, signifying Turkey's narrow understanding of peacekeeping. Since its initial significant contribution to the UN Protection Force (UNPROFOR) in Bosnia and Herzegovina, Turkey's involvement has transformed from an active to a passive participation. As of March 2018, Turkey has 133 troops participating in UNPKOs and is ranked 68th among the 124 troop-contributing countries (police, UN military experts on mission, staff officers and troops). This reflects the country's low-profile UN peacekeeping policy and its increasing autonomy in the field of international security.

Turkey also contributes to regional organisation peacekeeping operations such as those organised by NATO and the EU. For instance, Turkey has contributed to all NATO-led operations in the Balkans since 1995: Implementation Force (IFOR) and Stabilization Force (SFOR) in Bosnia and Herzegovina, KFOR in Kosovo, and Essential Harvest, Amber Fox and Allied Harmony in Macedonia. After the end of Operation Allied Harmony in Macedonia, Turkey also sent 11 personnel to the new military crisis management operation launched by the EU under the name 'Concordia', which was later replaced by the EU Police Mission 'Proxima', to which Turkey currently contributes eight personnel. Added to this, 101 Turkish police officers are serving in the International Police Task Force (IPTF) in Bosnia and Herzegovina and the UN Mission in Kosovo. Since 2003, Turkey has contributed to the EU Police Mission in Bosnia and Herzegovina, the EU's first civilian crisis management operation, with 14 personnel. Turkey also contributed to European Union Force (EUFOR) Bosnia and Herzegovina EUFOR-ALTHEA which replaced NATO's SFOR operation in Bosnia and Herzegovina. 23 gendarmerie officers also serve with the Integrated Police Unit (IPU).

Turkey has suffered significant negative effects from spillover from the Syrian war and the increasing security threats emanating from ISIS and YPG. This situation has gradually turned Turkey to a self-peacemaker and an autonomous security-provider country. Turkey's two successive military operations in Syria, Euphrates Shield and Operation Olive Branch, clearly illustrate this new trend in Turkey's conflict management in which Turkey turns from being a reluctant and passive actor at the global level into a self-peace provider and active actor at the regional level. Turkey's active contribution to NATO and EU peacekeeping operations in the Balkans is also a good indicator of Turkey's selective peacekeeping policy. Here it must be remembered that some countries such as China have followed a different path in terms of peacekeeping in recent years. On one hand, China has become an increasingly important UNPKO troop contributor in recent years and has become committed to developing a new role and conception for itself in international peace and security. On the other hand, it pursues an autonomous security-providing policy in its neighbourhood, especially in the South China Sea. This contradiction clearly shows that peacekeeping policies are not totally independent from countries' national and regional interests and that a selective strategy is still a matter of fact when it comes to peacekeeping.

Mediation

Far from being a traditional mediator, Turkey can be considered a newcomer to mediation. In fact, Turkey's first mediation efforts go back the Iraq–Iran war (1980–1988). Although Turkey pushed the limits of its mediation, it was not successful. During the Yugoslavia crisis,

Turkey acted as a mediator between Bosniak and Croat forces which resulted in the 1994 Agreement establishing the Croat–Bosnian Federation.[46] In the post-Yugoslavia crisis era, Turkey's efforts to manage the conflict endured, resulting in Turkey becoming one of the most active peacemakers in the Balkans, particularly in Bosnia, through activities such as peacekeeping, mediation, monitoring and post-conflict contributions. Turkey also increased its status as an effective mediator during the first JDP era (2001–2011) with its own brand of mediation in interventions in crises in the neighbouring regions of the Balkans, Caucasus and Middle East. In 2010, Turkey established the tripartite consultation mechanism between itself and leaders of Serbia and Bosnia and Herzegovina aiming to facilitate communication and the consolidation of peace in the region.[47]

Turkey's mediation attempts during the first decade of the 2000s was also completed by its continuing efforts at the ideational and institutional levels. During this era, Ankara sought to make Istanbul a centre for mediation in resolving international crises[48] by taking international initiatives such as the 'Mediation for Peace' initiative jointly launched by Finland in September 2010 in New York under the auspices of the UN. This initiative resulted in the creation of the 'Friends of Mediation Group',[49] an international initiative founded under the auspices of the UN on 24 September 2010. In addition, Turkey organised a series of international conferences on mediation: 'Enhancing Peace through Mediation' in 2012, 'Keys to Effective Mediation: Perspectives from Within' in 2013, 'The Increasing Role of Regional Organizations in Mediation' in 2014, and the 'Istanbul Conference on Mediation' with the theme 'Surge in Diplomacy, Action in Mediation' in 2017.[50]

As Table 3 showcases, most of Turkey's mediation efforts have been concentrated on the conflicts in the Middle East. Africa appears second in terms of concentration of mediation efforts among all the regions where Turkey's mediation was carried out. The African region is followed by Asia, where Turkey acted as a mediator in two specific cases: Government of Philippines–Moro Islamic Liberation Front and Kyrgyzstan. The geographic distribution of Turkey's mediation proves Turkey's increasing motivation for acting as a mediator in the ongoing conflicts in its neighbourhood regions most specifically. However, it has a weak mediation actorness in its extra-regions. In terms of success of its mediation efforts, Table 3 illustrates Turkey's limitations in acting as an effective mediator in resolving international crisis.

Furthermore, the Arab revolts in late 2010 and the rapid turn of domestic, regional and international conditions created some contradictions in Turkey's own brand of mediation in the making. Turkey's position, stuck between being involved in the conflicts and being a third

Table 3. Scaling Turkey's mediation efforts in terms of geography and success/failure.

Conflict	Year	Geography of the conflict	Success of mediation
Iraq	2005, 2010	Middle East	Success
Israel–Syria	2008	Middle East	Failure
Lebanon	2008	Middle East	Success
Government of Philippines–Moro Islamic Liberation Front	2009	Asia	Failure
Iran	2010	Middle East	Failure
Kyrgyzstan	2010	Asia	Success
Palestine	2011	Middle East	Success
Sudan–South Sudan	2011	Africa	Failure
Eritrea	2011	Africa	Failure
Somalia–Somaliland	2013	Africa	Success
Syria	2017–2018	Middle East	Failure

Table 4. Decoding Turkey's international conflict management: actorness, approaches and tools.

Cases	Actorness	Approaches	Tools
Yugoslavian Crisis	Active	Accommodation	Peacekeeping
Kosovo	Active	Mix of accommodationist and threat-based	Peacekeeping
Afghanistan	Active	Accommodationist	Peacekeeping
Israel–Palestine	Active	Accommodationist	Mediation
Israel–Syria	Active	Accommodationist	Mediation
Serbia–Croatia	Active	Accommodationist	Mediation
Afghanistan–Pakistan	Active	Accommodationist	Mediation
Somalia–Somaliland	Passive	Accommodationist/ deterrence	Mediation
Syria	Active	Mix of accommodationist/ deterrence and threat-based	Mediation/peace enforcement

party, gradually rendered its possible mediator role inefficient. As Turkey began to lose its neutral image in the eyes of its neighbours and allies in the aftermath of the Arab revolts and the severing of relations with some Middle Eastern countries such as Egypt, Israel and Syria, its international mediator role was considerably weakened. Added to this, its volatile relations with its Western allies, in particular the US and EU, and its rapprochement with Russia and Iran in the context of the Syrian war deteriorated Turkey's neutral in-between image. The growing democratic backlash in the country in the last two years following the 15 July military coup attempt also led to the weakening of Turkey's impartial and justice-oriented image abroad, and as a result made Turkey's mediation more questionable in terms of efficiency and in lower demand.[51] All these developments clearly prove the interconnectedness between mediation and foreign policy. For a successful mediation, as seen in Turkey's mediation in Myanmar, other factors such as the activism of NGOs in third-party countries and their developed business connections in the conflicting country also need to be taken into account.[52]

As a new trend in Turkey's current mediation, it must be noted that Turkey's mediation approach has shifted from a more structural and holistic understanding to a more biased one. In recent years Turkey's new mediation also changed content with its use of more hard-power security-laden tools rather than using soft-power security laden tools.[53] In short, with the Syrian war, Turkey's mediation became more selective and geographically narrowed, less cosmopolitan, and more pragmatic, as clearly seen in its contribution to the trilateral Astana, Sochi and Ankara process with Russia and Iran for the resolution of the Syrian conflict. In Syria, Turkey clearly shifted from an outsider with neutral mediator status to an insider partial mediator.

Peace enforcement

Turkey has actively participated in a number of peace enforcement missions since it assumed its first peace enforcing role in the Korean War under the United Nations Command between 1950 and 1953. Turkey's contribution to the UNPROFOR in the former Yugoslavia, KFOR and SFOR in Bosnia, UNAMIR in Rwanda, and UNOSOM I and II in Somalia are also examples of its active peace enforcement activities. These operations first started as peacekeeping and later merged with peace enforcement operations. In parallel to its low-profile contribution to peacekeeping during the Cold War, Turkey's support of peace enforcement under the UN mandate also remained moderate.

In the post-Cold War era Turkey actively participated in various UN-mandated or non-UN-mandated peace enforcement operations. Turkey contributed to the peace enforcement activities of the UN during Operation Desert Shield 1 by implementing supportive activities such as closing the Kirkuk pipeline, taking part in military and economic embargos against Iraq, and allowing coalition forces to use its airspace. However, Turkey's contribution to Operation Desert Shield did not include sending fighting troops to Iraqi territory. Turkey also participated in the UNPROFOR in Bosnia and contributed approximately 1500 personnel. After the operation was replaced by NATO and later the EU, Turkey continued to contribute to the peacekeeping missions (IFOR, SFOR, KFOR and ALTHEA in Bosnia and Herzegovina, Kosovo and Macedonia) and played an effective peace enforcement role in both ending the conflict and managing the post-conflict era. Somalia was another important case where Turkey actively took part in an international peace enforcement operation under the UN UNISOM I and II missions. With the 2001 UNSC decision attributing to NATO the mandate of an international military coalition called ISAF to provide security in Afghanistan, Turkey conducted ISAF's command during two terms and actively participated in every ISAF process, including military operations, military and non-military security-sector reform, governance, humanitarian and development aid, and other nation-building activities.

In addition to these missions under the auspices of the UN and other regional organisations, Turkey has also conducted its own autonomous peace enforcement operations in Syria. Euphrates Shield Operation was initiated in August 2016 and completed in March 2017, and was followed by operation Olive Branch in January 2018. The geographical concentration of Turkey's peace enforcement missions prove Turkey's selective peace enforcement strategy based on a prioritised support to missions in its neighbourhood rather than in other, extra-regional areas. Another finding with regards to Turkey's peace enforcement relates to the shift observed in recent years in Turkey's peace provider role, from a collective peace-providing actor to an autonomous peace-provider actor.

Adjudication

Turkey has long been reluctant to apply to international adjudicative mechanisms in its conflict management strategies. Turkey's ongoing Aegean and Cyprus disputes with Greece appear to be the most important cases in which international adjudication mechanisms may be implemented. However, the possibility of voluntary submission to an international arbitration with the aim of settling these issues remains slim.[54]

Although the settlement of the Cyprus issue on the basis of negotiations has appeared possible on several occasions since the mid-2000s, various domestic and international issues have affected the peace process, bringing it to a deadlock. Over recent years, the Cyprus dispute has extended to the extraction and use of natural resources,[55] which has further complicated the issue. The prospect of any adjudicative dispute settlement in the Cyprus case remains slim.

On the other hand, the use of international arbitration has smoothly increased in Turkey, especially for international disputes on energy, trade, finance and business. For instance, Turkey brought Iran and Russia to the International Court of Arbitration for its gas purchases on several occasions. However, Turkey's conflict management strategy remains reluctant and low profile in terms of international adjudicative mechanisms. Since the Republican era, the only case brought to the Permanent Court of International Justice by Turkey was the 1927 Lotus case against France.

Conclusion

This study clearly illustrates the shift observed in the historical trajectory of Turkey's conflict management since the Cold War years from *passive* to *active* actorness. In certain cases, and depending upon the regional and international conjuncture, Turkey also uses a mix of these two strategies in its conflict management. While it has generally acted as a conflict prevention actor by avoiding actively taking place in any regional or international conflicts in its surroundings during the Cold War and in the immediate post-Cold War years, since the mid-2000s Turkey began to adopt a more 'proventive' stance (in the term of John W. Burton) in its efforts to manage conflicts. With the aggravation of the Syrian crisis and the rise of the ISIS threat since 2015 most specifically, Turkey gradually adopted a mix of preventive and proventive conflict management strategies. Turkey's two recent military operations in Syria, Euphrates Shield and Olive Branch, are good examples of Turkey's adoption of a mix of preventive and proventive strategies – or, in other terms, passive and active conflict management. In the Horn of Africa in particular, Turkey again employs this double strategy. With the apparition of development cooperation as a niche diplomacy tool in Turkey's foreign policy, active conflict management has gained strength and has begun to be actively used as a complement to Turkey's current conflict strategies.

In terms of conflict management approaches, it can be argued that Turkey is more inclined to be an accommodationist actor using both traditional and non-traditional diplomatic means in cases where it has not been directly affected by the negative consequences of the conflict. As clearly seen in the Syrian crisis, in regional crises having negative ramifications for Turkey's national interests, Turkey does not avoid adopting threat-based and deterrence-based conflict management approaches. Turkey occasionally uses the adjudicatory approaches of the recognition and appeal of a system of norms and a legal structure. However, as seen in its conflict management approach to the Syrian crisis, Turkey seeks to conform to international law, most specifically the UN charter, in its two recent military interventions in Syria.

Regarding the use of conflict management tools, this study showcases that Turkey uses mediation and peace enforcement more actively than peacekeeping and adjudication. Whilst Turkey stands reluctant to participate in the UN's peacekeeping operations and sends a very low number of troops to UN peacekeeping compared to other rising powers (especially the BRICS [Brazil, Russia, India, China, and South Africa]), it has shown greater interest in mediation as an effective instrument of conflict management, especially after the first decade of the 2000s. However, Turkey's mediation has changed context and content, especially after the Syrian crisis, and Turkey has become an insider partial mediator using more hard-power-laden mechanisms than soft-power-laden mechanisms. Another tool which has been frequently used by Turkey, especially in managing regional crises, is peace enforcement. Here it must be remembered that Turkey has become an important peace-enforcing country in recent years mainly due to the increasing number of peace operations it launched against Northern Syria as a pivotal regional country. In the Syrian context most specifically, Turkey acts either alone or with a group of states in ad hoc coalitions with the aim of containing and ending the crisis. Adjudication appears to be the least used conflict management tool by Turkish authorities. Of course, this does not mean that Turkey rejects international norms and the international organisations' guidance and roles in resolving the crisis. As an example, after the 2013 Ghouta chemical attack Turkey showed a favourable stance to the application of the principle of Responsibility to Protect (R2P) as a way to remove the Syrian regime by the use of force.

These findings make it clear that Turkey acts more as a regional conflict management actor than a global one. The Syrian crisis also made Turkey an autonomous peace provider, and a more threat- and deterrence-based security actor heavily relying on coercive military tools. In other words, with Syria Turkey has gradually become a more peace-enforcement-oriented actor rather than a peacekeeper or a mediator. On the other hand, Turkey's active participation in the Geneva talks, since the very beginning, as well as the Astana, Sochi and Ankara talks are all indicators that it will not exclude any diplomatic effort for the resolution of the Syrian crisis. These talk processes, most specifically, can also be considered a joint mediation effort carried out with the other two regional actors actively involved in the Syrian crisis, Russia and Iran. In Africa, in contrast, Turkey seems to be adopting a mix of deterrence and accommodationist strategy via the use of mediation tools most specifically.

Last but not least, if located globally as a conflict management actor one can see that Turkey shows less inclination to participate in UN peacekeeping operations and does not seek to use peacekeeping to increase its international status and recognition, unlike the rising powers in the BRICS grouping, many of which (eg China, Brazil) have recently raised the number of their troops active in UN peacekeeping. Together with Brazil, Turkey appears one of most motivated states in acting as mediator. Together with China and Russia, Turkey seems to be one of the rising powers using peace enforcement mechanisms the most in recent years. Regarding adjudication, all BRICS members seem to be more attached than Turkey to the recognition of international law in defending the principle of sovereignty and non-interventionism.

Disclosure statement

No potential conflict of interest was reported by the author.

Funding

This project was funded by Marmara University Scientific Research Project Coordination Unit-BAPKO's A Type project entitled 'Assessing Turkey's Changing Conflict Management Role after the Cold War: Actorness, Approaches, and Tools'.

Acknowledgements

The author would like to thank Şaban Çaytaş and Hakan Mehmetçik for their technical help and the three anonymous reviewers for their constructive comments.

Notes

1. Maoz et al., *Multiple Paths to Knowledge in International Relations*.
2. Dunn, *From Power Politics to Conflict Resolution*; J. Burton and Dukes, *Conflict: Readings in Management and Resolution*.
3. Butler, *International Conflict Management*.
4. Wall et al., "Conflict and Its Management."
5. J. Burton, *Conflict: Resolution and Prevention*.
6. Dunn, *From Power Politics to Conflict Resolution*.
7. Bercovitch and Sigmund Gartner, "Empirical Studies in International Mediation."
8. G. Burton, *Rising Powers and the Arab–Israeli Conflict*.
9. Von Hippel and Clarke, "Something Must Be Done."
10. Bercovitch and Regan, "Mediation and International Conflict Management."
11. Byman and Waxman, *Dynamics of Coercion*.
12. MacFarlane, "Humanitarian Action and Conflict," 43.
13. Lyon, "Between the Integration and Accommodation of Ethnic Difference."
14. Crocker, Hampson, and Aall, *Turbulent Peace*, 8; Butler, *International Conflict Management*, 14.
15. Butler, *International Conflict Management*, 3.
16. Diehl and Lepgold, *Regional Conflict Management*, 10.
17. Dixon, "Third-Party Techniques for Preventing Conflict Escalation."
18. Bercovitch and Fretter, *Regional Guide to International Conflict and Management*.
19. Diehl and Lepgold, Regional Conflict Management, 273–9.
20. Reychler, Peacemaking, *Peacekeeping and Peacebuilding*.
21. Zartman and Touval, "International Mediation," 437–8.
22. Wilkenfeld et al., *Mediating International Crisis*.
23. Butler, *International Conflict Management*, 121.
24. Bercovitch, *Studies in International Mediation*.
25. Gent and Shannon, "Bias and Effectiveness of Third-party Conflict Management Mechanisms."
26. Gungor, "Analysis of Turkey's Approach to Peace Operations."
27. Ibid.
28. Romano, "The Proliferation of International Judicial Bodies: The Pieces of the Puzzle," 729.
29. Bercovitch and Regan, "Mediation and International Conflict Management."
30. Butler, *International Conflict Management*; Dixon, "Third-Party Techniques for Preventing Conflict Escalation."
31. Sazak and Woods, "Policies and Role of Turkey on Peacebuilding."
32. Sayari, "Turkish Foreign Policy in the Post-Cold War Era."
33. Cowell, "Turkey Faces Moral Crisis Over Bosnia."
34. Özcan, "Turkish Foreign Policy under the AK Party."
35. Aras, *Turkey's Mediation and Friends of Mediation Initiative*.

36. "Virtuous Power New Defense Doctrine."
37. Sazak and Woods, "Policies and Role of Turkey on Peacebuilding."
38. Theophylactou, "Geopolitics, Turkey's EU Accession Course and Cyprus."
39. Köse, "Rise and Fall of the AK Party's Kurdish Peace Initiatives."
40. Hill, Kirişci, and Moffatt, "Armenia and Turkey."
41. Akpinar, "Turkey's Peacebuilding in Somalia"; Aras, *Turkey's Mediation and Friends of Mediation Initiative*.
42. Ayata, "Turkish Foreign Policy in a Changing Arab World."
43. Özerdem, "Turkey and Peacebuilding in Africa."
44. Akpınar, "Turkey's Peacebuilding in Somalia."
45. For a detailed analysis of Turkey's contribution to peacekeeping, see the newly published database entitled Turkey's Peacekeeping Efforts Contribution Dataset "TUBAKOV," http://www.uik.org.tr/tubakov/en/
46. Park, *Modern Turkey*, 137.
47. Beriker et al., *Turkey as a Mediator*, 29.
48. "Turkey Seeks to Be International Mediation Center."
49. The aim of this initiative is to promote the use of mediation in the peaceful settlement of disputes, conflict prevention and resolution and to help of the development of mediation; http://sam.gov.tr/wp-content/uploads/2012/12/SAM_Papers_No.4-Dec12.pdf ;https://peacemaker.un.org/friendsofmediation
50. Ministry of Foreign Affairs of Turkey, "Mediation", 2018. http://www.mediation.mfa.gov.tr/default.tr.mfa
51. Beriker et al., *Turkey as a Mediator*, 34.
52. Aras, *Turkey's Mediation and Friends of Mediation Initiative*.
53. Köse, "Türk Dış Politikasının Ortadoğu'daki Yeni Kimliği ve Çatışma Çözümlerini Keşfi."
54. Acer, *Aegean Maritime Disputes and International Law*.
55. Hoffmann, "From Small Streams to Pipe Dreams."

Bibliography

Acer, Yucel. *The Aegean Maritime Disputes and International Law*. Abingdon, UK: Taylor & Francis, 2017.
Akpınar, Pınar. "Turkey's Peacebuilding in Somalia: The Limits of Humanitarian Diplomacy." *Turkish Studies* 14, no. 4 (2013): 735–757. doi:10.1080/14683849.2013.863448.
Aras, Bülent. *Turkey's Mediation and Friends of Mediation Initiative*. SAM Papers. Ankara: Center for Strategic Research, 2012.
Ayata, Bilgin. "Turkish Foreign Policy in a Changing Arab World: Rise and Fall of a Regional Actor?" *Journal of European Integration* 37, no. 1 (2015): 95–112. doi:10.1080/07036337.2014.975991.
Bercovitch, Jacob (ed.), *Studies in International Mediation*. New York: Palgrave Macmillan, 2012.
Bercovitch, Jacob, and Judith Fretter. *Regional Guide to International Conflict and Management from 1945 to 2003*. Washington D.C: CQ Press, 2004.
Bercovitch, Jacob, and Patrick M. Regan. "Mediation and International Conflict Management: A Review and Analysis." *In Multiple Paths to Knowledge in International Relations: Methodology in the Study of Conflict Management and Conflict Resolution*, 249–272. 2004.
Bercovitch, Jacob, and Patrick M. Regan. "Mediation and." In Zeev Maoz, Alex Mintz, T. Clifton Morgan, Glenn Palmar, and Richard J. Stoll (eds.), Multiple Paths to Knowledge in International Relations, Lanham, MD: Lexington, 249–272.
Bercovitch, Jacob, and Scott Sigmund Gartner. "Empirical Studies in International Mediation: Introduction to a Special Issue of International Interactions." *International Interactions* 32, no. 4 (2006): 319–328.
Beriker, Nimet, Arunjana Das, Sebnem Gumuscu, Ayse S. Kadayifci-Orellana, Havva Kok, Imdat Oner, and Dennis J. D. Sandole. *Turkey as a Mediator: Stories of Success and Failure*. Minneapolis, MN: Lexington Books, 2016.
Burton, Guy. *Rising Powers and the Arab–Israeli Conflict since 1947*. Minneapolis, MN: Lexington Books, 2018.
Burton, John. *Conflict: Resolution and Provention*. Basingstoke, UK: Macmillan, 1990.

Burton, John, and Frank Dukes. *Conflict: Readings in Management and Resolution.* New York: Springer, 1990.

Butler, Michael J. *International Conflict Management.* London; New York: Routledge, 2009.

Byman, Daniel, and Matthew Waxman. *The Dynamics of Coercion: American Foreign Policy and the Limits of Military Might.* Cambridge, UK: Cambridge University Press, 2002.

Cowell, Alan. "Turkey Faces Moral Crisis Over Bosnia." *The New York Times,* July 11, 1992, sec. World. https://www.nytimes.com/1992/07/11/world/turkey-faces-moral-crisis-over-bosnia.html

Crocker, Chester A., Fen Osler Hampson, and Pamela R. Aall. Turbulent Peace: The Challenges of Managing International Conflict. United States Institute of Peace Press, 2001.

Diehl, Paul F., and Joseph Lepgold, eds. *Regional Conflict Management.* Lanham: Rowman & Littlefield, 2003.

Dixon, William J. "Third-Party Techniques for Preventing Conflict Escalation and Promoting Peaceful Settlement." *International Organization* 50, no. 4 (1996): 653–681. doi:10.1017/S0020818300033543.

Dunn, David J. *From Power Politics to Conflict Resolution: The Work of John W. Burton.* New York: Springer, 2004.

Gent, Stephen E., and Megan Shannon. "Bias and Effectiveness of Third-party Conflict Management Mechanisms." *Conflict Management and Peace Science* 28 (2011): 124–144.

Gungor, Ugur. "The Analysis of Turkey's Approach to Peace Operations." PhD diss., Bilkent University, 2007. http://www.thesis.bilkent.edu.tr/0003253.pdf

Hill, Fiona, Kemal Kirişci, and Andrew Moffatt. "Armenia and Turkey: From Normalization to Reconciliation." *Turkish Policy Quarterly* 13, no. 4 (2015): 127–138.

Hoffmann, Clemens. "From Small Streams to Pipe Dreams – the Hydro-Engineering of the Cyprus Conflict." *Mediterranean Politics* 23, no. 2 (2018): 265–285.

Köse, Talha. "Rise and Fall of the AK Party's Kurdish Peace Initiatives." *Insight Turkey* 19, no. 2 (2017): 89–115. doi:10.25253/99.2017192.08.

Köse, Talha. "Türk Dış Politikasının Ortadoğu'daki Yeni Kimliği ve Çatışma Çözümlerini Keşfi." In *Türk Dış Politikası Yıllığı 2010,* 2011. Ankara: Seta Yayınları, 2010.

Lyon, Aisling. "Between the Integration and Accommodation of Ethnic Difference: Decentralization in the Republic of Macedonia," 2012.

MacFarlane, S. Neil. "Humanitarian Action and Conflict." *International Journal* 54, no. 4 (1999): 537–561.

Maoz, Zeev, Alex Mintz, Clifton T. Morgan, Glenn Palmer, and Richard J. Stoll. *Multiple Paths to Knowledge in International Relations: Methodology in the Study of Conflict Management and Conflict Resolution.* Lanham, Maryland: Lexington Books, 2004.

Ministry of Foreign Affairs of Turkey. "Mediation." 2018. http://www.mediation.mfa.gov.tr/default.en.mfa

Özcan, Mesut. "Turkish Foreign Policy under the AK Party." *Insight Turkey* 19, no. 2 (2017): 9–19. doi:10.25253/99.2017192.01.

Özerdem, Alpaslan. "Turkey and Peace Building in Africa: Leadership, Youth and Conflict Transformation." *Cesran* 14, Special Issue (2018): 6.

Park, Bill. *Modern Turkey: People, State and Foreign Policy in a Globalised World.* Abingdon, UK: Routledge, 2013.

Reychler, Luc. *Peacemaking, Peacekeeping and Peacebuilding, The International Studies Encyclopedia.* Oxford: Wiley-Blackwell, 2010.

Romano, C. "The Proliferation of International Judicial Bodies: The Pieces of the Puzzle." *NYU Journal of International Law and Politics* 31 (1999): 709–752.

Sayari, Sabri. "Turkish Foreign Policy in the Post-Cold War Era: The Challenges of Multi-Regionalism." *Journal of International Affairs,* 2000, 54, no. 1, 169–182.

Sazak, Onur, and Auveen Elizabeth Woods. "Policies and Role of Turkey on Peacebuilding." Policy Brief Series, IPC, 30 October 2015, Project: "Rising Powers and Innovative Approaches to Peacebuilding." www.RisingPowersandPeacebuilding.org.

Theophylactou, Demetrios A. "Geopolitics, Turkey's EU Accession Course and Cyprus: Power Balances and 'Soft Power' Calculations." *Southeast European and Black Sea Studies* 12, no. 1 (2012): 97–114. doi:10.1080/14683857.2012.662346.

"Turkey Seeks to Be International Mediation Center." VOA. Accessed April 26, 2018. https://www.voanews.com/a/turkey-seeks-to-be-international-mediation-center-140605183/171034.html

"Virtuous Power New Defense Doctrine: Turkish President." *Hürriyet Daily News*. Accessed April 26, 2018. http://www.hurriyetdailynews.com/virtuous-power-new-defense-doctrine-turkish-president-17784

Von Hippel, Karin, and Michael Clarke. "Something Must Be Done." *World Today* 55, no. 3 (1999): 4–7.

Wall, James A., Ronda Roberts Callister, James A. Wall, and Ronda Roberts Callister. "Conflict and Its Management." *Journal of Management*, 21, no. 3 (1995): 515–558.

Wilkenfeld, Jonathan, Victor Asal, Kathleen J. Young, and David M. Quinn. *Mediating International Crisis*. London; New York: Routledge Series, 2005.

Zartman, I. William, and Saadia Touval. *"International Mediation."* In *Leashing the Dogs of War: Conflict Management in a Divided World*, edited by Chester A. Crocker, Fen Osler Hampson, and Pamela Aall, 437–454. Washington, DC: United States Institute of Peace Press, 2007.

Rising powers and the horn of Africa: conflicting regionalisms*

Abigail Kabandula and Timothy M. Shaw

ABSTRACT

Rising powers are evolving centres for varieties of conflict as well as development. With a focus on the complexities of the Horn of Africa, we juxtapose Jan Nederveen Pieterse[1] on what is rising – States? Inter-regionalisms? Diasporas? Economies? Companies? New technologies? – with the late Jim Hentz[2] on non-traditional security (NTS) challenges on the continent. NTS factors include fragile states/ungoverned spaces, migrations and viruses, which continue to undermine contemporary state and governance structures inside and around Africa. In turn, NTS challenges demand alternative and creative ways to address them. We show how the Horn of Africa illustrates all these and other emergent factors in differing proportions over time, including the diversity of diasporas, both intra- and extra-regional. Further, we argue that rising powers internal and regional transnational tensions could impact human security for the foreseeable future. Thus, affecting the prospects for meeting Sustainable Development Goals (SDGs) in the Global South.

Introduction

Rising powers are at the centre of contemporary global politics and economics because they offer alternatives to the established global order. Understandably so, the global system is in flux as US global hegemony declines, and nationalist (populist) movements increase in Europe and the US, forcing Western powers to prioritise domestic politics. The ongoing domestic turmoil and undiplomatic views of current US regime give impetus to middle and rising powers like BRICS (Brazil, Russia, India, China, South Africa) and Turkey to continue seeking alternatives and deepen partnerships in trade, development, peace and security with countries in the Global South. After the transformation of the global economy from Euro-American concentration, unprecedented demand for mineral and energy resources has propelled African geopolitical significance owing to its vast natural resources,[3] which makes it economically attractive for many rising economies like Turkey as well as BRICS.

---

*We primarily consider Somalia, Sudan, South Sudan, Djibouti, Ethiopia and Eritrea as Horn of Africa countries.

With a focus on the complexities of the Horn of Africa, we juxtapose Pieterse[4] on what is rising – States? Inter-regionalisms? Diasporas? Economies? Companies? New technologies? – with Hentz[5] on non-traditional security (NTS) challenges on the continent. We explore two questions: what does the growing engagement of rising powers like Turkey entail for peace and security in the Horn of Africa region? And, will growing inter-regional relations facilitate/ exacerbate (in)security? We argue that while rising powers have made significant contributions to overall trade and development in Africa, recent political engagement and regional expansion/ inter-regionalism have contributed to the fragility of the Horn of Africa, thereby making the region susceptible to both intra- and inter-state conflicts. At the same time, conflict management processes, state stabilisation (Somalia) and human security have also been undermined as NTS policies that would encourage these aspects of security are given less priority.

NTS issues are foreground causes of both state and human insecurity as acute water and food shortages with a rapidly growing population increases the likelihood of armed conflict either intra- or inter-state as people scramble to survive on scarce resources due to climate change effects. We posit that heightened Turkish (and allies) military activities in the Horn could lead to militarisation of the region which inevitably reduces the priority previously given to NTS issues such as water, energy and food (WEF nexus).[6] Further, we show how the Horn, like most parts of Africa, faces new and complex NTS issues including terrorism, 'new wars' and climate change impacts. We also demonstrate how the advent of globalisation, particularly information technologies, has intensified and complicated NTS threats that demand measures to promote security across the continent and, specifically, the region. At the same time, information technologies have encouraged the growth of spaces where states have limited, weak, contested or absent authority. Cyberspace, offshore and shadow banking institutions have been most challenging for states to exert control because of the rise of powerful non-state actors: transnational corporations and individuals that contest and sometimes undermine state authority and legitimacy. Rising and middle powers have contributed to the economy; increased military engagement in the region has unleashed a complex of inter-regional relations and security challenges that further undermine both state and human security.

Twenty-first century (in)security conceptions

Traditionally, security policy and epistemology have been dominated by realist views that focus on protecting the state from external military threats and ensuring its survival.[7] Based on the Westphalian notion of statehood, traditional security upholds national sovereignty, territorial integrity and political independence as vital values to protect and ensure state survival. Threats to these values also threaten national security. Traditional security measures rely on hard power approaches such as military action or economic and political sanctions.[8] Even though of little significance to realists, civil wars are sources of internal threat to the state.

The global reconfiguration after the Cold War[9] and environmental changes created challenges that demanded a shift in thinking about security and security threats – who/what is secured and by whom? In the early 1990s many countries in the Horn, like others in sub-Saharan Africa and the globe, experienced civil war, genocide, poverty, drought, disease and inequality, particularly in post-colonial states. All these phenomena did not fit within the realist state-centric security model, yet the security of the state was undermined especially in internal conflict, more specifically new wars.[10] To reflect these global changes, the 1994 United Nations Development Program (UNDP) Human Development Report (HDR) broadens the notion of security, threats and actors responsible for producing and resolving insecurity. The report notes that in the contemporary world, insecurity arises from worries about daily life. Hence it proposes a shift in the referent for security, creating a human-centred security defined as 'safety from the constant threats of hunger, disease, crime and repression ... and protection from sudden and hurtful disruptions in the pattern of our daily lives – whether in our homes, in our jobs, in our communities or in our environment'.[11] The central argument for human security is that the individual within the state should be free from want and fear. Human security takes a liberal view by emphasising the rights of the individual to realise their full capabilities[12] economically, politically and socially.

Together with critical security studies, the Welsh, Paris and Copenhagen schools, feminist security studies[13] plus human security make up NTS studies. As the name suggests, NTS studies challenge the realist state-centred notion of security by expanding the security referent object – who and what to be secured – the actors – who provides security – and security threats. Security is socially constructed to an objective reality. Therefore, the referent object could be individuals, groups of people, the economy, technology or the environment. NTS concepts attest to the complexity of (in)security in the twenty-first century, simultaneously pointing to multifaceted security challenges that face contemporary Africa. NTS also highlights the significance of continuous transformation of the continent's security and development agencies to address both human and state security as they mutually reinforce each other as the following section illustrates.

Twenty-first century non-traditional security threats in Africa

Hentz, Duffield and Williams extensively discuss NTS challenges in Africa today.[14] We find that prevalent NTS threats in the Horn of Africa include fragile or failed states, new wars, terrorism, human and drug trafficking, and effects of climate change – famine, drought and disease. While we cannot sufficiently address each of these threats in detail, we highlight new wars/civil wars, state fragility/failed states, terrorism and climate change effects on the region. We also note the interlinkage of these threats within the process of neoliberal globalisation, and how the interlinkage strains and sometimes renders multinational – i.e. Africa Union (AU), United Nations (UN) or Regional Economic Communities (RECs) – peace and security efforts security futile. Threats such as civil war often do not occur in isolation. They are context specific often linked to the political, social and economic activities of people in the country or region. For instance, due to instability and protracted conflict, countries at war experience poor economic growth, which may lead to increased unemployment, general suffering, poverty, terrorism and subsequently lack of development. Further, we highlight the transnationality of the threats, conflict, state fragility and climate change effects in the Horn and the broader Eastern Africa region.

Non-traditional security, globalisation, conflict and terrorism

Neoliberal globalisation generated socio-political and -economic forces that expanded global interaction and integration of people, states, companies and governments through international trade, investment and advances in information technology.[15] Globalisation has intensified and complicated NTS threats and measures to promote security. Information technology globalisation has rendered time and distance obsolete. The development of information technology has connected the world in ways never imagined and Africa, too, has benefited from this process. The internet and cell phone technology has connected millions across the continent and they are using this technology in unique ways. Technologies such as M-Pesa[16] in East and Horn of Africa allow people to receive money on their phones almost instantly without a bank account. Travel within and out of the Horn as well as the continent is easier, faster and safer with the development of safer modes of transportation. Equipped with the power of new technology, people can access goods and services within the country, region and abroad. Therefore, economically, Africa is performing well.

However, the impact of new information technology on security in Africa is a double-edged sword. On the one hand, information technology has increased the visibility of NTS threats including human rights violations allowing for a multiplicity of actors – individuals, Non-Governmental Organisations (NGOs), Intergovernmental Organisations (INGOs) and the private sector – to respond. Ordinary people are more conscious of their human rights and identifying human rights violations. Citizens can easily mobilise local networks using new technology and social media outlets such as Facebook, Twitter and WhatsApp to organise support for social movements to protect human security. The Arab Spring in 2011 was partly successful because of effective social media mobilisation at local, national and global levels. The result was a revolution leading to the overthrow of abusive dictators in North Africa and the Middle East. In this sense, globalisation in information and communication technologies (ICTs) has positive effects in addressing NTS threats and promoting human security on the continent.

On the other hand, globalisation exacerbates NTS threats and strains measures to address insecurity. The effects of globalisation are felt at local and community levels as new social forces change traditional ways of life, cultures and language, plus erode traditional livelihoods and economies. The erosion, in some cases, has caused identity crises arising from uncertainty and anxiety in daily life as people's political, economic and psychological activities are dislocated. Religious extremism manifesting as terrorism and perverse violence are some ways of coping and self-affirmation.[17] These insecurities are transported to the global level through global interaction and interconnection aided by new technologies. Insecurity can travel through the spread of extremist ideologies and long-distance projection of violence with new technology such as drones.[18] One of the most effective terrorist recruitment tools is the internet. Terrorists across the world including Al-Shabaab in the Horn (and East Africa) use various virtual portals to propagate radical 'religious' ideas for recruitment purposes.

Further, information technologies can prolong and intensify civil wars and encourage state failure. Information technologies such as the internet and offshore banking institutions enable non-state actors to acquire resources to continue war[19] and make it difficult to protect civilians. Non-state actors with illegal control of local resources such as gold and diamonds can trade on the international black markets and use the money to pay for guns. They are also able to keep and access their funds in international off-shore banks where they are protected from state regulation. Insurgencies in Somalia (2006 to present) and Nigeria (2009 to present) are cases in point.

The Horn is greatly impacted by terrorism emanating from Somalia. Al-Shabaab transnational networks spread across the entire region making Somalia, Kenya and Ethiopia the epicentres of terrorism in east Africa.[20] Al-Shabaab and other non-state armed groups in the region have benefited from the revolution in information technology to strengthen, expand and sustain their insurgency. Al-Shabaab today is a fundamentally different group from that of 2006. Utilising readily available and sophisticated information technology, the group continues to recruit online through social media. Yet even more worrying is the group's continued ability to acquire funds at home and abroad. There are various methods in which the groups fund itself, including kidnapping, illegal sales of ivory, extorting local businesses, foreign governments, charities, Somali diaspora and individual donations.[21] Having lost control of its major local trade at Kismayo and Bakara market in Mogadishu, and suffered general disruption of its charcoal trade by AMISOM and Somali forces, Al-Shabaab's local revenues have declined significantly, forcing it to rely on transnational fundraising.[22]

Diaspora finances have been a significant source of funding for the general Somali population. It is estimated that US$500 million to US$800 million per year in remittances are sent to Somalia.[23] It is hard to determine how much goes to funding Al-Shabaab. The dedication and resilience of the Somali diaspora to continue supporting the youth insurgency suggests deep-seated motivations that ought to be understood and integrated into transnational security measures to realise peace and security in the country. Considering the number of people willing to fundraise or make personal contributions, it is imperative to understand how and why the diaspora sends funds to Al-Shabaab. Since the US Department of Justice crackdown on Al-Shabaab financiers, there are fewer to none cases of Al-Shabaab fundraising reported in the recent past. However, this does not mean that money is not being sent to Al-Shabaab. It could mean that people have found ways of evading the authorities or detection through shadow banking – another aspect of globalisation and information technology.

Shadow banking is broadly defined as 'credit intermediation involving entities and activities (fully or partially) outside the regular banking system'.[24] Shadow banking enables organised crime networks such as terrorist organisations to move money without detection. Minimally or fully regulated facilities such as a pre-paid store, debit cards, M-Pesa and virtual currencies like Bitcoin and crypto currencies can be used without any documentation or identification to load and carry large sums of money across borders without detection. The lack of documentation when loading or acquiring the money makes it almost impossible for authorities to track such transactions.

In May 2016, the International Consortium of Investigative Journalists (ICIJ) – a global network of over 200 investigative journalists – gained access to 11.5 million Mossack Fonseca Incorporated client files. Popularly known as the Panama Papers, the documents contain personal and financial information of their client's offshore holdings. *The Guardian* on 30 November 2016 reported that the European Union's law enforcement agency (Europol) identified about 3469 individuals and companies in Panama Papers as credible matches for suspected terrorists, cybercriminals and cigarette smugglers. While none of the individuals were explicitly linked to any terrorist groups, financial as well as legal experts have shown the possibility of financing terrorism through offshore accounts and shell companies. University of Utah professor Shima Baradaran Baughman asserts in an article on the *Conversation* on 12 April 2016 that terrorists can easily mask their true identities from law enforcement through shell companies, given the ease of creating such a company.

Al-Shabaab allegedly receives financial and military support from foreign governments such as Eritrea, Iran, Saudi Arabia, Syria, Qatar and Yemen. In 2012, it was reported that Eritrea through its embassy in Nairobi was giving about US$80,000 per month for 10 years to members of Al-Shabaab.[25] While the September 2015 SEM report finds no evidence of Eritrea supporting the group, it does not mean that it did not receive funding. As alluded to, it is increasingly difficult to trace money used in criminal activities in the current era of shadow banking and sophisticated communication services. Eritrea's illegal trade with arms dealers in Somalia, its military support to armed groups such the Tigray People's Democratic Movement (TPDM), active involvement in the informal economy controlled by the People's Front for Democracy and Justice (PFDJ) and lack of financial transparency[26] may suggest some truth in the allegation by the Somali government of its continuing support to Al-Shabaab.

The discussion above shows that twenty-first century NTS threats are complex and inter-linked, with growing regional dimensions. The advent of globalisation has exacerbated NTS threats and reduced the legitimacy and ability of the state to govern and protect its people by shifting the centres of authority to multiple places. This change suggests that traditional security instruments, structures and mechanisms that focus on securing the state are inadequate to deal with current security threats. The nature of NTS threats to both the state and human security demand a transformation and adaptation of African security structures and measures to current needs for them to be effective.[27] Which means the focus on state security, especially through military means, is insufficient to bring about sustainable peace, security or development.

The challenge of fragile states in the Horn

Fragile or 'failed' states are increasingly seen to contribute to regional and global insecurity. A state is considered fragile, weak or failing if it does not guarantee public order (through legitimate use of force) within its borders and fails to support the international system and global order.[28] Contentious though it may be, the Fund for Peace (FFP) fragile states index is helpful in visualising the extent of the state fragility in the Horn. In 2017, all Horn of Africa countries were either on alert or already fragile as Figure 1 shows.

Fragile states are seen to harbour security threats with national, regional and international implications including terrorism, nuclear proliferation, transnational organised crime, armed conflict and refugee flows.[30] Organised crime seems to flourish in failed states because of generalised insecurity. This insecurity threatens the security of

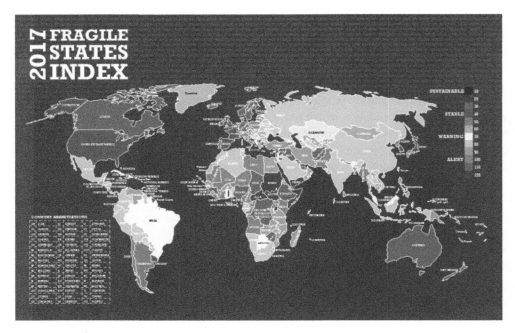

Figure 1. Fragile states. Sources: Fund for Peace.[29]

neighbouring states as refugee flows and criminal networks linked to belligerents establish cross-border networks. Information technology aids criminal activities in fragile states as it enables the export of local or regional conflict and insecurity to the global level. Improved communication makes it possible for entrepreneurs of violence to link and mobilise through the internet, radio and cell phones. As a result, twenty-first century Western aid is channelled towards security or the fight against terrorism in failed states such as Somalia and Mali because they ultimately present potential security threats to global security (or homeland security in the case of US).[31]

Water, energy, food and climate nexus

Civil war, state fragility and terrorism, together with rising water, energy and food (WEF) shortages, are complicating security in Africa in general and the Horn region specifically as disputes over water, land and other natural resources threaten to escalate into intra- and inter-state conflicts. In the last 20 years, the 'resource curse'[32] has been a leading explanation for causes of armed conflict in Africa. However, the effects of climate change are thwarting any notion of sustainable peace and security by threatening people's livelihood due to water, energy and food shortages. Otherwise known as the water, energy, food and climate 'nexus' (WEF-climate nexus), are complex relationships among water, energy and food exacerbated by myriad and unpredictable effects of climate change.[33]

Juxtaposing the WEF-climate nexus with rapid population growth and urbanisation as Figure 2 shows, and an expanding middle class, sub-Saharan Africa faces critical and uneven shortages of water, energy and food due to severe droughts.[34] Simultaneously, the demand for food, energy and water has increased due to population growth and developmental needs. The decline in freshwater resources due to erratic rainfall affects food, water and energy supplies, employment and income.[35] Acute water and food shortages with a rapidly growing population increases the likelihood of armed conflict either intra- or inter-state as people scramble to survive on the limited resources available. This, in turn, increases the need for conflict management processes and peacekeeping operations to bring about order, peace and security.

This is the case with Nile River conflict: a macro-regional dispute in East Africa. Egypt has threatened war with any country that jeopardises its water security – access to the Nile River[37] – despite the pre-emptive diplomacy of the Nile Basin Initiative based in Entebbe. Other nations benefiting from being upstream on the river are Ethiopia, Uganda, Sudan, South Sudan, Kenya, Congo DR and Tanzania.[38] Egypt is heavily dependent on the Nile River for its freshwater supply and has had supremacy over the Nile River since 1929. However, reduced waters in the Nile and erratic rains have caused the other five countries, notably Ethiopia, to demand more access to and use of the Nile River and its tributaries for national development.

Like Egypt, Ethiopia's main water supply comes from the Nile. A CNN article on 6 March 2015 reported that Ethiopia had begun constructing a US$5 billion Grand Ethiopia Renaissance Dam (GERD) located on the Blue Nile (the main water supply for the Nile). The article noted that, when completed, the dam could generate up to 6000 megawatts of electricity for domestic and export markets. Egypt responded by accusing Ethiopia of

Sub-Saharan Africa Urban Agglomerations Map 2010

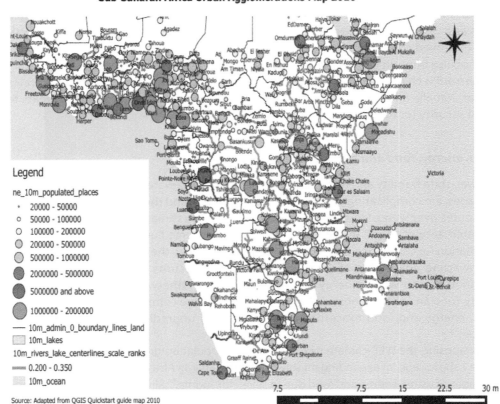

Figure 2. Sub-Saharan Africa population map. Sources: Wanjiku C. Kihato and Singumbe Muyeba.[36]

jeopardising Egypt's water needs. Negotiation between Ethiopia and Egypt on the GERD ensued, mediated by Sudan.[39] While endorsement of the construction was a significant milestone, tensions over the governance of the Nile waters remained. Below, we show how rising power engagement in the Horn exacerbates NTS threats including the one over the Nile River waters.

Inter-regionalisms

The Horn of Africa has become a centre for rising power plays. Not surprising, the region is strategic, it is a gateway to the continent of Africa, the Middle East and a passage to Europe. Thus, it offers many economic and security benefits. Turkey, a member of NATO (North Atlantic Treaty Organization), is the rising power whose interests in the region have changed the Horn's political, economic and security landscape. While Turkey has made many positive contributions to the region's economy through trade, investments and humanitarian aid, especially in Ethiopia and Somalia, its current political and security engagement with the region has made the Horn more volatile. In the following sections, we show how geopolitical tensions and regional rivalries resulting mainly from Turkish (allies and adversaries) involvement in the region risk militarising the region, thereby impacting human security and non-traditional security which are more defining to the people. Therefore, we posit that rising powers manoeuvres in the Horn of Africa serve to militarise the region thereby reinforcing more state-centric conceptions of security concentrated on territorial disputes and not broadly on human security.

Turkey's renewed engagement in Africa, 2005 onwards

Following recent heightened Turkish involvement in the Horn, we, like many scholars of Africa, ask why and what is Turkey's interest in Africa? Mostly, why is it heavily involved in the Horn, a region marred by civil war and tense inter-state relations? In this section, we explore some of the reasons why Turkey is engaged in Africa, especially the Horn, and subsequent inter-regional ties. Whereas Turkish relations with African countries dates to before the Ottoman Empire, its current engagement can be traced to 2005.[40] Ozkan and Akgun[41] note that the coming to power of the Justice and Development Party commonly also known as AKP (Adalet ve Kalkmma Partisi) in 2002 is the most defining moment in Turkish foreign policy reorientation. Under the AKP, Turkey has taken incredible steps to restructure its political and economic policies and to improve Turkey's global image by actively participating in global matters outside the European Union. Nonetheless, it appears that Turkey has focused most of its attention on the Middle East and Africa. Africa, in particular, has a renewed significance in Turkish politics and foreign policy especially in relation to competition for the BRICS, and especially China.

In 2005, Turkey proclaimed a 'year of Africa' and begun to renew ties with the continent. In the same year, Recep Tayyip Erdogan, then prime minister, also made a momentous visit to Ethiopia and South Africa, the first for a Turkish prime minister.[42] Turkey also established formal ties with AU and obtained observer status. That year the AU declared Turkey one of its strategic partners. Other strategic partnerships were formed with Intergovernmental Authority on Development (IGAD) – the main regional body for the Eastern Africa region – and the Economic Community of West African States (ECOWAS) in West Africa. Also, Turkey positioned itself as a development assistance partner – a status previously dominated by Western countries. It joined African Development Bank in 2008 and increased its diplomatic representation by opening more embassies, from 12 (2009) to 39 (2016).[43] Therefore, one may argue that the current Turkish involvement in Africa is primarily an AKP agenda and is leadership driven. Which then brings an interesting political dimension to Turkish-Africa relations post-AKP and Erdogan, more especially that the latter is seemingly obsessed with Turkey under the former Ottoman empire glory.

Nonetheless, scholars and pundits alike, including Korkut and Civelekoglu,[44] agree that 2011 marked a significant turning point in Turkish-Africa relations. Turkey moved from focusing on developing cordial ties to making substantial investments and humanitarian aid contributions. Some may argue that Erdogan truly believes he can make a difference in Africa. He once wrote in an Al-Jazeera op-ed that 'Many people in the world associate the African continent with extreme poverty, violent conflict and a general state of hopelessness. The people of Turkey have a different view. We believe Africa deserves better'[45] Following a severe drought in Somalia in 2011, Erdogan travelled to Somalia not only for humanitarian purposes but also to 'try to destroy the perception that no one can go to Mogadishu' (BBC, 19 August 2011). Donelli argues that this event brought the crisis in Somalia onto the international scene.[46] Turkey was among the few non-African and perhaps the only rising power to send significant humanitarian assistance to Somalia. A total of US$115m was raised by the Turkish public and US$350m in collaboration with other Muslim countries (BBC, 19 August 2011).

Turkish engagement in Africa has progressively strengthened, even though restricted to the Horn and mainly Muslim countries: Somalia, Djibouti and Sudan. One explanation for Turkey's interest in the Horn is the region's strategic geographical location: its easy access between the continent and the Middle East via the Red Sea and the Gulf of Aden. Turkey's involvement in the region has significantly changed its economic, political and security architecture. Some analysts and scholars[47] posit that Turkey is primarily driven by economic and strategic interests in the Horn. Like other rising powers, Turkey also depends on constant engagement with external markets for its economic growth.

From 2008, Turkey has pursued economic opportunities with Africa in trade and investments. Similar to the BRICS, Turkey's economic interests extend across the continent. Its primary focus has been the Horn of Africa because it is a gateway to the entire continent for Turkish imports and exports and easy access to the Middle East. Therefore, Turkey is strategically placing itself not only to extract natural resources from Africa but also to sell its finished products. Thus, controlling the means of transportation via the main channels on the Red Sea and Gulf of Aden is essential.

Korkut and Civelekoglu[48] see Turkey's activities as a strategic regional power play. They argue that building political assets in international relations across the world including Africa is important for regional powers. Antonopoulos et al. see Turkish manoeuvres in the Horn as a strategic move to expand its political influence and advance new forms of control and domination (inter-imperialism).[49] Their argument has merit given the infamous Gulf crisis which started in June 2017 when a coalition led by Saudi Arabia (United Arab Emirates, Bahrain, Mauritania and Egypt) severed diplomat ties and imposed trade and travel bans on Qatar. These actions came after Saudi Arabia accused Qatar of supporting terrorism, which it argued is a violation of a 2014 agreement with the Gulf Cooperation Council (GCC) the *Gulf News* reported on 2 April 2018. Turkey and Iran support Qatar in the crisis. Also, Turkey has had a history of disagreements with the Saudi Arabia and UAE over Iran and the Muslim Brotherhood.

Somalia, Sudan and Djibouti triage

Nonetheless, it is the events between September and December 2017 that escalated tensions in the fragile Horn of Africa region. In September 2017, Turkey opened its largest military base outside its borders in Somalia's capital Mogadishu. On 1 October 2017, Al-Jazeera reported that the base is worth US$50m, covering four kilometres, and is intended to strengthen the Somali army by training 10,000 soldiers, up to 1500 soldiers at a time. The base can be construed as a signal of the close relationship between the two countries, and an increasing Turkish presence in the region.

Further, in December 2017, Sudan and Turkey entered into a US$650m agreement to rehabilitate the Red Sea port island of Suakin in north-eastern Sudan. *Asia Times*, on 2 January 2018, observed that the agreement came with exclusive docking rights for Turkish civilian and military vessels on the west coast. The agreement also details fighting terror in the East and Horn of Africa regions. This agreement is particularly significant because it gives Turkey a military presence in the Red Sea via Sudanese territorial waters, though masked as counter-terrorism and protection for military ships. There were a number of agreements signed between the two countries in mining, agriculture, energy and health sectors. However, the leasing of an ancient island on the Red Sea – Suakin or Sawakin (Arabic) – home to several ancient buildings from eighteenth-century Ottoman Empire when Turkey colonised Sudan for 'investment and tourism purposes' has sparked an unpreceded chain reaction in the region like the Gulf crisis.

Almost immediately following the Sudanese agreement, Turkey was invited to open a military base in Djibouti, the small Horn of Africa country closest to the Middle East. Reports that the strategically located country may be home to another foreign military base – US, France, Japan, China and Saudi Arabia already have bases – came after Djiboutian President Ismail Omar Guelleh visited Turkey. However, it was Djibouti's ambassador to Turkey Aden H. Abdillahi who announced the open invitation. He remarked, 'possible steps from Turkey to build a military base in the country would be welcomed' (*Daily Sabah*, 29 December 2017).

Turkey's adversaries – Saudi Arabia and UAE – are alarmed by the swift Turkish expansion in the Horn, yet they are mostly angered by Suakin Island restoration and possible military presence. They have interpreted the move as a calculated ploy to station troops close to Jeddah, the Saudi city nearest to Sudan. According to the *Asia Times* of 2 January 2018, Saudi Arabia believes Qatar is the actual beneficiary of Turkey's presence on the island because they do not think Turkey has the money to finance Suakin's rehabilitation. Turkey has had strained relations with the duo over Qatar, Iran and the Muslim Brotherhood. As such, the pair is concerned about Turkish military expansion given its close ties with Iran and support for Qatar.

Since the Gulf crisis started, Turkey has stationed more troops in its Qatari military base. The *South China Morning Post* on 18 January 2018 indicated that Turkey intends to increase its troops to 3000 in 2018. Adding to the tension is Turkish suspicion of UAE, as of 7 November 2017 Voice of America reported Erdogan accusing UAE of supporting a failed coup to oust him in July 2016. Nonetheless, on 28 December 2017, Egyptian based media PressTV reported Erdogan categorically denying that his country is constructing a naval base on the Sudanese Island. He reiterated that Turkey plans to restore Ottoman-era ruins in the area. Further Saudi Arabia and UAE also value the Horn for its strategic location to expand their capabilities in the Gulf of Aden and the Red Sea to support operations in Yemen.[50] The Saudis are engaged in a proxy war with Iran in efforts to counter the Iranian-backed al Houthis in Yemen. Critical Threats on 26 February 2018 noted that the UAE have since acquired a military base in Djibouti and a 30-year lease of Berbera port in self-proclaimed independent Somaliland. The agreement was modified in March 2018 to include Ethiopia as a co-investor with 19%, while Somaliland and the UAE returned 30 and 51% ownership respectively.[51] As such, analysts assert that the UAE has used the war in Yemen to project power in the Gulf.[52]

Recent Turkish engagement in the Horn has opened an already fragile region to intense, complicated geopolitical rivalries and possible inter-state conflicts with implications for human security. The Sudanese-Turkish agreement comes after the two countries had improved their relations. Sudan contributed 6000 troops to the Saudi-led intervention in Yemen. In return, Saudi Arabia requested the US to lift economic sanctions on Sudan. Therefore, the Sudanese-Turkish agreement was both a comment on improved relations as well as on Saudi strategy to dominate the Gulf. Despite the agreement, President Omar al-Bashir insists that his country will keep its troops in Yemen. Whatever Turkey's true intentions for the Horn may be, what is certain is that its activities have changed the geopolitical and security of the region. The 2017 Gulf crisis has expanded into the area as the Saudis and their allies rush to counter Turkish-Qatari influence in the region. In fact, the whole continent has in some way been caught up in the crisis and power politics.

The Gulf crisis in the Horn

The rivalry between Turkey and the Gulf States has expanded into mainland Africa as the Saudi coalition rushes to establish relations with African countries to counter Turkish expansion. James Dorsey in the *South China Morning Post* on 18 January 2018 observed that competition for influence among the Gulf States includes the Sahel, Central and West Africa. He further notes that Qatar's Sheikh Tamim bin Hamad Al Thani visited six West African countries in 2017 to garner support for his country in the crisis. More importantly, the extension of the Gulf crisis to the Horn has fuelled already tense inter-state relations with the potential to trigger regional conflicts and to undermine Somalia's already weak federal system. After Eritrea and Djibouti supported the Saudi coalition and reduced ties with Qatar, Dorsey observes that Qatar withdrew its 400-troop peacekeeping contingent from the Red Sea island of Doumeira. Eritrea seized the opportunity to grab the island which Djibouti also claims as its own. This action has the potential to spark an inter-state conflict over the Island.

Turkey's improved relations with Sudan has caused unease in Egypt. Egypt became suspicious and anxious about the new relationship given that it already had strained relations with Sudan over a border dispute in the region of Halayeeb and the Nile River waters. On 28 December 2017, PressTV reported that Sudan complained to the United Nations that a maritime agreement reached in 2016 by Egypt and Saudi Arabia encroached on Sudanese waters. Sudan has also accused Egypt of deploying troops and warplanes to the Sudanese side of the border. However, after reports that Egypt, with the help of UAE, had sent troops to Eritrea, Sudan closed its border with Eritrea. Likewise, Egypt is angered by the Turkish presence in Suakin. Egypt fears that Sudan might rekindle its claim to the disputed Halaib Triangle on the Red Sea. For over 60 years, the two countries have quarrelled over the territory, each claiming it to be theirs. Egypt took control in the 1990s when it deployed troops to safeguard the territory and end Sudanese claims. However, with Turkish military support, Sami Moubayed in the *Asia Times* on 2 January 2018 argues that Egypt fears Sudan may reconsider its claim.

Further, Gulf States' power politics in the Horn have reignited an already intense cross-border water conflict centred on access to the Nile River. Egypt has capitalised on the ensuing Sudanese-Turkish-Qatari partnership to rekindle its fight over the Nile River, dam construction and disputed border with Sudan. The extremity of the Egyptian perspective is encapsulated in Egyptian columnist's words remarking, 'Sudan is violating the rules of history and geography and is conspiring against Egypt under the shadow of Turkish madness, Iranian conspiracy, an Ethiopian scheme to starve Egypt of water, and Qatar's financing of efforts to undermine Egypt' (*Daily News,* 28 December 2017).

While Somalia has benefited tremendously from the Turkish and UAE counterterrorism support and humanitarian aid (the latter mostly from Turkey), the rivalry between the two countries has undermined its loose federal system. The Gulf crisis has exacerbated tensions between Somalia and its federal states, Somaliland and Puntland. The Somali federal government (SFG) under President Farmajo has remained neutral throughout the crisis. However, the Saudis are using financial aid to pressure Somalia to cut ties with Qatar. They offered

US$80 million for the country to cut diplomatic relations with Qatar and threaten to pull out all financial aid if Somalia remained neutral in the crisis. When Somalia insisted on being neutral, the UAE recalled its ambassador to Somalia and deported Somali citizens as punishment for its neutrality. Earlier in 2017, Saudi Arabia rewarded Somalia with US$50m in aid for cutting relations with Iran. Though, the semi-autonomous states support the Saudi-led coalition against Qatar. Somaliland and Puntland announced their support for the UAE and Saudi Arabia and re-proclaimed their independence from Somalia in June 2017.[53] President Farmajo's government criticised the two states for cutting ties with Qatar. The fallout between the SFG and its states is the latest disagreements resulting from Turkey and UAE engagement in the country. At the start of 2017, the UAE signed a 30-year contract to lease the Port of Berbera in Somaliland against the consent of the SFG who called for its cancellation. The UAE is using the port to further their cause in Yemen. Yemeni al Houthi movement retaliated by threatening to bombard Berbera after UAE military ships docked at the port.[54] The tension has exposed weaknesses in the Somali federal system as well as intensified strained relations between the central government and federal states with an impact on African Union (AMISOM) state-building process.

More generally, rising powers' involvement in the Horn has facilitated geopolitical tensions and regional rivalries that risk militarising the region and impacting human security by reinforcing more state-centric conceptions of security concentrated on territorial and border disputes. As alluded to previously, the Horn, like many parts of Africa, faces complex NTS problems such as new wars, climate change impacts, transnational organised crime and terrorism that have contributed to its fragility and impacted human security adversely. Therefore, adding regional rivalry and geopolitical tensions to state fragility will encourage state-centric security measures that would impede progress and focus on NTS matters that are vital to human security. States are likely to focus more on securing their borders and territories, and strengthening their armies to protect themselves against an imminent adversary. Eritrea is a case in point. The country has been under a state of emergency since 1998 due to fear of an Ethiopian invasion. As a result, Eritrea spends a large portion of its GDP, about 13.6%, on defence.[55] While diplomatic relations between the two countries have resumed,[56] Eritrea is unlikely to reduce its military spending to focus on urgent NTS matters because Djibouti still poses a threat over Doumeira. Further, it still has poor relations with Sudan following the latter's border closure after it was reported that Egypt had sent troops to Eritrea in 2018. Therefore, rising powers' political and military engagement in the Horn has not only enabled further regional fragility, it has also jeopardised human security by creating a conducive environment for militarisation.

Impact of Turkish engagement in the Horn on China

Turkish expansion in Africa comes at a time when BRICS investments in Africa have declined for many reasons.[57] Rising powers like Turkey have seized the opportunity to increase their trade and investments on the continent. A decade ago, Chinese companies won almost all infrastructure projects; but now with Turkey in the region, Chinese companies are facing stiff competition. Turkey has geographical (legacy of the Ottoman empire) and religious (predominately Muslims countries) advantages over China which come into play when granting contracts.[58] Hence Turkish businesses, investments and trade have increased tremendously in the region. As noted in the *Financial Times* on 28 June 2012, Yapi Merkezi, a Turkish construction company, gets about 60% of its annual US$800m revenues from the Horn. Turkey's exports to Africa increased from US$1.5 billion in 2001 to US$10.3 billion in 2011, and the overall trade volume rose from US$4 billion in 2000 to US$19 billion in 2011.[59] However, despite the increasing trade volume, Rudincova argues that Turkish investments in Africa hardly compare to those of China, India or former colonial powers.[60]

Nevertheless, Turkish business and relations in the Horn have impacted the Chinese directly. Turkey's latest ties with Djibouti, in particular, threatens Chinese investments. Djibouti is home to the Bab el-Mandab, a vital maritime trade route in the Aden-Suez Canal passage. Over 20,000 ships pass through this route that connects the Gulf of Aden to the Red Sea. It is also an important trade route for Asia and Europe. China depends on this route not just for its trade with Africa, but also with Europe. About US$1 billion of its everyday trade with the European Union is dependent on the route.[61] Therefore, China is determined to secure the route and cement its presence in Djibouti as it pushes the Belt and Road Initiative forward. In July 2018, Djibouti opened a US$3.5bn Chinese funded free-trade zone. When completed, the zone will be the biggest in Africa.[62] With the UAE out of Djibouti following the latter's seizure of Doraleh port, China only has Turkey to worry about. The Turkish *Daily Sabah* reported on 29 December 2017 that Djibouti had agreed to open a special Turkish economic zone that will allow and encourage Turkish businesses to establish industries in the region, at the same time creating a gateway for Turkish goods into the continent. When fully operational, the special economic zone, together with other Turkish investments in the Horn, threaten to decrease Chinese trade and investments in the foreseeable future.

We have shown how the Horn has myriad insecurities, coalitions, actors and competing levels of regionalisms. Turkey's increased presence in Africa, especially in the Horn, has unleashed a complex network of inter-regional relations and security challenges. Concurrently, the region is becoming militarised. The latter has serious consequences for sustainable peace and security in the region. A move toward militarisation will overshadow human security and NTS challenges which are central to much of the insecurity in the region, thus affecting the prospects for meeting Sustainable Development Goals (SDGs) in Africa and the broader Global South.

Conclusion

We have argued that Africa in the twenty-first century remains a competitive source of natural resources and a lucrative investment destination. BRICS and other rising powers such as Turkey have developed and strengthened economic, development and humanitarian partnerships across the continent, thereby making significant contributions to its overall development. However, growing rising power engagement in the political and security processes of the Horn has led to rising inter-regional relations that facilitate and exacerbate insecurity in the fragile region. By unravelling the security and geopolitical complexities of the Horn, we have shown how recent Turkey (allies and adversaries) political engagement and regional expansion have contributed to the fragility of the Horn, making the region susceptible to both intra- and inter-state conflicts. At the same time conflict management processes, state stabilisation in extremely fragile states like Somalia and human security have also been undermined as NTS policies that would encourage these aspects of security are given less priority.

Further, we have argued that Turkish military activities with strategic Horn countries risk militarisation of regions which will inevitably reduce the significance formerly given to NTS issues such as water, energy and food (WEF nexus), rapid population growth and terrorism. We have shown how NTS issues are foreground causes of both state and human insecurity by increasing the likelihood of armed conflict either intra- or inter-state as people scramble to survive on the limited resources available. Further, we also demonstrated how the advent of globalisation in information technologies has intensified and complicated NTS threats and measures to promote security on the continent and the region. At the same time, we also show how information technologies have contributed to weakening the state and obscuring its legitimacy. Cyberspace, offshore and shadow banking institutions are challenging for states to exert control because of the rise of powerful non-state actors: transnational corporations and individuals that contest and sometimes undermine state authority and legitimacy. Therefore, we posit, even though rising powers have contributed to overall economic growth and development in the broader African continent, increased military engagement in the Horn region has brought about complex inter-regional relations and security challenges that will further undermine both state and human security in the region; consequently, affecting the prospects for meeting SDGs in Africa.

Acknowledgements

The authors would like to express their gratitude to Jason McSparren for reading and commenting on the initial draft, Professor Stacy VanDeveer and the Department of Conflict Resolution, Global Governance and Human Security for their continuing support.

Notes

1. Pieterse, "Global Rebalancing," 22–48.
2. Hentz, "Introduction," 3–8.
3. Ozkan, "What Drives Turkey's Involvement in Africa?" 533–540.
4. See note 1 above.
5. See note 2 above.

6.   For further information on WEF Nexus, see Bizikova et al., *The Water-Energy-Food Security Nexus* and Bazilian et al., "Considering the Energy, Water and Food Nexus."

7.   Morgenthau and Thompson, *Politics Among Nations;* Jervis, "Realism," 971–992; Waltz, *Theory of International Politics.*

8.   Karns and Mingst, *International Organizations,* 45.

9.   Besada et al., "African Solutions for African Problems," 1–15.

10.   Duffield, *Global Governance and the New Wars,* 1–10.

11.   United Nations Development Program, *Human Development Report,* 3.

12.   Sen, *Development as Freedom.*

13.   For a discussion on these schools of thought, see Peoples and Vaughan-Williams, *Critical Security Studies.*

14.   For Hentz, see note 2 above; for Duffield, see note 10 above; Williams, "Thinking about Security in Africa," 1021–1038.

15.   Williamson, "Globalization," 1–7; Muyeba, *Globalization and Africa,* 31–36; Stiglitz, *Making Globalization Work,* 3–25.

16.   See Vodafone South Africa on how M-Pesa works at: http://www.vodafone.com/content/index/what/m-pesa.html

17.   McRae, "Human Security," 14–27.

18.   Stiglitz and Kaldor, "Protection from Violence," 91–93.

19.   Axworthy, "Human Security and Global Governance," 19–23; see note 14 above.

20.   Aning and Abdallah, "Confronting Hybrid Threats," 20–37.

21.   Masters and Sergie, *Al-Shabab.*

22.   Kambere, "Financing Al Shabaab."

23.   Ibid.

24.   Claessens and Ratnovski, *What is Shadow Banking?* 3.

25.   See note 23 above.

26.   Letter dated 22 September 2015 from SEM addressed to the chair of the Security Council.

27.   Kabandula and Shaw, "African Multinational Forces," 2–4.

28.   Schneckener, "Fragile Statehood, Armed Non-State Actors," 23–40.

29.   Map available at: http://fundforpeace.org/fsi/analytics/fsi-heat-map/

30.   Cook and Downie, "Rethinking Engagement in Fragile States."

31.   Duffield, "Human Security," 11–38.

32.   Collier and Hoeffler, "Greed and Grievance in Civil War," 563–595.

33.   World Economic Forum, *Water Security.*

34.   Drime and Gandure, "Food Security," 181–197.

35.   See note 29 above.

36.   Kihato and Muyeba, "Challenges and Prospects of African Urbanization."

37.   Kimenyi and Mbaku, "Limits of the New Nile Agreement."

38.   Okoth-Owiro, "The Nile Treaty"; Kimenyi and Mbaku, "Governing the Nile River Basin."

39.   Kimenyi and Mbaku, "Limits of the New Nile Agreement." Kameri-Mbote, "Water, Conflict, and Cooperation."

40.   Ozkan, "What Drives Turkey's Involvement in Africa?" 533. Donelli and Levaggi, "Becoming a Global Actor," 93–115.

41.   Ozkan and Akgun, "Turkey's Opening to Africa," 525–546.

42.   Donelli, "The Ankara Consensus," 3.

43.   Ibid.

44.   Korkut and Civelekoglu, "Becoming a Regional Power," 187–203.

45.   Erdogan, "Turkey: Africa's Friend, Compatriot and Partner". https://www.aljazeera.com/indepth/opinion/2016/06/turkey-africa-friend-compatriot-partner-160601070207148.html

46.   See note 42 above.

47.   Korkut and Civelekoglu, "Becoming a Regional Power," 193. Ozkan, "Turkey's Politcial-Economic Engagement with Africa," 217–223.

48.   Ibid.

49.   Antonopoulos et al., "Somalia: Turkey's Pivot to Africa," 9.

50.   Ibid.

51.   See Somaliland Mission to the US press release at: http://unpo.org/article/20682
52.   See *The Economist* article on "Red Sea Scramble" at https://www.economist.com/middle-east-and-africa/2018/07/19/the-uae-is-scrambling-to-control-ports-in-africa
53.   See Kantack, *Critical Threats*, 26 February 2018, article entitled "The New Scramble for Africa" available at https://www.criticalthreats.org/print/ana_5a9462b12fff6
54.   Ibid.
55.   See Global Security.org website on Eritrea military expenditure https://www.globalsecurity.org/military/world/eritrea/budget.htm
56.   For further discussion, see Bruton, *Foreign Affairs*, "Ethiopia and Eritrea Have a Common Enemy" at https://foreignpolicy.com/2018/07/12/ethiopia-and-eritrea-have-a-common-enemy-abiy-ahmed-isaias-afwerki-badme-peace-tplf-eprdf
57.   See a discussion by Olander, Staden and Shinn on the changing landscape of foreign investment in Africa titled "As BRICS Slow Investments in Africa, Turkey Ramps Up" at http://www.chinafile.com/china-africa-project/brics-slow-investments-africa-turkey-ramps
58.   Ibid.
59.   Kaya and Warner, *Turkey and Africa*, 2.
60.   Rudincova, "New Player on the Scene," 204.
61.   Ibid.
62.   See note 51 above.

Bibliography

Aning, Kwesi, and Mustapha Abdallah. "Confronting Hybrid Threats in Africa: Improving Multidimensional Responses." In *The Future of African Peace Operations: From Janjaweed to Boko Haram*, edited by Cedric De Coning, Linnea Gelot and John Karlsrud, 20–37. London: Zed Books, 2016.

Antonopoulos, Paul, Oliver Villar, Drew Cottle, and Aweis Ahmed. "Somalia: Turkey's Pivot to Africa in The Context of Growing Inter-Imperialist Rivalries." *Journal of Comparative Politics* 10, no. 2 (2017): 4–15.

Axworthy, Lloyd. "Human Security and Global Governance: Putting People First." *Global Governance* 7 (2001): 19–23.

Bazilian, Morgan, Holger Rogner, Mark Howells, Sebastian Hermann, Douglas Arent, Dolf Gielen, and Pasquale Steduto. "Considering the Energy, Water and Food Nexus: Towards an Integrated Modelling Approach." *Energy Policy* 39, no. 12 (2011): 7896–7906.

Besada, Hany, Ariane Goetz, and Karolina Werner. "African Solutions for African Problems and Shared R2P." In *Crafting an African Security Architecture: Addressing Regional Peace and Conflict in the 21st Century*, edited by Hany Besada, 1–15. Burlington: Ashgate Publishing Company, 2010.

Bizikova, Livia, Dimple Roy, Darren Swanson, Henry D. Venema, and Matthew McCandless. *The Water-Energy-Food Security Nexus: Towards a Practical Planning and Decision-Support Framework for Landscape Investment and Risk Management*. Winnipeg: International Institute for Sustainable Development, 2013.

Claessens, Stiji, and Lev Ratnovski. *What is Shadow Banking?* Washington D.C: International Monetary Fund, 2014.

Collier, Paul, and Anke Hoeffler. "Greed and Grievance in Civil War." *Oxford Economic Papers* 56, no. 4 (2004): 563–595.

Cook, Jennifer G, and Richard Downie. *Rethinking Engagement in Fragile States*. Washington, D.C.: CSIS Africa Program, 2015.

Donelli, Federico. "The Ankara Consensus: The Significance of Turkey's Engagement in Sub-Saharan Africa." *Global Change, Peace & Security* 30, no. 1 (2018): 57–76. doi:10.1080/14781158.2018.1438384

Donelli, Federico, and Ariel Gonzalez Levaggi. "Becoming Global Actor: The Turkish Agenda for the Global South." *Rising Powers Quarterly* 1, no. 2 (2016): 93–115.

Drime, Scott, and Sithabiso Gandure. "Food Security." In *Region-Building in Southern Africa: Progress, Problems and Prospects*, edited by Chris Saunders, Gwinyayi A. Dzinesa, and Dawn Nagar, 181–197. London: Zed Books, 2012.

Duffield, Mark. "Human Security: Linking Development and Security in an Age of Terror." In *New Interfaces between Security and Development: Changing Concepts and Approaches*, edited by Stephan Klingebiel, 11–38. Bonn: German Development Institute (DIE), 2006.

Duffield, Mark. *Global Governance and the New Wars: The Merging of Development and Security*. London: Zed Books, 2001.

Erdogan, Recep Tayyip. 2016 "Turkey: Africa's Friend, Compatriot and Partner". Op-Ed. *Al-Jazeera, Qatar*. Accessed June 20, 2018. https://www.aljazeera.com/indepth/opinion/2016/06/turkey-africa-friend-compatriot-partner-160601070207148.html

Hentz, J. James. "Introduction: African Security in the Twenty-First Century", in *Routledge Handbook of African Security* edited by James J. Hentz, 3–8. New York: Routledge, 2014.

Jervis, Robert. "Realism in the Study of World Politics." *International Organization* 52, no. 4 (1998): 971–992.

Kabandula, Abigail, and Timothy M. Shaw. "African Multinational Forces in the Twenty First Century: Challenges, Progress and the Future." Paper Presented at Institute for Strategic Research (IRSEM) The Changing Character of Africa's Armed Forces, International Conference Paris, October 5–6, 2016.

Kambere, Geoffrey. "Financing Al Shabaab: The Vital Port of Kismayo." *Combatting Terrorism Exchange (CTX)* 2, no. 3 (2012): 40–48.

Kameri-Mbote, Patricia. "Water, Conflict, and Cooperation: Lessons from the Nile River Basin." January 2007. Accessed January 4, 2016. https://www.wilsoncenter.org/sites/default/files/NavigatingPeaceIssuePKM.pdf.

Karns, Margaret P., and Karen A. Mingst. *International Organizations: The Politics and Processes of Global Governance*. Boulder: Lynne Rienner Publishers, 2010.

Kaya, Karen, and Jason Warner. *Turkey and Africa: A Rising Military Partnership?* Fort Leavenworth: Foreign Military Studies Office, 2013.

Kihato, C. Wanjiku, and Singumbe Muyeba. *The Challenges and Prospects of African Urbanisation: Forging Africa's Economic Growth Through Sustainable Policies*. Cape Town: African Centre for Cities, 2015.

Kimenyi, S. Mwangi, and John M. Mbaku. *Governing the Nile River Basin: The Search for a New Legal Regime*. Washington: Brookings Institution Press, 2015.

Kimenyi, S. Mwangi, and John M. Mbaku. *The Limits of the New Nile Agreement*. Washington D.C: The Brookings Institution, 2015.

Korkut, Umut, and Ilke Civelekoglu. "Becoming a Regional Power while Pursuing Material Gains: The Case of Turkish Interest in Africa." *International Journal* 68, no.1 (Winter 2012–13):187–203.

Masters, Jonathan, and Mohammed A. Sergie. *Al-Shabab*. New York: Council on Foreign Relations, 2015.

McRae, Rob. "Human Security in a Globalized World." In *Human Security and the New Diplomacy: Protecting People, Promoting Peace*, edited by Rob McRae and Don Hubert, 14–27. London: McGill-Queen's University Press, 2001.

Morgenthau, Hans, and Kenneth Thompson. *Politics Among Nations: The Struggle for Power and Peace*. 7th ed. New York: Alfred Kopf, 1985.

Muyeba, Singumbe. *Globalization and Africa in the Twenty-First Century: A Zambian Perspective*. Bloomington: Author House, 2008.

Okoth-Owiro, Arthur. *The Nile Treaty: State Succession and International Treaty Commitments: A Case Study of the Nile Water Treaties*. Nairobi: Konrad Adenauer Foundation, 2004.

Ozkan, Mehmet. "Turkey's Political-Economic Engagement with Africa." In *Emerging Powers in Africa: A New Wave in the Relationship?* Edited by Justin Van der Merwe, Ian Taylor, and Alexandra Arkhangelskaya, 217–23. London: Palgrave Macmillan, 2016.

Ozkan, Mehmet. "What Drives Turkey's Involvement in Africa?" *Review of African Political Economy* 37, no. 126 (2010): 533–540.

Ozkan, Mehmet, and Birol Akgun. "Turkey's Opening to Africa." *The Journal of Modern African Studies* 48, no. 4 (2010): 525–546.

Peoples, Columba, and Nick Vaughan-Williams. *Critical Security Studies: An Introduction*. 2nd ed. London: Routledge, 2015.

Pieterse, Jan Nederveen. "Global Rebalancing: Crisis and the East–South Turn." *Development and Change* 42, no. 1 (2011): 22–48.

Rudincova, Katerina. "New Player on the Scene: Turkish Engagement in Africa." *Bulletin of Geography. Socio-economic Series* 25, no. 25 (2014): 197–213. DOI: http://dx.doi.org/10.2478/bog-2014-0039 .

Schneckener, Ulrich. "Fragile Statehood, Armed Non-State Actors." In *Private Actors and Security Governance*, edited by Alan Bryden and Marina Caparini, 23–40. Geneva: LIT & DCAF, 2006.

SEM. *Letter dated 22 September 2015 from the members of the Monitoring Group on Somalia and Eritrea addressed to the Chair of the Security Council Committee pursuant to resolutions 751(1992) and 1907 (2009) concerning Somalia and Eritrea*. New York: United Nations, 2015.

Sen, K. Amartya. *Development as Freedom*. Oxford: Oxford University Press, 2001.

Stiglitz, E. Joseph. *Making Globalization Work*. New York: W.W. Norton & Company, 2006. 10, ER2, JULY 2017

Stiglitz, E. Joseph, and Mary Kaldor. "Protection from Violence." In *the Quest for Security: Protection without Protectionism and the Challenge of Global Governance*, edited by Joseph E. Stiglitz, and Mary Kaldor, 91–93. New York: Columbia Press, 2013.

United Nations Development Program. *Human Development Report 1994*. New York: Oxford Press, 1994.

Waltz, N. Kenneth. *Theory of International Politics*. First. New York: McGraw-Hill, 1979.

Williams, D. Paul. "Thinking about Security in Africa." *International Affairs* 83, no. 6 (2007): 1021–1038.

Williamson, John. *"Globalization: The Concept, Causes and Consequences. Keynote Address to the Congress of the Sri Lankan Association for the Advancement of Science held in Colombo."* Colombo: Peterson Institute for International Economics, December 15, 1998.

World Economic Forum. *Water Security: The Water-Food-Energy-Climate Nexus*. Washington D.C: Island Press, 2011.

Pragmatic eclecticism, neoclassical realism and post-structuralism: reconsidering the African response to the Libyan crisis of 2011

Linnéa Gelot ⓘ and Martin Welz ⓘ

ABSTRACT

This article analyses the role of the African Union (AU) during the Libyan crisis of 2011. It addresses the question of why the AU has not played a central conflict manager role in that crisis. Inspired by pragmatic eclecticism, we take a theoretical detour to answer this question. Through a neoclassical realist and post-structuralist lens, we provide a novel eclectic reconsideration of the crisis response and we also highlight shared ground between both perspectives. Our theoretical and empirical discussion moves along the categories 'primacy of power', 'discourses' and 'leader images'. We highlight the ability of dominant powers to influence the unfolding of events with material forms of power but also through immaterial ones such as the advancement of a dominant discourse on a cosmopolitan liberal order related to the responsibility-to-protect.

This article analyses the inability of the African Union (AU) to lead on conflict management during the Libyan crisis of 2011 and provides a novel reading of the unfolding events and contradictions that this case resulted in. The question that we explore is, 'Why was the AU unable to advance its mediation plan as part of conflict management in Libya in 2011?' For some, the crisis rendered the notion of 'African solutions to African problems' redundant due to the AU's lack of internal cohesion,[1] while others emphasised the role of outside powers in obstructing the AU's Libya mediation plan.[2] Both views share the understanding that Africa's rise in international conflict management was curbed through the AU's inability to claim the lead mediator role in the Libyan crisis. However, the explanations of ineffective African contributions to international conflict management, which are linked to different theoretical perspectives, have attributed different weight to key factors including material or capacity-based,[3] morality or legitimacy-based[4] and legality-based.[5] As such, a realist reading of the Libyan crisis, which would emphasise material power, appears helpful at first glance to explain the events. At the same time, such a perspective has been critical of the regime-change approach on the grounds that great power national interests were not so crucially at stake as to accept the risks and costs.[6] A realist reading would also fail to fully account for the legitimation strategies of great powers. A post-structuralist reading on the other hand would argue that African positions on Libya reflect the long-standing objections to major powers claiming to act as an international community as they advance their self-serving agendas in Africa.[7] However, such a perspective fails to explain the determining weight of material elements of power. Moving beyond either of these perspectives, we argue that international conflict management in Libya in 2011 can be explained through three moves: a predominance of power justified in the name of a cosmopolitan liberal end, the formation and advancement of a legitimating discourse, and invoking an enemy image of Gaddafi.

With an explorative ambition, we develop an 'eclectic typology'[8] and identify contact zones between post-structuralism and neoclassical realism that helps us to address our empirical goal. Like others before us, notably Sterling-Folker and Shinko's contribution to traverse the realist–post-structuralist divide,[9] we intend to show how insights from these two theoretical perspectives can offer novel perspectives that satisfy both researchers and practitioners in the pursuit of analysing the AU's failure to secure a key mediator role in the response to the Libyan crisis. This is because such joint perspectives are more inclusive – admittedly at the expense of parsimony. We also seek to convey how, despite different epistemological commitments, the premises and findings by both theoretical accounts of a specific case may fruitfully speak to one another. We do not aim to merge or synthesise these traditions and we are mindful of 'the strengths and trade-offs of the approaches' and the 'recognition of the particular intellectual gains generated by these traditions in relation to substantive problems'.[10]

We propose a typology of three contact zones, which we term 'primacy of power', 'discourses' and 'images of leaders', and show how both perspectives provide strong explanations of these features. With our typology we aim to explore how both neoclassical realist and post-structuralist arguments can be used to deconstruct the predominant narrative's advancement of liberal cosmopolitan motivations behind the intervention in Libya, strongly related to the principle of the responsibility-to-protect (R2P). Analytical eclecticism enables us to convey a novel understanding of why the African mediation plan was so unwelcomed and make visible the complexity of the issue, without conforming fully to metatheoretical or methodological tenets characterising individual research traditions.[11] Moreover, we can reveal and connect the wide range of explanatory factors with regard to our case study that operate at various levels of analysis over different time horizons in shaping political outcomes that are of consequence to actors coping with real-world problems.[12] First, we spell out the three contact zones from a theoretical perspective, and then apply our theoretical arguments to the empirics on which our research focus rests, namely the Libyan crisis.

An eclectic typology

Our first category 'primacy of power' is inspired by Sterling-Folker and Shinko, who find common ground between post-structuralism and realism on the premise that political power is rooted in struggle.[13] The second category 'discourses' draws on Der Derian's reminder that post-structuralism is best understood not as a coherent theory but rather as an umbrella term 'for a host of activities like discourse analysis, genealogy, deconstruction and intertextualism'.[14] We explore post-structuralism understood as a critical engagement and see if we can find echoes in a neoclassical realist reading of the same case. The third category 'images of leaders' grew out of our engagement with neoclassical realism and its stance that the domestic sphere matters for international political outcomes. When referring to neoclassical realism, we mean the latest variant within the rich realist tradition as presented by Ripsman, Taliaferro and Lobell because of their inclusion of domestic-level variables in explanations of international politics.[15] We open up this realist variant to an eclectic reading and exploration of contact zones between that perspective and post-structuralism. When referring to post-structuralism we have drawn on the works of Milliken, Foucault, George and Campbell particularly for their analysis of discourses, the role these play for foreign policymaking and their link to post-structuralism's critical task, namely to show 'how the textual and social processes are intrinsically connected to illustrate, in specific contexts, the implications of this connection for the way we think and act in the contemporary world'.[16] In purposefully selecting main theoretical tenets relevant for our eclectic typology, we are mindful that we do not do justice to all theoretical streams within the rich literatures of realism and post-structuralism.

Primacy of power

Realism views international politics 'as a never-ending struggle among states for power and influence in a world of finite resources and uncertainty about each other's intentions and capabilities'.[17] Relative material power is primary in international politics and hence constitutes an independent variable that shapes the foreign policy options of states. Power is understood as inherent in states and primarily expressed in materialist terms, i.e. coercive capabilities, structurally modified by geography and technology.[18]

That said, classical realists Morgenthau and Hobbes, on whom neoclassical realism draws, were deeply interested in varied sources and forms of power and their contextual conditions. Morgenthau argued that power comprised anything that established and maintained domination of man over man, and whereas we tend to think of capability to inflict physical violence first, other more insidious forms of power may well include subtle psychological ties (ideological or cultural control over minds) and may well be seen as variables depending on time and context.[19]

Post-structuralists consider power as pervasive and resulting in disciplinary relations of domination. Instances of power struggles can thus be studied as clashes of perspectives or interpretations of reality that far precede instances of overt or coercive state uses of material power.[20] Power may also be productive and creative of identity and subjects. Drawing on Foucault's governmentality perspective, Abrahamsen advances a conception of power as, 'work[ing] through systems of knowledge and discursive practices to provide the meanings, norms, values and identities that not only constrain actors, but also constitute them. In this sense, human beings, or the subject, are not only power's intended target, but also its effect'.[21]

The Foucauldian conception of power as relational, fluid, networked and non-linear entails staying tuned to the possibilities for resistance to structural domination.[22] Post-structuralists study where and how resources might be found to resist or reconfigure existing physical and ideational structures. A core strength of post-structuralist thought is therefore its ability to reveal and 'denaturalise' power's many usages and to open up space for the marginalised voices and forms of subjugated knowledge.[23]

While realists depart from measurable material power vested in the state, to be wielded by political elites in the name of state survival under conditions of international anarchy, post-structuralists consider power to be relational, residing in multiple locations (material and immaterial). It is reproduced through multiple micro-strategies at the local, domestic and global level. Going back to classical realist roots, we also find a conception of power in immaterial as well as material capabilities. Ideational power, for instance, was not foreign to Carr who studied in-depth what he called 'the power over public opinion'.[24] Sterling-Folker and Shinko have explored these diverging understandings of power as a contact zone between realism and post-structuralism, and they find that, '[i] n both instances, power is seen as a resource that when it is employed is capable of simultaneously maintaining structures and inducing historical change. However, what wields power and why it does so are seen to be different'.[25]

For post-structuralists, power constrains and limits, it produces and creates. Among power's products are discourses, which (re)produce power struggles and act as vehicles for them. Post-structuralists hold that in order to overcome the realist world-view, one has to explore the 'reality of human struggles to make life go on'.[26] Neoclassical realists similarly stress power struggles and their relational character, yet focus on great power/state actors and specific strategically important situations more deserving of explanation than others. Power has effects, to the extent that uses of power involves a minimum of two actors.[27] On the whole, neoclassical realist analyses remain strongly wedded to material power usage both in the international and domestic domains. Capabilities and objects that signal power are used to impose the will or preference of one actor on another. Resistance to such power usage can disrupt the balance of power, prompting the need for more use of power towards balancing purposes.[28]

From this brief discussion, we sum up that for neoclassical realists and post-structuralists alike, power struggles can maintain structures but can also induce historical change. Power takes many forms and has multiple sources (material and non-material) and can work as a capability to produce identities and subjects.

Discourses

Post-structuralism is concerned with how power and discourses are intertwined. The core premise is that while a 'real world' of objects independent of our knowledge exists, it is only through meaning-making that these objects become real or knowable to us human beings.[29] Post-structuralists study the interconnections between material and immaterial factors, since discourse 'is not equivalent to "ideas"; discourse incorporates material as well as ideational factors'.[30] What this means for post-structuralism and how it might be done is explored for example in its engagement with the new materialism debate.[31] Discourses, as argued by Milliken, are most often studied as textual and social 'structures' of signification;[32] 'processes' productive of subjects and objects (make intelligible some ways of being in and acting towards the world, define subjects authorised to speak, define knowledgeable practices); or 'sites' revealing the play of practice or the production of common sense (implementing practices, ways of legitimating these, political consequences and the efforts to fix social structures of meaning despite them being inherently dynamic or unstable). The potential for power through discourses is that a certain common sense is endorsed, while other ways of portraying or perceiving reality become seen as meaningless, impracticable and inadequate or otherwise disqualified. Discourses, therefore, act to enable, exclude, differentiate, structure, label and make hierarchies/relations among identities, practices and objects.[33]

These powerful effects lead post-structuralists to study the creation of hegemonic discourses, and to analyse their structuring of meaning as connected to legitimating and implementing practices. Since discourses require active (re)production, the efforts made to (de)stabilise them makes up an important research focus.[34]

Neoclassical realists would agree that relative material power is reflected in and partly wielded by the different discourses about the same event promoted by differently positioned world leaders, considering their assumption that morality and ethics are the products of power.[35] Powerful leaders/states define what actions are morally and ethically appropriate, and powerful political rhetoric will then delimit and structure the feasible foreign policy options of the weaker states. In this way, rhetoric embodies potential action. What powerful actors consider morally and ethically appropriate will shape expectations around and inform state action, and constitute what might be termed a 'strategic frame'. Powerful structures of social meaning suppress opposing political choices. This suggests that neoclassical realism and post-structuralism share an engagement with the power effects of knowledge production and the relationship between knowledge and action.

Neoclassical realism analyses the connections between foreign policy and domestic politics through a set of variables.[36] In other words, the domestic sphere matters since action on the world political stage is supported or hampered by domestic factors. Public opinion, herein broadly referring to positions citizens take on specific policies, has a stronger legitimacy effect on foreign policy in democratic states than in authoritarian states. Yet at the same time one must not forget that authoritarian leaders often need to 'omnibalance', i.e. fight threats from within the state and external ones. Hence, such leaders face severe limits to their foreign policy action.[37] With its assumptions about state level variables, neoclassical realism provides the analytical tools to study how the foreign policy executive engages in constant efforts to fix strategic frames or social structures of meaning directed at domestic constituencies as well as the international peer community.

Images of leaders

Lastly, we explore the commitment inherent in post-structuralism and neoclassical realism to what we understand as an 'ethnography' of foreign policy behaviour. Both perspectives aim to ground contextually all accounts of state power yet they admit (to varying degrees) the formidable constraints on change and transformative politics.[38] They part views over how a more nuanced reading of sovereignty helps to analyze actual state practice.

Neoclassical realism points to 'leader images' as a key variable at the state level. Individuals have core beliefs, images and values that together form cognitive filters, which frame how they perceive information and how they respond to stimuli. Cognitive filters in turn underpin a set of ideas which guide foreign policymaking: scientific ideas which 'tell us about how the world works [… and] establish the boundaries of possibility for state strategies by describing and interpreting the relations of empirical realities in the international system'; intentional ideas which 'are normative suggestions that seek to establish goals for foreign policy'; and lastly operational ideas, referring to 'scientific or normative statements that recommend the means by which a certain end should be pursued'.[39]

In contrast to neoclassical realists, whose ontological assumption is that an objective reality is processed by leaders through their cognitive filters and responded to *ipso facto*, post-structuralists assume that any representation of reality is necessarily an interpretation of that reality. In other words, there is no 'objective truth' but only different accounts of truth articulated through different discourses and believed by different people. Different interpretations of events not only contribute to our understanding of the event, or shape the response, but also constitute them. Narratives transport and shape knowledge, whose production is therefore not only a cognitive matter, but also has normative and political effects.[40]

Post-structuralism divulges the play of power within the macro-(to micro-)practices inside state structures. Among several alternative readings of foreign policy studies, Campbell's notion of 'narrativised reality' helps to show that all foreign policy actors (and analysts) are ethically implicated in state policy-making and implementation.[41] In this work, the objective vantage point from which to judge decisions as right or wrong is unsettled, as is the vantage point from where to judge the intentions of world leaders (in order to better predict their likely foreign policy actions). When privileged narratives and perceptions emerge regarding the intentions of others in the international climate, and as friends/foes dichotomies emerge, that it is on the basis of these social constructions that decision-makers justify policy prescriptions and solutions.

Neoclassical realists share grounds with post-structuralists that ideas and images can be subject to change over time. One major difference is that the historical process of discursive formation is not studied by neoclassical realists and overall they play up the restrictive conditions barring against historical change.[42] When world leaders and foreign policy executives develop images of their counterparts, among other factors based on their cognitive filters, these images structure how leaders perceive information including the distribution of power and how they respond to external stimuli.[43] Neoclassical realism would argue that the images and filters underpinning the reception, (non-) acceptance and sampling are tied to scientific, intentional and operational ideas.[44] This means that state policies are entrenched in actions deemed morally and ethically appropriate as well as considered to be the best response to a systemic stimulus which at the same time elicits support of the domestic audience. Neoclassical realists pay little attention to the roots of these ideas and images.[45] In contrast, post-structuralism has been devoted to uncovering such origins, their reconfiguration/reconstruction, their potential attainment of discursive dominance, as well as the forms of resistance they engender.

In our view, post-structuralism and neoclassical realism are both well suited for close-knit and contextual readings of foreign policy behaviour. Neoclassical realists concede that foreign policymakers can never fully overcome some level of doubt of ambiguity in decision-making processes (complex political and material processes at domestic, state as well as international levels constrain and in part also shape state preferences and manoeuvring space) and that there is always uncertainty about the actions of other states in the international system. Such beliefs can change, but rarely do: '[l]eaders hold to these master beliefs rather tenaciously and are very reluctant to change them'.[46] Post-structuralism explores the emergence and (re)reshaping of these ideas and images. Nonetheless, both perspectives share grounds in the acceptance that historicity and positionality of actors matter. They both reject the proposition of objective parameters to judge good from bad foreign policy. Thus, both traditions consider the importance of the role of psychology, language and rhetoric in social construction of (contingent) images, for instance, of good and bad leaders, policies, or interventions.[47] Neoclassical realists include psychological factors into their analysis[48] and post-structuralism can be said to take an interest in this development as the 'homo abscanditus', the view that the human being has been bizarrely obscure in IR theory,[49] moves closer to the centre of gravity.[50]

Our typology is not intended to conceal or minimise differences in epistemological or ontological commitments. Nor do we develop a conclusive list of factors that can potentially explain our case. Rather, inspired by analytical eclecticism, we negotiate between IR theories[51] to explain which crucial factors mattered most in a specific context.[52]

The Libyan crisis: AU and African conflict management

In the preceding theoretical discussion, we have limited ourselves to three contact zones – primacy of power, discourses and leader images – and identified shared elements as well as aspects of these theories which fruitfully speak to one another. In this section, we state that a complementary reading of our empirical case from a neoclassical realist and post-structuralist perspective sheds light on more facets of the Libyan crisis than a single perspective does on its own. This allows us to more fully engage with our core empirical research question of why the AU was unable to advance its mediation plan despite its attempts to play a central role.

Primacy of power

On the night of 17 March 2011, amidst an ongoing civil war in Libya, Gaddafi threatened residents of Benghazi, Libya's second city, and said he would finish the battle by that same night. Reminiscent of the rhetoric during the Rwandan genocide, Gaddafi dismissed the rebels and protestors as 'rats' and 'cockroaches'. Several world leaders, most prominently Barack Obama, Nicolas Sarkozy and David Cameron, characterised the Benghazi situation as a looming genocide.[53] The UN Security Council passed Resolution 1973 on the same day. That resolution allowed taking 'all necessary measures [...] to protect civilians and civilian populated areas under threat of attack in [Libya]'[54] and imposed a no-fly zone over Libya. This resolution was not only approved by Britain, France and the US, while China and Russia abstained, but also by the three African countries (Gabon, Nigeria and South Africa – hereafter 'A3') serving as non-permanent members of the UN Security Council at that time.[55]

Representing the great powers in the intervening coalition of states, Obama, Sarkozy and Cameron proffered a liberal cosmopolitan case for the coercive military operation in Libya.[56] 'Unity' among the major powers, and backed by a broad coalition of countries including the Arab world, underpinned a so-called humanitarian action that would endure until Gaddafi had been removed from power. The League of Arab States helped the intervening coalition's course symbolically from within the region when it requested the UN Security Council to authorise a no-fly zone.[57] Like the intervening states, the United Nations Security Council as a whole relied on the League of Arab States to build the case of unity behind Resolution 1973.[58] This action was framed as a necessary step in Libya's pathway to peace. The message was that global moral forces had to stand united against evil. Additionally, that decisive decision-making in the UN Security Council had heeded calls for protection by thousands of Libyan civilians. Gaddafi was depicted as an intolerable obstacle in Libya's development and his removal therefore justifiable within a liberal cosmopolitan political framework.[59]

Following the adoption of Resolution 1973, France brought together a coalition of the willing in Paris on 19 March 2011, to decide upon military strikes and to establish a no-fly zone over Libya as requested by the UN Security Council. The NATO-led military operation started shortly thereafter. For some, Gaddafi's 'armed forces were no match for superior NATO air power and rebel forces on the ground, which were assisted by elements of coalition special forces',[60] thus bluntly highlighting the material dimension of power as highlighted in neoclassical realist theory. The intervening coalition and the rebels moved ahead until the rebels, gathered under the umbrella called National Transitional Council (NTC), seized the Libyan capital, took control over Libyan politics and were recognised by several states as the sole legitimate representative of Libya. NATO's intervention was authorised by reference to liberal cosmopolitan arguments to 'promote' and help fast-track liberal democratic development in a fragile state. In effect, when the great powers declared the NTC as the legitimate representative of Libya they 'performed' a discursive regime change before it had occurred on the ground. Few were publicly debating the history of relations between the NTC and the interveners prior to the intervention.[61]

The decision to intervene (and recognise the NTC) rested on the urgency to remove Gaddafi, not on the basis of longer-term strategic planning among the interveners for the political future of Libya led by the NTC.[62] Even though Gaddafi had abandoned his plan to acquire nuclear weapons and cooperated with the West in its counter-terrorism activities, he was through the neoclassical realist lens perceived to be a factor of insecurity (see below). The civil war in Libya opened a window of opportunity to eliminate a risk factor. In the neoclassical realism logic this meant that the state of preparation to balance his (potential) global/regional ambitions would be over. Against this background, the intervening coalition at no point perceived the AU to be a competent mediator in the crisis. A French EU official argued that the AU comprises the old and far from democratic elites and that there has to be a new generation of African leaders before one could trust the AU in such a role.[63] In Western capitals a strong image was that African leaders were guided in their position vis-à-vis Gaddafi by his historical anti-imperialist and financial benefactor role, some among them had dubiously acceded power and hence could not openly speak out against him at the AU level.[64] Holding on to such an image, interveners were able to overlook that the A3 in effect took a critical stance towards Gaddafi. This therefore closed down the opportunity to find shared diplomatic ground with the A3 and deal with the AU akin to a strategic partnership. However, agreement on a principled position was linked in the dominant narrative to also signify unity on the strategy going forward. Yet, once the initial unity to rebuke Gaddafi crumbled, those questioning the necessity of regime change were derided by the coalition partners. From this perspective, the more immanent a threat or an opportunity, the more restrictive a state's strategic environment becomes, effectively delimiting policy choices.[65]

Post-structuralism's treatment of power helps to appraise and deconstruct the strategies used by the interveners to justify their use of material power. The post-structuralist perspective brings out that the AU and its members were not only constrained by the discursive strategies used by major powers. They were also, through the A3 that backed the Security Council's adoption of forcible measures, initially persuaded by the appeal to cosmopolitan norms. Geopolitics, clothed this way, was a play of power where African actors had a place as coalition partners as long as the hegemonic vision of what was to be done prevailed. Among power's effects, in this case, was a depiction of the AU as uncooperative and a non-credible conflict manager in Libya.[66] In this analysis, power works to create identities and new disciplinary relations of domination. AU officials accused non-African states of obstructing the implementation of the AU mediation plan and their chances of getting concessions from Gaddafi.[67] Pushing back at major powers for their neglect of African perspectives, they resisted the formation of a dominant narrative and attempted to carve out some influence for the organisation, in an illustration of how both the powerful and less powerful are the subjects of power.

The African high-level mediation panel on Libya set up by the AU prior to the intervention argued that mediation, alongside multilateral intervention, was preferable since the Arab Spring would likely lead to destructive regional instability.[68] Apart from Benghazi's residents, they also emphasised the protection of those African migrants defected from Gaddafi's security forces and now tortured or executed by Western-backed militias. This was not solely a regime survival argument. Notably, post-1995 Gaddafi had become less of a source of instability than he had previously been, putting into question the interveners' risk analysis as a persuasive motive for the war to unseat him.[69]

The A3 did not back the view that Gaddafi must be forcibly overthrown, despite their approval of Resolution 1973. South Africa, for instance, subscribed to the urgent need to protect civilians, but rejected the validity of a forceful regime change.[70] In trying to find an effective, yet sustainable, solution to the crisis, and following the mantra 'African solutions to African problems', South Africa faced a dilemma. From their perspective, the AU lacked a united African position towards Gaddafi,[71] which later on spurred a contentious discussion about the credibility of African unity.[72] Hence, South Africa unilaterally negotiated for pro-hibition of boots on the ground (in order to lessen fears of the resented type of foreign interference on the continent) and for implementing the AU roadmap as basis for a political solution. By the time the no-fly zone proposal was on the table, and discussed at AU heads of state level on 10 March, other options became harder to raise and to discuss. It was already anticipated that the Resolution 1973 would pass and the remaining manoeuvring space was to amend and introduce caveats, but not throwing it out.[73] Raising the need for high-level mediation and implementation of the AU roadmap was met with disbelief – the idea seemed out of sync with the needs and the urgency – now that the no-fly zone was a concrete pro-posal. South Africa's negotiators were talking to BRICS members as well as the non-aligned movement, discussing the risk of abuse on the one hand;[74] but clearly, Gaddafi had gone too far on the other. South Africa, along with China and Russia, only after the fact lamented the abuse of the resolution's reference to 'all necessary measures' (such as instances of NATO attacks on disputable targets) and were derided internationally for having 'shifted sides'.

The analysis of the power politics involved in the initial crisis response reveals a multitude of sources of power, including material aspects but also regionally provided legitimacy and the dominance of a discourse of rightful action which we focus on in the following section. The changing environment not only limited the foreign policy options of the interveners but in turn also those of other states. African states opposing the intervention were discred-ited and their options limited.

Discourses

The dominant narrative that took shape on the international intervention in Libya in 2011 emphasises that R2P had at last been activated and implemented by the UN Security Council. R2P symbolises a liberal belief in progress, the capacity of individuals to learn lessons and design and reform institutions to enable individual freedom and reduce risk of violence, for instance to end genocides. After Resolution 1973 was adopted, the case was being made that the R2P principle was universal, and the tone was triumphant.[75] Much scholarly debate has helped reinforce the discourse about liberal cosmopolitan norms justifying military action by major powers, in this case aiming to support progressive liberal democratic change in the North African region.[76] When scholars contentedly observe that Libyans had 'taken their fate into their own hands'[77] to topple Gaddafi during the 2011 crisis, this acts to embed Libya's history writing within a liberal cosmopolitan linear discourse whereby change is driven first and foremost by liberal Libyan subjects demanding modernity, democratic rights and freedoms.

Cameron, Obama and Sarkozy argued that 'it is impossible to imagine a future for Libya with Qaddafi in power'.[78] They began to advance a discourse whereby air strikes were necessary on humanitarian grounds, thus legitimating exceptional combat measures. Among the effects of this discourse was that Libya's sovereign equality could be 'suspended'. However, such a liberal-infused discourse contains an inconsistency. When values of democratisation and sovereign equality seem to stand in opposition, liberal prescriptions tend to reinforce the former at the expense of the latter. Despite an 'equalitarian regime'[79] internationally, a global hierarchy allows for liberal regimes to legitimate illiberal practices when facing exceptionalism (tyranny, terrorism, supreme threats).[80]

Neoclassical realism would stress that the powerful states and their leaders define which actions are morally and ethically appropriate based on the assumption that morality and ethics are the products of power. From the interveners' perspective, the morally and ethically appropriate position was linked to the R2P principle at the expense of regime change. Effectively, from a neoclassical realist perspective, opposing or critical voices to the morally and ethically appropriate stance stood no chance of being heard, giving the interveners' capabilities.

Several AU member states voiced objections both to Gaddafi's crackdown on opposition and to the link constructed in the dominant narrative between an R2P approach and regime change. From the post-structuralist perspective, African actors were attempting to destabilise the discourse by the coalition partners in the process. Reactions to counter-discourses in turn indicate active efforts to reproduce the discourse, and once the military intervention had begun, political alternatives in opposition of regime change were treated as suspect and dangerously naïve. Grovogui argues that the AU roadmap 'in favor for peaceful resolution so infuriated Western powers that they excluded it altogether from the subsequent processes of the resolution of the conflict'.[81] This illustrates that discourses have other powerful effects, and the discourse on the Libya crisis defined subjects authorised to speak (coalition partners), established actionable knowledge on the crisis management effort, and acted to exclude and make hierarchies/relations among the willing conflict management governors.

Neoclassical realism and post-structuralism both find that powerful states can advance and work to maintain discourses that determine what is morally and ethically appropriate. Post-structuralism links power and discourses, while neoclassical realism argues that morality and ethics are products of power, which has material and non-material foundations. In exercising state power, foreign policy executives utilise their power resources but must also exclude diverging voices lest these unhinge, destabilise, the hegemonic discourse. For Britain, France and the US, marginalisation of the AU was necessary since its position challenged the prevailing interpretations of humanitarianism and necessity.[82] With the exception of Morocco, the only African state that was not part of the AU at that time, there was no African diplomatic presence at the Paris summit, during which the gathered leaders agreed to intervene in Libya.[83] The AU's attempts to broker a deal with Gaddafi and the NTC were effectively thwarted by the UN and other players in the Libyan crisis, notably France, Britain, the US and the League of Arab States. The interveners' use of material power continued and they refused to stop their airstrikes and thus blocked the way for an *ad hoc* committee of African Heads of State and Government, mandated by the AU, to travel to Libya to discuss their roadmap with Gaddafi and the NTC.

A discourse about the need for a humanitarian military intervention to protect Libyan civilians initially gained regional legitimacy from the League of Arab States and the three African states on the UN Security Council. Unity, however, crumbled as soon as forcible regime change appeared as the 'illiberal twin' of that discourse.[84]

Leader images

The images of Gaddafi projected by the foreign policy executives of the great powers have in part been informed by their predecessors' memories and experiences, and by the institutional cultures in which they work. The importance given to leader images by neoclassical realism and the commitment to historicising dominant representations in post-structuralism leads us to interrogate the images of Gaddafi in world politics. This is important since the mobilising strength of the dominant narrative in the context of the 2011 intervention in Libya depended on an image of Gaddafi as incorrigible tyrant.

Gaddafi's revolutionary politics of the 1970s were considered insignificant or non-threatening in Western capitals, due to both ex-colonial historical linkages and commercial advantage.[85] His revolutionary ideology, Arab nationalism, and his adventurist anti-imperialist foreign policy by the late 1970s, however, became infamous in London, Paris, Washington and elsewhere for its backing of 'radical' national liberation movements and terrorist groups near and far.[86] Since Libya's independence, the core forces of its foreign policy have been perceived to be international confrontation and 'strategic' anti-imperialism. Gaddafi's claim to power and basis for some level of domestic legitimacy was his ability to portray himself as a defender of the weak. Hence, his political survival depended on inventive power strategies to ensure a certain level of economic well-being for Libyans and to delegitimate decision-makers in the West.[87]

By the late 1970s, Gaddafi was widely perceived as a 'deviant dictator'. In 1979, the US administration put Libya on their list of terrorist sponsors. By the mid-1980s, US President Ronald Reagan militarily confronted Libya by bombing Gaddafi's home in 1986 in revenge for Libyan involvement in the bombing of La Belle nightclub in West Berlin. Washington argued that a rogue state had to be contained and isolated, including with the use of punitive measures such as economic embargo, covert action and military force.[88] After the Lockerbie affair in 1988 and the bombing of a French airplane over Niger in 1989, Washington and London took the steps that resulted in the UN Security Council's multilateral sanctions regime on Libya. In other European capitals, however, commercial linkages mitigated against a deepening of the sanctions regime.[89]

The change in image does not belie that external powers' relations with Gaddafi prioritised commercial (oil) interests and geostrategic interests, down-playing or neglecting issues such as the Libyan regime's democratic credentials or the freedoms and basic human rights of its citizens. As Zoubir argues, Gaddafi was labelled 'rogue' in an act of provocation more so than as an established fact within western foreign and defence ministries. This rogue image was necessary to support a valid justification domestically (as well as internationally) for

Washington's containment of Gaddafi.[90] He shows how the US incrementally accepted a policy of rapprochement because a reintegration process was already underway between Libya and much of the rest of the international community. This reflects the power strategies at play in constructing dominant narratives, a key focus of post-structuralism.

By the mid-1990s Gaddafi gradually became portrayed as a 'rehabilitated rogue'.[91] Tripoli adjusted its foreign policy and decided to support the western intervention to reverse Iraqi occupation of Kuwait. The Organization of African Unity (OAU), the AU's predecessor, and the League of Arab States offered Libya some international legitimacy by questioning the legality of the sanctions regime, and supporting Libya's plea to have the two Libyan suspects of the Lockerbie bombing tried in a neutral country. In January 1999, Nelson Mandela visited Gaddafi to persuade him to negotiate with the UK and the US over the Lockerbie affair. A diplomatic track towards normalisation of relations was attempted, and secret dialogues with Gaddafi's regime were intensified. Washington and London negotiated two primary aims: Libya's compliance over the Lockerbie affair and its abandonment of its weapons of mass destruction programme.

After 9/11, the Bush administration's talks with Libya deepened, since the US needed all the 'Arab allies' it could get to extract terrorism intelligence. Gaddafi, eager to gain international recognition, supported the US invasion in Afghanistan.[92] In December 2003, Gaddafi announced his government's intention to abandon its weapon of mass destruction programmes. Now international reformist statesman, Gaddafi welcomed Blair on an official visit in Tripoli in March 2004 and by June 2004 normalised relations with the US were established.

Notwithstanding this rapprochement, the old image of Gaddafi remains in the shadows of Western decision makers. Such images very rarely change as neoclassical realism and political psychology inform us,[93] and Gaddafi's international appearances (he, for instance, tore a copy of the UN Charter while speaking at the General Assembly and he called himself 'king of kings' at a meeting of the Arab League) does not easily adjust them. Commercial realities (oil, economic reforms) and geopolitical interests (migration across the Mediterranean, counter-terrorism, knowledge exchange about nuclear capability) now dominated the agenda in Western capitals. Leaders adopted a novel language and policy towards Gaddafi despite their deep seated suspicions towards him. As Gaddafi's positions and politics did not harm Western priorities at that point in time, the major powers could risk that gap and allow a different narrative on Gaddafi, that of rehabilitated rogue, to emerge and settle. This image even provided an immaterial type of power capability, but was recalibrated once the Libyan crisis unfolded.

Both neoclassical realists and post-structuralists counter the linear liberal view on history and stress the enduring and pervasive material and immaterial power struggles, which enable the strong and powerful to coerce/discipline others. Their explanations centre on geostrategic motives and commercial interests – economic realism – as opposed to arguments that delegitimate Gaddafi's aberrant 'governance reforms' or his regime's misfit in regard to the (liberal expectation of) growth of international social norms. Neoclassical realism reveals how Western business actors and domestic institutions weigh in on foreign policymaking, also at those most 'anarchical' diplomatic low-points in Libya–Western relations. Post-structuralism considers the politics of roguing/deroguing to be part of great powers mobilising support internationally, also for policies with illiberal consequences.[94]

Benefits of eclecticism: a pragmatic conclusion

We consider the AU's unsuccessful bid to lead on Libyan crisis response in 2011 as both the peak and the nadir in the recent history of African international management efforts. Several African states were affronted by the way the interveners, supported by Arab states, dealt with the crisis, and the crisis presented the AU–UN–EU tripartite partnership on peace and security with a serious credibility challenge.[95] The struggle to voice a collective African position contributed to the AU's shrinking ability to be at the helm of Libyan crisis management. The notion of African solutions to African problems came under attack also from within Africa and pushed the AU into a process of self-interrogation and reform initiatives.[96] Yet, our reading stresses various forms of power resting with the interveners and expressed in material terms, as well as in discourses, as the key explanation. Our findings point in the direction that history can repeat itself and further constrain the AU's efforts in cases where strong interests or values of major powers are at stake. This has clear repercussions on Africa's rise in political terms.

Our eclectic neoclassical realist and post-structuralist approach of the case allowed seeing the power and identity struggles that are transported by the hegemonic narrative. It calls forth a critical reflection on the scholarly debates regarding the putative triumph of the R2P in Libya and the proclaimed necessity to remove Gaddafi forcibly to ensure freedom and protection to the Libyan people. Our analysis suggests that geopolitical interests were the drivers behind the intervention and that the strategic considerations during the coalition's imposition of the no-fly zone were decisive in hardening the narrative's emphasis on necessity (to remove Gaddafi). An enduring strategic interest has been to secure continued access to Libya's oil and cooperation over 'irregular' migration.[97] The cosmopolitan liberal framework served as a productive vehicle for the argument that democratisation and economic liberalisation in Libya could be fast-tracked by the great power intervention, and that the NTC was the safest bet towards a stable trade partner and a gradually more transparent and democratic government.[98] Our analysis further interconnects the historical questions that manifested in the interveners' approaches to Libya, with the intense power strategies needed to sustain the privileged narrative regarding the intervention, such as deriding the AU,[99] on other occasions the West's 'African partner' whose peace and security institutions great powers have funded and legitimated.

We find the eclectic approach particularly valuable with regard to our analysis of the dominant discourse that defined what actions were considered morally and ethically appropriate. The ethical components of the predominant narrative are crucial enablers of power according to both perspectives. Neoclassical realists would argue that policy must be justified on the basis that legitimacy had been secured from both domestic constituencies and in line with systemic/rule-driven global governance. Post-structuralists would argue that the narrative on humanitarian military intervention for Libya is situated within a specific global order context, and reflects the geopolitical realities and power hierarchies of the time. The distinction between rightful action and irresponsible action offered a way to clothe a decision in legitimacy. Together post-structuralism and neoclassical realism emphasise how the great powers were able to use their material power (especially military capabilities) as well as ideational power to discredit divergent voices and discourses, such as the argument by the AU that diplomacy and regional involvement in the mediation process was crucial for regional stability.

With regard to leader images, we have illustrated how for neoclassical realists leaders base foreign actions around their images. Post-structuralism takes this further by showing how such images are always in construction and contextual, and how the power strategies to fix images are incessant and incomplete. Our analysis demonstrates that neoclassical realists and post-structuralists share a commitment to historicising and interrogating the image of Gaddafi as incorrigible tyrant. Neoclassical realism explains that global power politics always entail major players more successfully using material and ideational resources to determine what is morally and ethically appropriate. Post-structuralism locates and denaturalises the multi-scalar processes through which such social constructions occur. Both lend support to the finding that the image of tyrannical Gaddafi helped shape a distinction between interveners' rightful humanitarian military response and the inadequacy of the AU mediation plan.

Neoclassical realism and post-structuralism share an engagement with historical constructions of particular political orders, and with exploring the foundation of order and political authority under the conditions of limitations on human knowledge, human reason and human nature. Their shared understanding of power as rooted in struggle reflects their commitment to a concept of the political, which stresses the conflictual, acutely aware of human communities' destructive as well as productive potential. Neoclassical realism lucidly lays bare the enduring forces of world politics, both ideational and material, and stays true to an explanatory purpose. It cogently factors in the primacy of power politics, and the determining weight of material constraints on global-level transformation. Post-structuralism more evocatively lingers in the fragility and uncertainty of orders-in-creation, to show how embattled social meanings produce power effects.

In sum, the empirical question of the AU's inability to advance its mediation plan in Libya benefits from analytical eclecticism that draws on contact zones between neoclassical realism and post-structuralism. Using such an approach helps us to bring forth a theoretically backed empirical argument that contributes to debates on Africa's rise through highlighting the deep-seated immaterial and material constraints facing African institutions when being involved in international conflict management.

Disclosure statement

No potential conflict of interest was reported by the authors.

Acknowledgements

We wish to thank the anonymous reviewers for their constructive engagement with draft versions of this article. We also thank Adrian Hyde-Price, Emel Parlar Dar, Jan Aart Scholte, Maria Stern, Nora Stappert and Johan Karlsson Schaffer for their feedback and helpful suggestions on working drafts and presentations based on this research. Thank you also to Chiara de Franco and all participants at the workshop of the Nordic Political Science Association (NOPSA) meeting in Odense 2017 for very valuable feedback. All remaining errors are ours. Many thanks to Nikole Erickson for proofreading. Linnéa Gelot gratefully acknowledges funding from Swedish Research Council project reference 2015-03476 and Martin Welz from the Center of Excellence 'Cultural Foundations of Integration' at the University of Konstanz.

ORCID

Linnéa Gelot ⓘ http://orcid.org/0000-0001-7634-8394
Martin Welz ⓘ http://orcid.org/0000-0002-4349-5133

Notes

1. Kasaija, "The African Union"; Sithole, "The African Union Peace and Security."
2. Grovogui, "Looking Beyond Spring"; Ping, "The African Union Role."
3. Kasaija, "The African Union."
4. Omorogbe, "The African Union"; Nnaeme and Asuelime, "The African Union's Questionable Legitimacy"; Grovogui, "Looking Beyond Spring."
5. Abass, "The African Union's Response."
6. Walt, "Learning the Right Lessons"; Luttwak, "Libya"; Kasaija, "The African Union", explains the inability of African states to pursue collective positions as a reflection of capacity shortages and lack of political will.
7. Grovogui, "Looking Beyond Spring."
8. Sil and Katzenstein, "Analytic Eclecticism."
9. Sterling-Folker and Shinko, "Discourses of Power."
10. Sil and Katzenstein, "Analytic Eclecticism," 414.
11. Ibid.
12. Ibid., 417.
13. Sterling-Folker and Shinko, "Discourses of Power."
14. Der Derian, "Philosophical Traditions," 192.
15. Ripsman et al., *Neoclassical Realist Theory.*
16. George, "Of Incarnation and Closure," 221.
17. Ripsman et al., *Neoclassical Realist Theory,* 31–57.
18. Schweller, "Deadly Imbalances," 17–18.
19. Morgenthau, *Politics among Nations,* 9.
20. Abrahamsen, "The Power of Partnerships."
21. Ibid., 1459.
22. Foucault, "Omnes et Singulatim"; Foucault, "What is Critique."
23. Sterling-Folker and Shinko, "Discourses of Power," 638.
24. Carr, *The Twenty Years' Crisis,* 120–30.
25. Sterling-Folker and Shinko, "Discourses of Power," 641–2. For the post-structuralist the productive possibility inherent in power use, such as resistance, can serve as a 'resource' to overcome or reconfigure structural constraints. We thank an anonymous reviewer for emphasising this point.

26. Ashley, "The Achievements of Post-structuralism," 244.
27. Sterling-Folker and Shinko, "Discourses of Power," 640; Kitchen, "Systemic Pressures."
28. Schweller, "Deadly Imbalances."
29. Laclau and Mouffe, *Hegemony and Socialist Strategy,* 108; Nabers, *A Poststructuralist Discourse Theory.*
30. Hansen, *Security as Practice,* 17.
31. Lundborg and Vaughan-Williams, "New Materialisms."
32. Milliken, "The Study of Discourse."
33. Milliken, "The Study of Discourse," 229; Ashley, "The Geopolitics," 410.
34. Milliken, "The Study of Discourse," 230.
35. Taliaferro et al., "Neoclassical Realism."
36. Ibid., 58–79.
37. David, "Explaining Third World Alignment."
38. Sterling-Folker and Shinko, "Discourses of Power," 639.
39. Kitchen, "Systemic Pressures," 129.
40. Goetze, "Bringing Claude-Lévi Strauss"; Devetak, "Post-Structuralism."
41. Milliken, "The Study of Discourse," 236; Campbell, *National Deconstruction,* 34.
42. Of course, the ontological assumptions differ starkly, not least on the existence of objective reality and the possibility of truth claims.
43. Zaller, *The Nature and Origins of Mass Opinion.*
44. Kitchen, "Systemic Pressures."
45. Ibid.
46. Ripsman et al., *Neoclassical Realist Theory,* 64.
47. Williams, *The Realist Tradition,* 32.
48. Ripsman et al., *Neoclassical Realist Theory,* 64.
49. Jacobi and Freyberg-Inan, *Critical Investigations,* 7.
50. Jacobi and Freyberg-Inan, "The Forum."
51. Behr and Williams, "Interlocuting Classical Realism and Critical Theory."
52. Sil and Katzenstein, "Analytic Eclecticism," 414.
53. Obama et al., "Libya's Pathway to Peace."
54. UN Security Council, *Resolution 1973.*
55. AU PSC Communiqué of the 261st Meeting had strongly condemned regime crackdown on protesters.AU Press Statement PSC/PR/BR.1(CCLXVIII), 23 March 2011 acknowledges the adoption of Resolution 1973.
56. Obama et al., "Libya's Pathway to Peace."
57. Ban Ki-Moon, "Address."
58. Deputy Ambassador of Libya Ibrahim Dabbashi had defected when he requested an emergency meeting of the UNSC, see UN doc S/2011/102. On the importance of defections from the Gaddafi regime, see Kasaija, "The African Union," 119.
59. Obama et al., "Libya's Pathway to Peace."
60. Hallams and Schreer, "Towards a 'Post-American' Alliance?" 323.
61. Breeden, "Nicolas Sarkozy."
62. Malloy and Treyz, "Obama Admits Worst Mistake."
63. Confidential interview by Martin Welz, senior official of the EEAS, Brussels, November 2013.
64. Kasaija, "The African Union," 123–4; McKaiser, "Annual Ruth First Memorial Lecture," 151.
65. Ripsman et al., *Neoclassical Realist Theory,* 52.
66. Maasho, "AU Says Non-Africans."
67. Ping, "African Union Peace and Security Council, "Statement""; Lamamra, 275th AU Peace and Security Council Ministerial Meeting.
68. de Waal, "African Roles."
69. Bøås and Utas, "Introduction."
70. Rossouw, "SA's 'No-Fly' Vote."
71. Confidential interview by Linnéa Gelot, senior AU official, Addis Ababa, April 2012.
72. AU, "Communiqué 595th Meeting."
73. Confidential interview by Linnéa Gelot, South African diplomat, Addis Ababa, April 2012.

74.   Adebajo, "The Revolt against the West," 1197.
75.   Evans, "Interview."
76.   Bellamy, "Libya and the Responsibility to Protect"; for a critical position, see Hehir, "The Responsibility to Protect," 39.
77.   Pargeter, *Libya*, 1.
78.   Obama et al., "Libya's Pathway to Peace."
79.   Reus-Smit, "Liberal Hierarchy," 72.
80.   Bigo and Tsoukala, *Terror, Insecurity and Liberty*, 2.
81.   Grovogui, "Looking Beyond Spring," 569; AU, *Communique of the 265th meeting*, para. 5.
82.   Mbeki, "Union Africaine."
83.   de Waal, "African Roles," 371.
84.   Policymakers, academics, the media, etc. have played a role in fixing the discourse by reinforcing the representation of the intervention as necessary to 'liberate' a nation, and as a 'universal' success, see the description in Engelbrekt, "Why Libya?"
85.   Joffé, "Libya and Europe," 85.
86.   Ogunbadejo, "Qaddafi's North African Design."
87.   Vandewalle, *A History of Modern Libya*, 170.
88.   Zoubir, "Libya in US Foreign Policy," 34.
89.   Ibid.
90.   Ibid., 33, 37.
91.   Ibid., 46.
92.   Vandewalle, *A History of Modern Libya*, 178.
93.   Ripsman et al., *Neoclassical Realist Theory*, 64; Zaller, *The Nature and Origins of Mass Opinion*.
94.   Bøås and Utas, "Introduction."
95.   Weiss and Welz, "The UN and AU."
96.   Mbeki, "Union Africaine"; Ebrahim, "Speech by Deputy Minister," 134; Gelot, "The Role and Impact."
97.   Gazzini, "Assessing Italy's Grande Gesto."
98.   Vandewalle, *A History of Modern Libya*, 202.
99.   Pargeter, *Libya*, 178–9.

Bibliography

Abass, Ademola. "The African Union's Response to the Libya Crisis: A Plea for Objectivity." *African Journal of Legal Studies* 7, no. 1 (2014): 123–147. doi:10.1163/17087384-12342043.

Abrahamsen, Rita. "The Power of Partnerships in Global Governance." *Third World Quarterly* 25, no. 8 (2004): 1453–1467. doi:10.1080/0143659042000308465.

Adebajo, Adekeye. "The revolt against the West: intervention and sovereignty." *Third World Quarterly* 37, no. 7 (2016): 1187–1202. doi:10.1080/01436597.2016.1154434.

African Union Peace and Security Council, "Communiqué 261st Meeting PSC/PR/COMM(CCLXI) Addis Ababa", *Ethiopia*, 23 February 2011.

African Union Peace and Security Council. "Statement by Amb Ramtane Lamamra, Commissioner for Peace and Security." 275th Au Peace and Security Council Ministerial Meeting Devoted to a Debate on the State of Peace and Security in Africa, Addis Ababa, Ethiopia, May 25–26, 2011.

African Union Peace and Security Council. "Communiqué 595th meeting of the Peace and Security Council on the role of the African non-permanent Members of the United Nations Security Council (A3) and the AU Permanent Observer Mission to the United Nations." Addis Ababa, May 28, 2016, PSC/PR/COMM.3(DXCV).

Ashley, R. K. "The Achievements of post-structuralism." In *International Theory: Positivism and Beyond*, edited by Steve Smith, 240–253. Cambridge: Cambridge University Press, 1996.

Ashley, Richard K. "The Geopolitics of Geopolitical Space: Toward a Critical Social Theory of International Politics." *Alternatives: Global, Local, Political* 12, no. 4 (1987): 403–434. doi:10.1177/030437548701200401.

Ban Ki-Moon. "Address to Stanley Foundation Conference on the Responsibility to Protect." *UN News Centre*, January 18, 2012. http://www.un.org/apps/news/infocus/sgspeeches/print_full.asp?statID=1433.

Bellamy, Alex. "Libya and the Responsibility to Protect: The Exception and the Norm." *Ethics and International Affairs* 25, no. 3 (2011): 263–269. doi:10.1017/S0892679411000219.

Behr, Hartmut, and Michael C. Williams. "Interlocuting classical realism and critical theory: Negotiating 'divides' in international relations theory." *Journal of Political Theory* 13, no. 1 (2016): 3–17. doi:10.1177/1755088216671735.

Bigo, Didier, and Anastassia Tsoukala, eds. *Terror, Insecurity and Liberty. Illiberal practices of liberal regimes after 9/11*. London: Routledge, 2008.

Bøås, Morten, and Mats Utas. "Introduction: Post-Gaddafi Repercussions in the Sahel and West Africa." *Strategic Review for Southern Africa* 35, no. 2 (2013): 1–15.

Breeden, Aurelien. "Nicolas Sarkozy and the Libya Investigation: The Key Questions." *New York Times*, March 23, 2018. https://www.nytimes.com/2018/03/23/world/europe/nicolas-sarkozy.html.

Campbell, David. *National Deconstruction: Violence, Identity, and Justice in Bosnia*. Minneapolis: Minnesota University Press, 1998.

Carr, Edward H. *The Twenty Years' Crisis: 1919-1939*. London: Papermac, 1995.

David, Steven R. "Explaining Third World Alignment." *World Politics* 43, no. 2 (1991): 233–256. doi:10.2307/2010472.

Der Derian, James. "Introducing Philosophical Traditions in International Relations." *Millennium* 17, no. 2 (1988): 189–193. doi:10.1177/03058298880170020601.

Devetak, Richard. "Post-Structuralism." In *Theories of International Relations*, edited by Scott Burchill, 183–211. Basingstoke: MacMillan, 1999.

de Waal, Alex. "African roles in the Libyan Conflict of 2011." *International Affairs* 89, no. 2 (2012): 365–379. doi:10.1111/1468-2346.12022.

Ebrahim I. Ebrahim, "Speech by Deputy Minister of International Relations and Cooperation, Mr Ebrahim I. Ebrahim, on the Occasion of a Public Lecture on 'Libya, the United Nations, the African Union and South Africa: Wrong Moves? Wrong Motives?', University of Pretoria, 15 September 2011." *Strategic Review for Southern Africa* 33, no. 2 (2011): 128–134.

Engelbrekt, Kjell. "Why Libya? Security Council Resolution 1973 and the Politics of Justification." In *The NATO intervention in Libya. Lessons Learned from the Campaign*, edited by Kjell Engelbrekt, Marcus Mohlin, and Charlotte Wagnsson, 41–62. London: Routledge, 2014.

Evans, Gareth. "Interview: The RtoP Balance Sheet After Libya." e-International Relations, September 2011. http://www.e-ir.info/wp-content/uploads/R2P.pdf.

Foucault, Michel. "Omnes et Singulatim: Towards a Critique of Political Reason." In *Power: Essential Works of Foucault 1954–1984*, Vol. 3, edited by J. D. Faubian, translated by R. Hurley, 298–325. New York: The New Press, 2000.

Foucault, Michel. "What is critique." In *M. Foucault, The Politics of Truth*, edited by S. Lotringer, 41–81. Los Angeles, CA: Semiotext(e), 2007.

Gazzini, Claudia. "Assessing Italy's Grande Gesto to Libya." Middle East Research and Information Project, March 16, 2009. http://www.merip.org/mero/mero031609.

Gelot, Linnéa. "The Role and Impact on the African Union." In *Political Rationale and International Consequences of the War in Libya*, edited by Dag Henriksen and Ann Karin Larssen. Oxford: Oxford University Press, 2016.

George, Jim. "Of Incarnation and Closure: Neo-Realism and the New/Old World Order." *Millennium* 22, no. 2 (1993): 197–234. doi:10.1177/03058298930220020901.

Goetze, Catherine. "Bringing Claude Lévi-Strauss and Pierre Bourdieu Together for a Post-Structuralist Mthodology to Analyse Myths." In *Myth and Narrative in International Politics: Interpretative Approaches to the Study of IR*, edited by Berit Blieseman de Guevara, 87–106. London: Palgrave Macmillan, 2016.

Grovogui, Siba N. "Looking Beyond Spring for the Season: An African Perspective on the World Order after the Arab Revolt." *Globalization* 8, no. 5 (2011): 567–572. doi:10.1080/14747731.2011.622868.

Hallams, Ellen, and Benjamin Schreer. "Towards a 'Post-American' Alliance? NATO Burden-Sharing after Libya." *International Affairs* 88, no. 2 (2012): 313–327. doi:10.1111/j.1468-2346.2012.01073.x.

Hansen, Lene. *Security as Practice*. London: Routledge, 2006.

Hehir, Aidan. "The Responsibility to Protect as the apotheosis of Liberal teleology." In *Libya: The Responsibility to Protect and the Future of Humanitarian Intervention*, edited by Aidan Hehir and Robert Murray. Basingstoke: Palgrave MacMillan, 2013.

Jacobi, Daniel, and Annette Freyberg-Inan. *Critical Investigations into 'Human Beings in International Relations'*. Cambridge: Cambridge University Press, 2015.

Jacobi, Daniel, and Annette Freyberg-Inan. "The Forum: Human Being(s) in International Relations." *International Studies Review* 14, no. 4: 645–665. doi:10.1111/misr.12012.

Joffé, George. "Libya and Europe." *The Journal of North African Studies* 6, no. 4 (2001): 75–92. doi:10.1080/13629380108718452.

Kasaija, Phillip A. "The African Union (AU), the Libya Crisis and the Notion of 'African Solutions to African problems'." *Journal of Contemporary African Studies* 31, no. 1 (2013): 117–138. doi:10.1080/0 2589001.2012.761463.

Kitchen, Nicholas. "Systemic Pressures and Domestic Ideas: A Neoclassical Realist Model of Grand Strategy Formation." *Review of International Studies* 36, no. 1 (2010): 117–143. doi:10.1017/ S0260210509990532.

Laclau, Ernesto and Chantal Mouffe 2001. *Hegemony and Socialist Strategy: Towards a Radical Democratic Politics*, 2nd Ed. London: Verso.

Lundborg, Tom and Nick Vaughan-Williams. "New Materialisms, discourse analysis and International Relations: a radical intertextual approach." *Review of International Studies* 4, no. 1 (2015): 3–25. doi:10.1017/S0260210514000163.

Luttwak, Edward N., Libya: it's not our fight, 21 March, Los Angeles Times.

Maasho, A. "AU Says Non-Africans Sidelining Libya Peace Plan." *Reuters*, April 26, 2011. https://www. reuters.com/article/libya-au-idUSLDE73P1BF20110426.

Malloy, Allie, and Catherine Treyz. "Obama Admits Worst Mistake of his Presidency." *CNN*, April 11, 2016. http://edition.cnn.com/2016/04/10/politics/obama-libya-biggest-mistake/.

Mbeki, Thabo. "Union Africaine: Une Décennie d'échecs." *Courrier Internationale*, September 27, 2012. http://www.courrierinternational.com/article/2012/09/27/une-decennie-d-echecs.

McKaiser, Eusebius. "Annual Ruth First Memorial Lecture, University of the Witwatersrand: Looking an International Relations Gift Horse in the Mouth: SA's Response to the Libyan Crisis." *African Studies* 71, no. 1 (2012): 145–157. doi:10.1080/00020184.2012.668298.

Milliken, Jennifer. "The Study of Discourse in International Relations: A Critique of Research and Methods." *European Journal of International Relations* 5, no. 2 (1999): 225–254. doi:10.1177/135406 6199005002003.

Morgenthau, Hans. *Politics Among Nations*. 4th ed. New York: Knopf, 1967.

Nabers, Dirk. *A Poststructuralist Discourse Theory of Global Politics*. London: Palgrave Macmillan, 2015.

Nnaeme, Charles C., and Lucky E. Asuelime. "The African Union's Questionable Legitimacy in Selected African Crises Regimes in 21 Century." *Journal of African Union Studies (JoAUS)* 4, no. 2–3 (2015): 77–100.

Obama, Barack, David Cameron, and Nicholas Sarkozy, "Libya's Pathway to Peace." *New York Times*, April 14, 2011. https://www.nytimes.com/2011/04/15/opinion/15iht-edlibya15.html.

Ogunbadejo, Oye. "Qaddafi's North African Design." *International Security* 8, no. 1 (1983): 154–178. doi:10.2307/2538490.

Omorogbe, Eki Yemisi. "The African Union, Responsibility to Protect and the Libyan Crisis." *Netherlands International Law Review* 59, no. 2 (2012): 141–163. doi:10.1017/S0165070X12000150.

Pargeter, Alison. *Libya: The Rise and fall of Qaddafi*. Yale: Yale University Press, 2012.

Ping, Jean. "The African Union Role in the Libyan Crisis." *Pambazuka News*, December 15, 2011. https:// www.pambazuka.org/governance/african-union-role-libyan-crisis.

Reus-Smit, Christian. "Liberal Hierarchy and the License to Use Force." *Review of International Studies* 31, no. S1 (2005): 71–92. doi:10.1017/S0260210505006790.

Ripsman, Norrin M., Jeffrey W. Taliaferro, and Steve E. Lobell. *Neoclassical Realist Theory of International Politics*. Oxford: Oxford University Press, 2016.

Rossouw, Mandy. "SA's 'No-Fly' Vote hits Turbulence." *Mail and Guardian Online*, March 25, 2011. http:// mg.co.za/article/2011-03-25-sas-nofly-vote-hits-turbulence.

Schweller, Randall. *Deadly Imbalances: Tripolarity and Hitler's Strategy of World Conquest*. New York: Columbia University Press, 1998.

Sil, Ruda, and Peter J. Katzenstein. "Analytic Eclecticism in the Study of World Politics: Reconfiguring Problems and Mechanisms across Research Traditions." *Perspectives on Politics* 8, no. 2 (2010): 411–431. doi:10.1017/S1537592710001179.

Sithole, Anyway. "The African Union Peace and Security Mechanism's crawl from design to reality." *African Journal of Conflict Resolution* 12, no. 2 (2012): 111–134.

Sterling-Folker, Jennifer, and Rosemary E. Shinko. "Discourses of Power: Traversing the Realist Postmodern divide." *Millennium* 33, no. 3 (2005): 637–664. doi:10.1177/03058298050330031801.

Taliaferro, Jeffrey W., Steven E. Lobell and Norrim M. Ripsman. "Introduction: Neoclassical Realism, the State, and Foreign Policy." In *Neoclassical Realism, the State, and Foreign Policy,* edited by Steven E. Lobell, Norrim M. Ripsman and Jeffrey W. Taliaferro, 1–41. Cambridge: Cambridge University Press, 2009.

United Nations. UN Ambassador Dabbashi Letter dated February 21, 2011. UN doc. S/2011/102, February 22, 2011.

United Nations Security Council. Resolution 1973, New York, March 17, 2011.

Vandewalle, Dirk. *A History of Modern Libya.* Cambridge: Cambridge University Press, 2012.

Walt Stephen M. "Learning the right lessons from Libya." *Foreign Policy,* 29 August 2011.

Weiss, Thomas G., and Martin Welz. "The UN and AU in Mali and Beyond, a Shotgun Wedding?" *International Affairs* 90, no. 4 (2014): 889–905. doi:10.1111/1468-2346.12146.

Williams, Michael C. *The Realist tradition and the limits of International Relations.* Cambridge: Cambridge University Press, 2005.

Zaller, John R. *The Nature and Origins of Mass Opinion.* Cambridge: Cambridge University Press, 1992.

Zoubir, Yahia. "Libya in US foreign policy: from rogue state to good fellow?" *Third World Quarterly* 23, no. 1 (2002): 31–53. doi:10.1080/01436590220108162.

Index

For Product Safety Concerns and Information please contact our EU
representative GPSR@taylorandfrancis.com Taylor & Francis Verlag GmbH,
Kaufingerstraße 24, 80331 München, Germany

Printed and bound by CPI Group (UK) Ltd, Croydon, CR0 4YY
08/05/2025
01864358-0018